W9-CHI-751

THE MEANING OF LIBERALISM

THE MEANING OF LIBERALISM

BY

J. M. ROBERTSON

WITH A FOREWORD BY THE
EARL OF OXFORD AND ASQUITH

SECOND EDITION
REVISED AND ENLARGED

KENNIKAT PRESS
Port Washington, N. Y./London

THE MEANING OF LIBERALISM

First published in 1925
Reissued in 1971 by Kennikat Press
Library of Congress Catalog Card No: 71-102582
ISBN 0-8046-0742-7

Manufactured by Taylor Publishing Company   Dallas, Texas

FOREWORD

MY old friend and colleague, John Robertson, has asked me to write a foreword to this new edition of his well-known work "The Meaning of Liberalism," and though no contemporary writer on political questions stands less in need of the commendation of others than he, I gladly assent to his request. The great increase in the numbers of the electorate since this volume was first published, accompanied as it has been by the emergence of the three-party system, has created a widened interest in political problems, to which Mr. Robertson is peculiarly qualified to appeal.

As a former Liberal Minister of the Crown, and as one of the most distinguished political and economic thinkers of the day, he has a special claim upon the attention of all serious students of national and international problems. They will find in this book, not dogmatic assertion or *ad captandum* rhetoric, but reasoned demonstration and suggestion conducted in a spirit of intellectual breadth and equity.

OXFORD

April, 1925.

PREFACE
TO THE SECOND EDITION

THE first edition of this book, issued in 1912, was nearly exhausted when there came the explosion of the World War, to alter profoundly the immediate issues of British politics for over a decade. To that war the Liberal Party was committed, no less by its deepest principles than by the statesmanship of its trusted leaders ; and for four tremendous years the normal educative tasks of Liberalism were wholly suspended, save inasmuch as necessary interferences with free trade, and proposals for unnecessary and injurious extensions of such interference, caused polemic.

During that period, however, the Labour Party so-called, zealously continued its special propaganda, with no regard to the war " truce " between Liberals and Conservatives ; and not even the appeal made at the end of 1918 by the Coalition Ministers for a combination of the middle and upper classes against the alleged tendencies of Labour politics availed to prevent the resulting increase in the parliamentary strength of the Party thus opposed. Indeed the very nature of that appeal did much to improve the position of those Labour leaders who had partly hampered the conduct of the war, and to re-unite them with the other Labour leaders who had heartily supported the national cause. Liberalism suffered accordingly.

The subsequent developments of Conservative party policy led, first, to the return of a Conservative Government which promised " tranquillity," and, within a year, to the defeat at the polls of that Government upon its attempt to be relieved of the very fiscal pledges which had won it a working majority. Then came the phenomenon of a Labour Party in office, as a result of the loyalty of the Liberal leader to the principles of the constitution, and his worthy refusal to combine the Liberal forces with those of Conservatism for the prevention of the experiment of a Labour Ministry.

For the opening thus loyally given him, the leader of
the Labour Party was at first duly grateful, avowing as he
did after some months of office that the heads of the other
parties had treated him generously. It was when Mr.
Macdonald had by his own startling unwisdom brought
his Ministry to the verge of its inevitable extinction that
he bethought him of charging upon the Liberal Party and
its leaders all manner of underhand misconduct towards
him all along. At the same time, while Mr. Baldwin
avowed that the Liberal leader had taken a wise and
statesmanlike course, the managers of the Conservative
Party used every plan in their power to persuade multitudes
of ill-informed electors, male and female, that the Liberal
Party was implicated equally with the Labour Party in
the dealings of the latter with Russian Bolshevism, inasmuch as the action of the Liberal leader had made a
Labour Ministry possible.

Thus, between the tactics of Labour leaders and those
of Conservative managers, alike unscrupulous, the Liberal
Party in Parliament has reached the lowest point of numeri-
cal strength in its history for a century past ; and, as is
now realised even by thoughtful Conservatives, the national
outlook has become newly disquieting in a high degree.

Conservatives of another description had actually been
calling for a merging of the depleted Liberal Party in their
own ranks. As that was precisely what the tacticians of
the Labour Party desired, the wisdom of the ideal scarcely
needs discussing. What the wiser Conservatives realised
was that, if the Liberal Party as such should disappear,
there must occur some day, in the ordinary course of party
vicissitude, a return of the Labour Party to power with a
working majority—the thing dreaded above all by all
Conservatives alike.

Before the actual episode of the Macdonald Ministry,
most Liberals would not thus have regarded a Labour
majority as a highly unstable thing ; though all competent
Liberals well knew the vital necessity of the Liberal Party
to resist the extremists of both the others. But within a
few months Mr. Macdonald had made it clear that he was
helpless under the pressures of *his* extremists ; and that his
compulsory abstention from the Socialist legislative
measures by the promise of which his party had won votes,

1ade it the more necessary for him to assent to measures of policy demanded by the Communist wing of his supporters.

In this conjuncture the need for the rebuilding of the Liberal Party as an effective force must be obvious to the more intelligent of the members even of the Labour Party, no less than to intelligent Conservatives. The majority of the Labour leaders, while vieing with their colleagues in vote-catching devices which may euphemistically be termed " bold," had no thought of any legislation that could properly be called revolutionary. Mr. Webb had proclaimed " the inevitability of gradualness " ; and Mr. Snowden, in the last stage of his party's belated advocacy of a Capital Levy, had avowed that such a levy could not be imposed against the wish of the moneyed classes. Little as was his power of persuasion in the matter, it was on persuasion alone that he avowedly relied.

But in the autumn of 1924 an astonished country saw the Cabinet of which Mr. Webb and Mr. Snowden were members agreeing to guarantee a loan of £30,000,000 to the Bolshevik Government ; while one of their colleagues in the Ministry proclaimed his conviction that such a loan would be fruitful of commercial gain to us even if it were never repaid. " The economics of Bedlam " had been a justifiable description of the teaching of Tariff Reform : it was now by special right transferable to the finance of the Labour Ministry. Whatever may have been the private opinions of Mr. Webb and Mr. Snowden, they assented to the policy dictated to Mr. Macdonald by the present Communist controllers of the Trade Union Congress.

Mr. Snowden, conscious of the pass to which his party had thus been driven, has recently denounced the controllers in question as its worst enemies. But personal chagrin has blinded Mr. Snowden to the fact that the Communists are only turning against him and his colleagues the tactics which he and they had employed against Liberalism during the War. As politicians, Mr. Snowden and Mr. Macdonald have been trained by Liberalism. Employing the vocabulary of Marxism to inflame class feeling and class hopes in the ranks of labour, they had found a way to turn the trade union organisation to the advancement of their own faction, well pleased to call it all the while " Labour " rather than " Socialist."

With the Liberal Party in the past they never had any
real quarrel. Well they knew that in the eight years before
the War it had achieved, in the interest of Labour, a series
of capital measures such as they themselves had not before
dreamt of seeing carried in twice the time. Neither gratitude nor concern for the common cause of political progress
ever withheld them from planning to turn the forces of
trade unionism to the " destruction " of the Liberal Party,
as they and their coadjutors fondly phrased their aspiration.
In their personal advancement they found the sanction for
their habitual description of Liberalism as an enemy of the
people's cause. It must indeed be disturbing to them to
find that their own Communists, in turn, propose to dis-
comfit the present leaders of the Labour Party, and to turn
the trade-unionist vote and money to their own advancement. But the development is exactly what was to be
expected.

If any hasty Liberals have in recent years hoped to see
the task of Liberalism competently carried on by a Labour
Party, so named in order to create and exploit class feeling,
they have surely now been disillusioned. From the first,
when constituted as a group antagonistic to Liberalism,
the Independent Labour Party has been irresistibly led
both to asperse Liberalism and to outbid it. Liberal
reforms, however wisely schemed, were hard enough to
carry even with the support of Labour. The wild plans of
the Labour Party, framed to capture votes from Liberalism,
inevitably bred large expectations. When even the official
ideals of Labour Ministers, to say nothing of their feeble
official schemes, were seen to shrink to constitutional programmes that obviously must wait indefinitely for fulfil-
ment, the extremists had their turn and took it. For the
time being the machinery of the British Trade Union
Congress is controlled by Communists, who " report " in
eulogy of the Bolshevik State, under which all semblance of
political liberty has ceased to exist save for the governing
oligarchy, all political opposition is " illegal," all printed
censure of State action is impossible, and leaders of strikes
are shot.

Liberals can now compendiously state their case against
the competing parties. Organised Conservatism has
wrought its part in making myriads of workers believe that

only to a Labour Party can they look for sympathetic treatment. The active spirits of Conservatism have once more revealed that *their* one serious ideal is Tariffism ; and the official dismissal of that policy after its defeat at the polls leaves no experienced politician in doubt that it will be resumed as soon as may be. A hope that it will be one day accepted by a sufficient section of the Labour Party is openly avowed, with a considerable measure of counten-.ance from tariffist Labour members.

Thus the future of British industry and commerce lies ostensibly at the mercy of 'two aggressive parties, one secretly longing to fleece the poor, the other openly hoping somehow to fleece the rich ; and both alike vitally incompetent to handle their problems. The Conservative Party cannot be trusted to maintain Free Trade ; the Labour Party is divided alike on that issue and on the application of its Socialist principles, everything tending to show that those of its leaders who have been in office find themselves coerced by the Communists behind them. They have thus completely discredited their own policy of luring votes away from Liberalism. The result thus far has been the handing back of power to reactionary Conservatism, perhaps for many years ; the complete arrest of progressive legislation ; and the demonstration of the unfitness of men trained in theoretic Socialism for actual government.

That has indeed been demonstrated with an amazing completeness by the Communist Government of Russia, which has effected the completest wreck of a civilization ever achieved in the modern world, bringing progressive penury upon a State once regarded as the most self-supporting in Europe. This has been done by applying to the Russian State the principles of Marxian Socialism, which prescribe revolution and dictatorship as the means of realising the ideal. The parliamentary leaders of the British Labour Party, playing with Marxian fireworks to attract Socialist support, profess never to have entertained the Marxian creed of revolution. The more dishonest has been their association with a Continental movement which it was their plain duty to repudiate. At a time when, alike in France and in England, men professing warm loyalty to the ideals of Socialism are earnestly repudiating Marxism as did Jaurès in effect before the War, and when the

xii 		THE MEANING OF LIBERALISM

old Marxism in Germany is adhered to, broadly speaking,
only by the Communists, the British Labour Party, clinging
under pressure to the Communist connection while
professedly repudiating Communism, still tactically invokes
Marx's name and seeks the Bolshevik alliance.

To those who, like the present writer, studied Socialism
in youth with moral sympathy, yet always found the
professed Socialists either idealists devoid of steady faculty
for practical politics, or revolutionists merely moved by
class envy, the evolution of Fabianism up to the point of
capturing the Trade Union movement has been an instructive spectacle. The old deficit of political judgment,
vainly supposed to be made good by assiduous wire-pulling,
has revealed itself to the full in the hour of chance success.
A lifetime of balancing between the two stools of à priori
theory and vote-catching expedients has produced a bench
of momentary Ministers whose theories are even less coherent
than their practice. A Premier Foreign Secretary who
had denounced the Bolshevik dragooning of Georgia, and
an Under-Secretary who in the days of Tsardom had called
on the British Government to flout the Tsar for his evil
home policy, have joined in proposing to finance the Soviet
and in explaining that its misdeeds of internal policy are no
affair of ours.

In this state of things, the effective revival of the Liberal
Party is visibly the sole hopeful means of guiding aright
the forces of political progress in Britain. Conservatism
cannot now be trusted to spare Free Trade save under
immediate fear of defeat ; and the Labour Party, with its
Communists always menacing its leaders from the rear,
can never be trusted to handle either foreign or home
affairs with sanity. Vainly do its nominal leaders seek
to keep support for a practically progressive policy by
sweeping promises as against the destructive programme
of the Marxists who really believe in Marx. They have
divided the progressive forces to their own undoing ; and
vainly do they denounce the wreckers behind them who
turn against them their own devices.

To be told by schemers thus outschemed that " the
Liberal Party is doomed " is to be newly convinced that it
is indestructible. There is but one doomed Party in British
politics, and that is the Socialist. For Socialism, as a

political programme, simply cannot work.   That much has been learned by the Socialists of Germany and Austria since they have been brought to the test of action ; that much has been fatally demonstrated by the Socialists of Russia, " architects of ruin," helplessly vacillating between a systematic Communism which can achieve only all-round bankruptcy, and a compromise which stultifies Communism. Before democracy in Britain lies the choice between that dire experience and a return to the Liberalism which for nigh a hundred years has steered the State through all its dangers.

Sorely shaken at once by past schism and by the ruinous tactics of the Labour wing, the Liberal Party must just re-build itself with an energy proportionate to the need. There is no other sane outlook for political progress ; and the men and women who, in the face of the proved incompetence of a Labour Ministry, continue to support its doubly discredited cause, are but labouring to evoke for themselves either such a Russian ruin as broke the hearts of earnest Socialists in Germany seven years ago, or a lifetime of sheer frustration.

Already the Labour Party, not only at election times, but in general, has through its adherents shown itself eager to make an end of free platform speech for other parties.   It is for all who profess the old ideals to renounce a movement which tramples them under foot.   The seceders have dealt ill by Liberalism.   It is for Liberals to deal more magnanimously by them, in conserving the common good. And everywhere one sees the shattered Party girding its loins anew to its great task.   We have seen of late the moving spectacle of an eager national effort to save a fine feature of the Metropolitan scene, the imperilled dome of St. Paul's.   But there is a greater dome than that of St. Paul's, to wit, the dome of the Commonwealth, the greatest structure, we would fain believe, ever yet raised by the hands of man.   It is to preserve that supreme possession, now visibly in peril, that the Liberal Party lives and moves, and has its being.

This little book, a product of pre-War politics, is now re-published with certain curtailments, amendments, and additions.   Sections dealing with Liberal policy in the matters of Woman Suffrage and Irish Home Rule have been retained foɹ historic reasons. But in so far as the theories and ideals of Liberalism as developed in the decade before the War are still set forth in the terms then fitting, the exposition, it may be hoped, has not lost all utility. Liberal principles have not changed ; and if this vindication be in general sound, it may still serve, as it was thought to do by some good Liberals at whose kindly instance the author originally wrote its different sections, to help young politicians to define their ground and shape their course.

The chief additions have been the section on the present aspect of the important problem of the House of Lords and the appendix of articles written two years ago in criticism of a newspaper exposition of Socialism by Mr. Snowden, for permission to reprint which the author has to thank the editor of the *Liverpool Daily Post*. That Mr. Snowden could offer no better refutation of those criticisms than a feeble personal flout is one of the many proofs of the unfitness of his party to lead the nation in either the theory or the practice of politics.

This unchanging irrationalism, on the part of a sect that supposes itself to proceed on an application of reason to the problem of social welfare, is perhaps the most significant aspect of modern Socialism. Owen reasoned. Marx, claiming to be alone scientific, dogmatised, denounced, and vaticinated, for two generations of hypnotised Germans. His latter-day British pupils, changing somewhat the purport of the prophecy, rely as confidently on the same elementary dialectic, substituting declamation for demonstration and aspersion for argument. They were doing the same thing forty years ago, when Hyndman debated with Bradlaugh. Mr. Snowden, propounding Socialism, and already at odds with his " Mountain," is about as rational as Robespierre. An exposure of his futility, happily, may help to secure for him a better end.

J.M.R.

July, 1925.

CONTENTS

PART III.—CAPITAL, BRAINS AND LABOUR

PART I
LIBERALISM AS A CREED

CHAPTER I

NATURAL DETERMINANTS

§ I

ACENTURY and a half ago, when Englishmen were mainly divided,[1] as now, in two factions, Hume declared that they were " at a loss to tell the nature, pretensions and principles of the two parties."[2] The same complaint is made to-day. " What do your Liberalism and Conservatism really mean ? " is a question sometimes put by vivacious women, caring for none of these things. Their attitude is excusable on the score that the question is surprisingly seldom put or answered methodically by either party leaders or journalists, though —perhaps because—new issues are constantly arising which invite general surveys and definitions. Daily is the battle waged between the parties, and the members of both feel that they know why they are so ; but systematic explanation of the whole drift of the struggle is not common ; and many politicians, even, are perhaps sceptical of the possibility of a sound systematic explanation. Looking at the similar conflict of Republicans and Democrats in the United States, they see no continuous clues, and they are apt to surmise that none are to be found. At home they see Liberalism and Conservatism alike chronically broaching new policies, on each of which men change sides ; and they are moved to think of the whole *processus* as a series of disputes none of which can be foreseen.

Certainly they can argue that party leaders in the past have not set forth any detailed creeds that will square with or elucidate the course of events. Leaders on both sides are for tactical reasons chary of going beyond immediate proposals and moral generalities ; and this suggests

[1] Written in 1912.
[2] Essay *Of the Parties of Great Britain*, ed. 1741.

an uncertainty about their own course which tends to discredit theoretic forecasts. Of most modern leaders, from Peel and Gladstone downwards, it can fairly be said that even at the middle of their career they had probably no inkling of what they would be doing about the close of it. And as the leaders named changed policies and directions, so, in our own day, we have seen a number of notable men on both sides renouncing party allegiance, and this usually for political, not personal reasons. True, but do these phenomena make definitions either less possible or less necessary?

The more seriously a man takes his politics, the more he will want to realise the nature of his position and his bias, and to foresee where the latter is likely to take him. The problem concerns us both morally and intellectually. There is something disturbing to the moral sense in the spectacle of transformations ill-explained; something that troubles the intelligence in the sense of either apparent or felt inconsistency; something uncomfortable, to say the least, in unexpected demands for an assent that has not been mentally prepared. All of these strains might conceivably be averted in some measure by a habit of thinking out party politics to their foundations in individual bias, social tendency, and the party tradition or heredity. And such a study was never more necessary than to-day. when policies develop and situations change more rapidly than ever, all parties visibly fulfilling some inner law of change. When all is said, each man must answer the main question for himself. But for obvious moral reasons parties also ought collectively to answer it; and while the answer given on one side cannot conceivably satisfy the other, it may be that a Liberal estimate of Liberalism, which involves an estimate of Conservatism, is capable of leading to counter-estimates which may not be unfruitful. However that may be, an attempt to elucidate historic Liberalism in terms of Liberal sympathies is here undertaken, with a sense of its necessity.

§ 2

It has been often remarked that Liberalism is not so much a creed or body of doctrine as a state of mind, an attitude towards men and towards civic life, which in a manner predetermines one's political judgments. To this summing up, probably, most thoughtful men would assent,[1] whatever be their politics, as they presumably would to the corollary that Conservatism comes under the same description.[2] Debate begins when we go about to analyse and describe the two states of mind in question. A reservation may by some be proposed with regard to the force of mere upbringing and association, and, above all, of class feeling. There are unquestionably many Liberal and many Conservative partisans whose allegiance to their parties is in the main hereditary or conventional, a habit of going with their class, their church, their trade ; and who, born to another status, would as readily have chimed in with the common politics of that. But to say this is only to say that " minds " are in large measure formed by training and usage. Where there is a strong innate bias of any kind, it tends to assert itself in defiance of upbringing and environment, yielding, in politics, rich Democrats or Conservative working men, who, so to speak, politically de-class themselves. But the majority of men, probably, acquire their opinions as a result largely of their social and general education, and only partly of an innate temperament ; and the attitude of mind set up by general intellectual experience or lessoning is not in practice distinguishable from that of natural bias Whether innate or instilled, a temper or frame of mind is established which makes a man broadly prone either to Conservative or to Liberal views and courses.

A real exception falls to be made in respect of the men in whom loyalty to party as such is a preponderating bias, overruling others. That there is such a primary " spirit of party," irrespective of other mental determinations, is very obvious in many historical instances, and as it is

[1] I have heard, for instance, a Conservative statesman avow having noted a " fundamental Radicalism " in Lord Randolph Churchill, and in Mr. Winston Churchill before his first change of party.

[2] In the article of Mr. Baumann entitled " Drifting Down Stream," in the *Fortnightly Review*, Feb. 1, 1911, it is argued that in making tariffism the main plank of its platform, his party has got away from a distinctive Conservative basis. Mr Baumann supports tariffism, but does not regard it as more a Conservative than a Liberal fiscal expedient.

found in all sorts of combinations, it is not be to pronounced in itself either Liberal or Conservative, unless we agree—which probably we shall not—to class it as one of the conservative elements that may co-exist with liberal bias of other kinds. It will probably be more accurate to see in it a form of the primary gregarious instinct, taking on a quasimoral colour while really eluding moral control. The " Blues " and " Greens " of the Roman and Byzantine circus,[1] in their psychology, approximated more, perhaps, to the exclusive gangs of scavenger dogs in modern Constantinople than to the political factions of the rest of Europe. But in the United States, where party distinctions are so often obscure for Europeans, the habit of sticking to one's party machine, whatever it may do, is marked enough to prove that primary partisanism is a lasting force in politics. Indeed, members of all political parties in Britain commonly impute it to their opponents.

Still, there is no room for doubt as to the potency of the higher determinant—the mental attitude, partly congenital or temperamental, partly class-bred. In every general election many men change their party allegiance, and in many, if not in most cases, the change is made in terms of a real political choice, though many seem to vote on motives varying between a mere wish to be on the winning side and a mere desire to see a change in the Government for change's sake. To know rightly, then, what Liberalism or Conservatism is—and we can hardly define the one without incidentally defining the other—we require to ascertain the psychic and intellectual marks of the main attitudes in question.

In making the attempt, we plainly run a risk of merely flattering ourselves. The current generalizations which satisfy public meetings of either colour, however broadly defensible, will not pass as scientific formulas. A good instance of such a generalization on the Liberal side is Gladstone's telling account of Liberalism as meaning " Trust in the people, tempered by prudence," and of Conservatism as " Distrust of the people, tempered by fear." Few Conservatives would accept the latter description of their policy, and it would perhaps have been difficult

---

[1] Though these are latterly held to have originated in deme-divisions.

even for Gladstone to prove that his own " prudence "
was never " fear." Conservatives have found cause to
" trust " the people on some points—support of a reckless
war policy, for instance—and Liberals a corresponding
ground for distrust. Some broad and general truth the
maxim must have, else it could hardly have given such
prolonged satisfaction even to one side, but even when
accepted, it leaves to be analysed the grounds of the
" trust " and the quality of the " prudence." A step
towards a more general agreement may be made by avowing
that in the Liberal as in the Conservative case there is
presumably a " defect of the ruling quality " to be reckoned
with. We must broadly connect with Liberalism the phase
of political faith which projects impermanent reforms and
outruns the people's power of response, even as we connect
with Conservatism the invincible distrust of popular
aspiration which ends in provoking revolutions. If the
Conservative will concede that such persistent distrust
means political incapacity, we have something of a basis
for a generally valid conclusion ; and the British Conservative may now perhaps be expected to concede it, seeing
that Mr. Balfour has recently pleaded the principle of
" Government by consent " as the true justification for
woman suffrage. At the same time, we must concede that
there may be incapacity in the Liberal direction—the incapacity which precipitates revolutions that cannot be
maintained.

On the strength of two such admissions, it might hastily
be concluded that the master-element in Liberalism is
desire for political change, and the master-element in
Conservatism the dislike of it. But that generalization
will clearly not fit the British Conservatism of the present
day ; and it will probably be found inadequate to the
explanation of either the Liberalism or the Conservatism
of any considerable period in any country. In the Rome
of the Gracchi, for instance, the revolutionary policy of
the two brothers, clearly lacking as it was alike in technical
and in practical wisdom, was on one side really " Conservative," in that it sought to restore an ancient state of
things which the " Conservative " party or class had,
with or without systematic purpose, uprooted. In our
own history, again, the earlier manifestations of what

we now call Liberalism were for centuries by way of demanding the restitution of ancient rights and the regeneration
of ancient laws. Conservatism certainly does often resist
innovation, but not necessarily *as such*, for it has its own
plans of innovation. It is a question of the *kind* of innovation desired. We have still to reach a general view of the
motives or tempers which constitute the bias.

§ 3

In seeking to make a sound induction, we of course
recognise at the outset that into every political movement
there enter different kinds of motive. Hotspur and Owen
Glendower are not kindred minds : they are merely political
associates. All practical politicians are aware that every
party has adherents on the score of some one conviction,
bias, grudge or grievance ; on the satisfaction or removal
of which they can readily revert to the other side. Some
Temperance reformers, for instance, adhere to the Liberal
party on the sole ground of their desire for a better control
of the drink trade, caring for no other Liberal measure,
and even disliking other Liberal tendencies. On the other
hand, some Conservatives have changed sides because of
loyalty to Free Trade ; while not a few Liberals in the
past generation turned Conservative because of dislike of
Home Rule, and some more recently in resentment of a
new tax to which a Liberal Ministry had subjected them.
In both types of case, some light may be thrown upon
the nature of Conservatism : temperamental dislike of
radical change might operate in either. But if this be
so, such a bias is strictly special to neither side. Conservatives do in fact nowadays accuse Liberals of sticking to
Free Trade from motives or instincts of what used to be
called Conservatism, thus repudiating what used to be
their own ostensible standpoint. Conservatism, we are
told, stands now for new ideas, Liberalism for old prejudices.
And it is not only in the matter of Free Trade that the
Conservative aggregate as a whole has cast off the semblance
of strict traditionalism. Claiming in the past to be the
" Constitutional " party, its members have of late shown
themselves zealous to break down one of the oldest of

the limitary principles of the Constitution—that, namely, of the sole right of the Commons to settle the national finance. In the Parliament of 1900, again, they destroyed at one blow, without any preliminary consultation of the electorate, the whole system of English School Boards ; and yet again, in the Parliament of 1886, they established a system of County Councils.

Either measure, had it been proposed in the Liberal interest, would probably have been zealously resisted by many Conservatives, if not by the party as a whole ; but the course of events has proved that mere constitutional dislike of radical or structural change is not now fundamental in " Conservative " character, if it ever was. On the sole signal of its leader, literally at a moment's notice, the Conservative party, at the second General Election of 1910, adopted *en masse* the principle of the referendum, concerning which the great majority of the electors had never heard any discussion.[1] It is safe to say that on the Liberal side such an instantaneous change of policy would have been impossible, and perhaps equally safe to say that had the proposal come from the Liberal side, it would have been opposed by the great mass of Conservatives. On the other hand, it is plainly fantastic to pretend that the Conservative party in Britain has become possessed by a consuming desire for social or political reform. If that were so, its older ideals, expressed in its deliberately chosen name, must have been entirely abandoned ; and so complete a reversal of the bias of a great party is inconceivable. Most of its later legislative measures which have aimed at social reform have been rather obviously motived by the immediate desire to " dish the Liberals," whether or not for ulterior reasons of a more presentable kind. Disraeli's Reform Bill and the Workmen's Compensation Act of 1897 are typical, and both were accepted with much reluctance by many, if not most, Conservatives. Disraeli's policy, and that forced on his successors by Mr. Chamberlain, were alike planned, pushed and complied with, in order to catch votes ; and the County Councils Act, which was planned partly to counterwork Home Rule, obviously tended to give power to the landed class

[1] This now appears to have been entirely abandoned by the Conservative party.

in county affairs. Thus far, we have not laid our finger
upon the mainspring of Conservatism.

Seeking it, one naturally turns to contemplate British
political history from the point at which parties clearly
take shape. The phenomena of Liberalism and Conservatism are of course to be studied through all human
history; and the political evolution of ancient Greece and
Rome, in particular, is too instructive to be ignored by
any one who seeks to shape for himself anything approaching
to a science of politics. But the present inquiry is one
which may no less help to throw light on ancient political
evolution than to derive light from it; and if we reason
soundly within the limits of British political experience,
our conclusions, we may hope, will be generally valid for
the politics of other nations. Our political history, by
common consent, presents a more steady development than
that of almost any other " progressive " country in the
modern world, and is thus the most readily intelligible.
In any case, it is that which the majority of Britons can
best understand; and it has been recorded with adequate
fulness and competence from various points of view.

Starting, then, from a point well within common knowledge, we can recognize something like the growth of a
Conservative side and a Liberal side in the contest which
begins in the seventeenth century in the Long Parliament;
and there, as now, it is clear that Liberalism is not mere
desire for social or political change, and that Conservatism
is not mere devotion to tradition. The Radicals of 1640
actually pleaded tradition against the policy of the king,
here standing to the ancient form of Liberalism—the
demand for a return to use and wont. The many innovations following upon that stand were not foreseen, and
were not motives. The king's oppressive practices were
in the main innovations, practically if not theoretically,
and in abetting these the Cavalier party were supporting
constitutional change.

We cannot suppose, however, that there emerged here
any new temperamental state or moving principle, any
more than we can suppose the members of the Conservative
party in our own day to have reversed their whole bias
in accepting " Tariff Reform." Nor can we suppose that
the mere heredity of the Caroline aristocracy counted for

much in generating their politics. They were, it is true, in large part a modern patriciate, which took its rise as such under the Tudors, the old Norman nobility having been in part destroyed in the Wars of the Roses, or humbled by the anti-papal policy of Henry VIII. and his Protestant children. But a generation or two seems to serve for the assimilation of a " recent " to an " ancient " aristocracy in all respects. The late Professor Gumplowicz, who sought to account for social phenomena in general in terms of " race," advanced to the conclusion that social status generates types in a manner indistinguishable from that of racial heredity. Aristocrats under Charles I. were presumably not psychically unlike aristocrats under Henry VI., save as regards their greater refinement and culture, and their political determinants were presumably similar in similar cases.

In the fifteenth and sixteenth centuries the political creed of the English nobility was tolerably simple. They fought the king if he sufficiently angered them, or fought each other in dynastic quarrels in which mere feudal loyalty was the sufficient motive. But in their attitude towards the common people, regarded either as *Jacquerie* or as Lollards, we have the germ of the Conservatism of the seventeenth century. It is a negative or counter motion. The clamorous peasants are spontaneously hated for their insubordination, their presumption, antecedently to any act of violence on their part. In the same way the middle-class critics of the king's doings in the Long Parliament are viewed as " upstarts " by men accustomed to deference for themselves, and to taking that as part of an unchallengeable system in which supreme deference is the appanage of the king. Their politics is thus primarily a matter of class feeling—one of the rudimentary forms of human antagonism.

Not that such feeling would override plain pecuniary interest. When Mary of England sought to regain from her loyal nobility and gentry some of the Church lands allotted to laymen by her father and brother, she could no more recover a rood than could Mary of Scotland in similar case. When Charles I. took steps that pointed towards a resumption by the Crown of the tithes in Scotland, he set against him there nobility and people alike, and fired the whole train of consequences which led to the Civil War. But where the interests of the landed class were not threatened, they spontaneously tended, as a body, to resent the presumption of small men and burghers who claimed to dictate to " their betters." Thus begins English " Conservatism," as a specific political force or aggregate. We are contemplating a passion, a prejudice, a movement of resentment towards the claims of others, not anything schematic, theoretic, or constructive. All that is strictly positive in the matter is the 'equally primordial concern for lucre, for acquisition, for power. And these two aspects of the Tory or Conservative party are found to survive all the permutations of its policy at the hands of its " tactical " leaders, from Bolingbroke to Balfour.

The doctrine of " divine right " was rather a product than a source of this tendency. It was indeed propounded under James I.;[1] but, as Hume noted,[2] it was not much stressed by the Cavaliers ; and it is after the Restoration that it becomes a standard doctrine among Royalists.[3] The Jacobite party is thus from first to last the simple reincarnation of the old resistance to the upstarts, the innovators, the men with constitutional theories, who had been able to carry their point when James II. presumed on the power of tradition so far as to set himself in antagonism to the Church of England. At the Restoration the triumph of the reaction had been overwhelming ; but James contrived at last so thoroughly to alarm the Anglican clergy that they, who had tolerated all other innovations made by him, rather than permit one which affected themselves assented to the revolution which dethroned him. Thereafter the frictions inevitably set up by the new rule tended to evoke the primary jealousy of " the foreigner," a passion always easily exploited for Conservative purposes ; and against this the sovereigns who were out of the direct line had to rely mainly on the self-interest of their original supporters—a self-interest that was singularly strengthened by the new National Debt, the holders of which were taught

---

[1] Gardiner, *History of England, 1603-42*, i. 370 ; *cp*. Stubbs, *Const. Hist.*, 4th ed., i. 593, and More's *Utopia*, bk. i.
[2] Essay *Of the Parties of Great Britain*.
[3] *See* refs. in the author's *Evolution of States*, Part vi., ch. iii., §2.

to expect its repudiation in the event of a Stuart Restoration.

For a long time, therefore, English party politics was a matter primarily of maintaining a new dynasty, and secondarily of the partisanship which grew up on the new footing. Neither Jacobitism nor Whiggism could be said to typify either the natural craving of the depressed mass for political status and better life or the upper-class resentment which such cravings provoke ; and when the new dynasty was well established, the pressing political problems were those of commercial and imperial policy. The masses were too ignorant and therefore too unorganized to obtrude effectually any class claims : a new social soil had to be created before that was possible. They lent themselves readily to the furious movement against Walpole's excise policy, later recognised as thoroughly sound, and established accordingly. On the plea of " Jenkins' ear," they lent themselves uproariously to the war of 1739 against Spain, later admitted by men of all parties to have been a folly, forced upon Walpole by an unscrupulous Opposition. They gave the natural assent of primitive patriotism to the policy of conquest ; and only in the stand made by the hereditary Whigs for a rational and sympathetic handling of the case of the North American Colonies did fundamental Liberal and Conservative tendencies come into typical conflict. Domestic Liberalism, in the modern sense, was only coming to its new birth.

§ 4

It is at the French Revolution that modern English Conservatism crystallizes in its typical form, under circumstances very unfavourable to Liberalism. All the aspirations towards parliamentary, electoral and fiscal reform which had been active before 1789 had to run the gauntlet of the reaction ; and the fatality of violence in the course of affairs in France inevitably threw most moderate men in England on the side of " law and order." Fox, with his blend of generous and factious instincts, had never been an ideal leader for Democracy ; and his leadership could avail little against the reversion of Burke

to the side of counter-revolution.   A greater and a stronger
than either could not have made head against a reaction
which was reinforced by the whole volume of normal
patriotism stimulated by the wars with France, and was
led by Pitt, who, beginning as a substantially Liberal
statesman, was irresistibly strong as the head of a quasi-
national combination of which Burke had become the
prophet.   Thus, in 1815, England was predominantly
Conservative in the original sense of that term, which,
when coined or fathered by Croker in 1830, appealed to the
great mass of prejudice and sentiment generated alike
by the atrocities of the Revolution, the execution of Louis
XVI., and the career of Napoleon.   In the new Liberalism
which emerges under the guidance and inspiration of such
writers as Bentham and James Mill, and such statesmen
as Huskisson on the Conservative side and Grey on the
Whig, we can hope with some confidence to ascertain the
bias, the attitude of mind, which is typically and essentially
Liberal.

It begins, then, as a reasoned recognition of injustices,
errors and maladjustments in the social and political
system, and a decision to remedy them as far as may be.
Emerging in men of the upper and middle classes, this
temper is not at all revolutionary.   A great Radical like
Thomas Paine, the force of whose critical and constructive
thinking was fully recognised and admitted by Pitt,[1] could
welcome the French Revolution at its outset in virtue of his
detachment from upper-class traditions and sympathies—
in a word, his freedom from administrative responsibility ;
and there can be no doubt that his powerful advocacy of
political rationalism at once fed revolutionary feeling in
England among those who remained hearty Democrats, and
built up the popular movement of democratic protest
which the less aggressive writers and the more progressive
statesmen sought to instruct and to guide.   But the
fortunes of Liberalism ultimately depended on the prac-
titioners, the obstetricians of progress, who contrived so to
regularize the forward pressure as to secure a working
power from the general assent of the more reasonable men,
the natural Liberals of the age.

[1] Conway's *Life of Paine*, 1 vol. ed., p. 139, *note.*

To say this is not in the least to disparage the agitators, the Radicals who aroused the demand, generating the new spirit that sought to come to birth. But for them there would have been no new birth at all, nothing for the obstetricians to do. Only the functions are different. The radical reformer has to learn, with Wordsworth, that

> " Life requires an *art*,
> To which our souls must bend."

That art is the art of legislation by consent, the winning of adequate assent to a given change. And that assent is, as aforesaid, a matter of reasoned and sympathetic recognition of error, anomaly and injustice in the established system of things, a readiness to apply well-calculated remedies, a sympathy with the aspiration of the masses who resent the gross political inequality of their lot.

This becomes very clear when we study in contrast the opposing attitude and temper. The men who fought the Reform Bill of 1832 were, in general, patently enough the men of hereditary or class-born prejudice, full of revengeful and terrified reminiscences of the French Revolution, hotly resentful of popular pretensions, fed on Burke and Mitford when they happened to be men of reading, more often scornful of all bookish thinking. Since, however, they included both the Squire and the Rector types, and men of culture as well as illiterates, we must look for their common ground, as for that of the Liberals, in an attitude of mind, a bias compounded of ways of feeling and ways of thinking. To sum it up as one of deficient sympathy would hardly be fair, inasmuch as it was and is exhibited by some men of even a superior human-kindness, ready to succour distress at their doors;[1] though it is always found, historically speaking, that Conservative parties exhibit the larger amount of normal brutality, however hard the demos may run them in times of revolution—the extremist type among the unlettered demos being in fact the intellectual analogue of the upper-class Conservatives, blindly seeking its interests against theirs.

[1] Mem., for instance, the young John Mill's account of Southey as " a man of gentle feelings and bitter opinions " (*Letters of J. S. Mill*, 1910, i. 13).

So genial a spirit as Sir Walter Scott was visibly swayed by the spectacle of this reaction in his own country-side, where he had not been so disturbed by the attitude of his own class. Wordsworth, in turn, reacted alike against the theory and the practice of the new popular movement, forgetting the mood of his own youth.

What determines the Conservative attitude in men of normal good feeling appears to be lack of that *intellectual* sympathy which is not only a different thing from every-day kindly feeling, but may even be possessed by some men who do not, generally speaking, care very warmly about their fellow-creatures. The difference is one of range of relation. In every group or class, good-natured people are spontaneously reciprocal as regards the group or class, and will probably maintain the good-natured attitude towards people of other classes as individuals. But where the intellectual element or discipline is lacking, their good-nature will leave them at best apathetic to the class-aspirations of the outsiders ; and this apathy determines their political activity. Without intellectual sympathy there cannot be any steady capacity for political justice, though a man capable of intellectual sympathy may now and then be no very zealous philanthropist.

Intellectual sympathy may be understood as depending on a certain concurrence of power of imagination with concern for logic and consistency. To have it, you must have the primary capacity to put yourself in the place of another, to reflect from his point of view, and to ask yourself how you would feel if you were so situated. The contrary disposition, which makes for Conservatism in all its forms, arises out of incapacity or dislike for such a mental exercise in all cases where it is called for by the formulated claims of rising or discontented classes, or the obtrusion of new theories of life or criticisms of established institutions or creeds. And this negative attitude necessarily fosters and is fostered by a good conceit of oneself, a constitutional sense of the native superiority of one's own judgment.

Some years ago[1] there appeared in one of the reviews an article by a Conservative of the class of educated country

[1] Written in 1912.

gentlemen, in which the writer told of his liking to discuss ordinary political matters with the village blacksmith, who often said shrewd and sensible things, but who, of course, was not to be listened to when he aired his views on Home Rule. Upon such a question as that he stood disqualified by his status and his training. It called for a large and high outlook to which the blacksmith could not attain. The writer, on the other hand, was perfectly sure that *he* had it, in respect alike of culture and natural capacity. He had never in his life, probably, doubted the plenary validity of his political judgment, never suspected his own bias, never questioned the normal political prejudices of his class. How he explained the contrary attitude of men at least as cultured as himself, one could only guess ; but it seemed certain that he did it by disparagement either of their judgment or of their good faith.

Of course this attitude of mind is not confined to professed Conservatives. It is to be seen in some ladies whose interest in politics began the other day, over the question of the suffrage. It is fairly typical again of members of the Fabian Society, a small and select body, who are on that account more fitted than other professed progressives to co-operate from time to time with Conservatism. In their case the consciousness of superiority of judgment, when not innate, is attained partly by a ritual of self-panegyric, partly by an accepted tactic of making out all previous political theorists, Benthamite or Marxian, Rousseauist or Bucklean, as necessarily the prey of error through being born before 1870. But such an acquired or cult-made frame of mind, happily, does not generate such repugnance to popular aspiration as does the more spontaneous bias of the Conservative. That involves, not merely the Squire's calm dismissal of the poor blacksmith's ideas on high State policy, but the widespread growth of hatred towards Home Rule and all Home Rulers which marked English political and social life in the decade from 1885 to 1895—a state of temper to be matched only by the kindred feeling against " pro-Boers " in the years 1899 to 1902. Such developments—in which, be it remembered, a number of former professed Liberals joined the Conservative ranks—belong to the nature of Conservative bias, and tell of its psychic roots, as they illustrate its tendencies.

§5

It would obviously be unjust to the average Conservative of any class to identify him with the aristocratic youth of Aristotelean Athens, who " took an oath to hate the demos." The largeness and complexity of the modern State preclude such simple forms of party ; and Conservatives are not wholly devoid of philosophy. Nor are Bishops, who pass for typically Conservative persons, to be supposed destitute of either charity or philanthropy. In their case, indeed, we must surmise that function and environment count for much in determining political attachment—or adhesion. It must take a good endowment of natural Liberalism to make a Liberal Bishop. And here we must make explicit note of a principle formulated at the outset of our inquiry—the extent to which class position deflects men's political characters. Social pressures, attractions, and compulsions, may swing to the Conservative side men who, otherwise, would tend to the side of reform and sympathetic innovation.

It is somewhat surprising to note, on a retrospect, how many Conservative leaders there have been who had, so to speak, no natural bent that way. Bolingbroke, in point of intellectual bias, was more fitted to lead innovators and reformers than to champion Tories ; even as his antagonist, Walpole, would make a tolerable natural leader for a Conservative class. In their case, in fact, the complications of the dynastic cause overlaid normal political bias ; and Toryism and Whiggism had a dynastic and primarily partisan rather than a psychological significance. But the younger Pitt was at the start, in some important respects, naturally at least as much of a Liberal as Fox and Burke, who thwarted him in his earlier Liberal courses ; Canning in turn was only by association and common anti-Jacobin prejudice, not by intellectual cast, a fit leader for Conservatism ; and Disraeli was still less so. Peel, whom Disraeli flouted and fought in the name of Conservatism, was even to the end much more of a Conservative in the old sense than his assailant ; the main part of his life having been lived in championship of primary Conservative resistance to such liberalizing movements as those of Catholic emancipation, reform of the franchise, and Free Trade.

How far Peel all along sympathized with the Conservative resistance on those heads it would take a long and careful analysis to ascertain. But it is clear that it was on the intellectual side that he was won over to Free Trade, of which he saw the logical strength while his young lieutenant, Gladstone, was still hostile by habit, class-sympathy, and training. And though Gladstone, once his intellect was convinced, was immovable in his allegiance to the new truth in virtue of his mastering conscientiousness, there was still a piquant paradox in the succession to the Tory leadership of Disraeli, who could live the Tory life only by reason of his lack of that moral sincerity which for his great opponent barred the way to an alliance with him.

In later times, whatever may be thought of the late Lord Salisbury, it is obviously class association rather than mental affinity that has made Mr. Balfour a Conservative. In him the faculty for intellectual sympathy seems to be countervailed by the combination of class bias with a turn for philosophical scepticism—that is, a constitutional lack of faith in any cause or principle. Had he been born in the working class he might very well have become a " tactical " labour leader. Typical Conservatives say as much of the late Lord Randolph Churchill. And the flagrant case of Mr. Joseph Chamberlain illustrates the extent to which mere class bias on the one hand may make a man take on the colour of Radicalism ; and how personal and political animosities, on the other hand, may carry him, with a certain baggage of retained Liberal ideas, into the camp of Conservatism, there to make him a leader by force of his pugnacity, his deficiency in scruple, and the predominance in him of those elements of passion, self-assertion and sheer partisanship which are so much more compatible with Conservative than with Liberal thinking.

§6

As has already been indicated and implied, a similar allowance must be made for the association with Liberalism of elements of character which do not constitute, under our definition, a Liberal bias. By the admission alike of Liberals and Conservatives—whichever side originated the statement —the primary fact in political Liberalism, in all ages, is the existence of a great mass of " have-nots," the servile or landless class in the pre-industrial stage, the unenfranchised in early democracies, the unpropertied and wage-earning classes in the modern industrial world. It is the insupressible needs of these classes for betterment, for education, for improved political and legal status, that in the main motive all democratic movements so-called. They crave liberation from all the social disabilities entailed upon them by their lot; and Liberalism broadly means sympathy with their cravings and a desire to help them. The have-nots, to begin with, are " Liberals " in their own interest ; and that is no more a guarantee of innate intellectual sympathy or open-mindedness for any man than is the mere possession of wealth or wealth-given culture. Obviously, the have-nots have one kind of special education in sympathy, in respect of their very poverty and their burdens. The mutual helpfulness of the poor, recognized by so many observers, is the product of their conditions : fellow-feeling for distress is generated by experience thereof.

But the class-consciousness of the have-nots is only, so to speak, part of the raw material of Liberalism. It is plainly impossible that the mere accident of poverty, inherited or incurred, can confer disinterestedness of character. It cannot reasonably be doubted that multitudes of the have-nots, be they Radicals or Socialists, would be normal Conservatives had they been born in the middle or upper classes. The hardness of a number of men who work their way to the capitalist status from that of the artisan is notorious ; and even among the wage-earning class the innate bias to Conservatism and the lack of openness to critical ideas are (with or without special educational fostering) often sufficiently pronounced to counteract all class bias and constitute the type of Conservative working man.

That type, whether produced by the activities of the church school, or by the kind of class feeling which sets a workman in opposition to the politics of a Liberal employer, or by the animosity of the beer-drinker to the party which seems to him to meddle unwarrantably with the drink trade, is more necessarily and naturally Conservative than a workman is Liberal whose ruling motive is a simple desire to tax wealth or fight the aristocracy. The higher Liberalism, the true political Liberalism, begins among the working class when the workman has realized that if born to wealth he *might* have been a Tory, and therefore seeks for a broadly-reasoned justification of democracy, thus substituting an intellectual for a passional impulse and attitude. When he can be reflectively sure that the acquisition of a fortune would leave him zealous in the politics which aims at freeing and helping his former comrades, he is become a sound Liberal, or, be it added, a comparatively intelligent Socialist. And not till then. We have but to recall the class-bred Radicalism of the earlier Mr. Chamberlain to realize how wanting in intellectual and moral root may be the democratism of class prejudice.

The foregoing avowal is the sufficient answer to the Conservative charge against Liberalism of " setting class against class." Mere class antagonism is assuredly demoralizing, inasmuch as it substitutes an unreasoned for a reasoned motive ; and the professed Liberal or Socialist who acts on the former is ethically on all fours with his Conservative antagonist, who normally begins and ends upon just such a motive. But class criticism is not class hatred ; and it is precisely the incorrigible class prejudice and narrowness of the majority of Conservatives that compels indictments of their class characteristics. Like every other party the Conservative includes many humane and worthy men ; but the party must be judged as such by its main types. In no other way can the facts of the case be brought home to men nurtured in self-sufficiency and hardened by class habit. Of all men, the average Conservative is the most class-formed, class-bound, and class-led : hence the broad accuracy of the generalization, " the classes and the masses." It is a permanently significant fact that, while constantly charging class-feeling against all who plead the cause of the mass, the Conservative not only

starts as such in a spirit of class interest and class resentment, but habitually appeals, in our current politics, to
cognate racial prejudices, such as jealousy of " the foreigner"
and dislike of " the Irish." The second General Election
of 1910 was largely fought by him upon such cries. [1]

Doubtless there is a risk of a counter class feeling being
generated by such cries as " People against Peers." Men
fighting against an entrenched and privileged class are apt
to forget that not birth and status but the conditions into
which one is born are the main determinants of political
bias. The permanent vindication of Liberalism as against
Conservatism must lie in the possession of general standards
and ideals which are founded in an inclusive as against an
exclusive bias, or rooted in a general sympathy and not in
antipathy, in aspiration and not in ill-will. The Liberal
movement or impulse starts in a simple desire for " better
life " for those who lack it ; and only when the movement
is resisted by the classes who already have the best of
things, does a class feeling against them tend to fix itself.
It is thus the fundamental class feeling of the typical
Conservative, whose ideal of " good life " is always exclusive,
always limitary, that " sets class against class." But this
can never be for the enlightened Liberal an excuse ; it is
only an explanation. A cause whose best inspiration is
good-will, and whose motive is good deeds, is always en-
dangered by the entrance of systematic malice, as distinguished from the necessary hard hitting of the political
mellay. And in so far as a fixed ill-will of class, however
generated, may enter into the mass of Liberal activity, it is
to be diagnosed as an alloy, partaking of the nature of the
thing combated.

But, given all these deflecting forces, all these qualifica-
tions of our general definitions, the broad facts of Conservative and Liberal bias become all the more clear. Great
parties do indeed subsist as such partly by force of pure and
simple partisanism—the tendency of the average combative
man to go on combating the bodies and the men whom he
combated in the past. Many a Conservative now supports
a tariff policy simply because his party in the lump has
adopted it ; and not a few Liberals are at once educated in

[1] So was the Election of 1918.

Liberalism by the pressure of colleagues and helped in their allegiance by simple reluctance to join their former foemen. Thus the Liberalism of to-day, no less than the Conservatism of to-day, has undergone transformation at salient points. New perceptions create new ideals and formulas ; time, as the rhyme says, " makes ancient good uncouth " ; but none the less Liberalism means a movement of liberation, of sympathetic beneficence, of social readjustment and reconstruction ; while Conservatism continues to mean fundamentally a resistance to those tendencies or to some of them. And all the distinctive proclivities of the two parties continue to be intelligible in terms of the primary general differentiation.

§ 7

Are we then left facing a " natural " cleavage which defies control, correction, or persuasion ? If " culture," so called, can leave multitudes of men lacking in what has been described as intellectual sympathy, is anything to be hoped for from criticism or even statement of their form of bias ? Conservatives, pointing to the representation of the Universities, claim that culture is on their side, prudently saying nothing of the difficulty of stating the common measure of the politics of the university, of Birmingham, and of the drink trade. Are we driven to reckon on a perpetual sunderance of great masses of similarly instructed men, determined mainly by promptings of interest and class prejudice, which operate irrespectively of argument, and are incapable of modification by any theoretic way of viewing things ? It is to be hoped that we are not. The aim of the present inquiry, at least, is such a view of the total strife as may suggest grounds for reconsideration to some readers. It proceeds on the assumption that all forces which can be cognized as intellectual, and even a number of impulses of temperament, are amenable to intellectual pressures.

It is indeed difficult to exaggerate the importance of the intellectual element in political sympathy. To dwell upon it is not to overlook the fact that sympathy is primarily temperamental, and is often strong in unintellectual people.

The point is that temperamental sympathy, common in youth, is apt, like optimism, to run thin with advancing years.   This, in fact, is the secret of the number of reversions from Liberalism to Conservatism among elderly men.   All of us, in approaching or attaining that status, are more or less conscious of an occasional flagging in the zest of political fellow-feeling and the zeal for reconstruction ; and it is only by the disciplined use of self-criticism that men thus flagging in zest for change can keep themselves in touch with the forever renewing spirit of aspiration in others.   Political wisdom is of the nature of science, and involves the habit of detachment, the capacity to realize political forces in terms of the whole play of things.

To surrender to personal apathy or lassitude, to vote for keeping things as they are when one has passed the first passion for betterment, is simply to join hands with those who never felt it, and whose resistance to the reformative appeal of others is the expression of pure primary egoism. It is told of Mr. George Norman, described as " the last patriarch of Benthamism, who, like his friend, Mr. Grote, inclined to Conservatism in his old age," that he thus expressed himself : " I only wish that Gladstone would leave us without organic changes for the next forty years."[1] The fatigued Benthamite was simply falling into the ordinary way of those who in his youth had resisted all the reforms craved by Bentham.   Thus to let " the elderly temper " usurp the place of judgment is to lapse alike morally and intellectually.   The rights of ill-starred humanity to the earnest consideration of all the rest are just as real when we are old as when we are young ; and to fail of realizing as much is to betray a certain obtuseness.

A contrary view is apt to be set up by the occasional spectacle of reaction in conspicuously studious men.   When a man of much reading goes over to the side of the public-house in politics, we are invited to see in the act the ascendancy of the spirit of " culture," the recoil of the instructed man from the blind extravagances of demagogy.   It would be hard, however, to find a case of the kind alleged which would not on scrutiny turn out to be either the wilting of a temperament or the recoil of an average egotist from a tax.

[1] Hon. Lionel A. Tollemache, *Recollections of Pattison*, 1911, p. 37.

An exception may be allowed for simple fear of social up-
heaval : we are still near enough to the French Revolution
to make such fears pass muster as reasoned apprehensions ;
but they, too, commonly stand for temperamental sub-
sidence. Against that, the only safeguarding " culture "
lies in the searching study of the problem in hand—the
problem of politics in all its aspects.

And this is usually the last study to be dreamt of by
those who fall away from Liberal to Conservative opinion.
The aged Benthamite who protested against " Gladstone's
organic changes " made the gloomy prediction : " Sooner
or later, there must be a struggle between *those who have
got,* and *those who want,* and I don't see how it is to be
settled except by the sword. But I suppose that those
who have got will win." [1] To this oracle the academic
Pattison gave an hasty assent. It expresses, however,
only the despair-engendering failure to attain a scientific
or evolutionary conception of politics—a failure as natural
and as facile to studious as to unstudious men when they
study everything except the complex problem in hand.
All literature, indeed, may minister to political wisdom ;
but mere literature will no more supply a science of the
problems of political life than it will yield a science of
astronomy or geology.

The common confusion as to the validity of " culture "
in political judgment is to be solved only by realizing at the
start that politics is the strife of wills, needs and ideals on
the area of political relations, and that general culture can
purify or transmute that strife only in so far as it transmutes
egoism and deepens fellow-feeling. Specific superiority
is to be reached (genius apart) only by the mastery of the
special science of human wills, needs and aspirations in the
political relation. It used to be common to speak of
" knowledge " and " ignorance " in these matters ; as if
the acquirement—even the nominal acquirement—of an
academic or general literary culture gave not only a right
to make laws for less fortunate people against their will,
but a real efficiency for all purposes of political judgment.
The mere working man was held nearly incapable of reasonable political opinions. In the egregious language of

[1] Tollemache, as cited.

Macaulay, " the higher and middling orders are the natural
representatives of the human race."[1]

Thus Bagehot, after declaring in the first edition of his
English Constitution that the working classes ought to have
the franchise, announced in the introduction to the second
edition, after the Reform Act of 1867, that he was " exceedingly afraid of the ignorant multitude of the new constituencies." If a reader had asked him, " Ignorant of
what ? " he would have been hard pressed to defend his
position. In his first edition he had affirmed that the
landed interest, which, he said, had far more power in the
House of Commons than any other, had a " fixed device "
to make its representatives " stupid."[2] Of the middle class,
again, which had greatly increased its representation since
1832, he had affirmed that its education, by the account of
an " excellent " judge, was " pretentious, insufficient and
unsound."[3] Such classes would seem in turn to have been
politicians to be " exceedingly afraid of." Both classes,
but in particular the first, had been concerned in imposing
on the country for seventy years, in defiance of the best
economic teaching available to them, a fiscal policy which,
in Bagehot's own opinion, had been wholly wrong and
highly injurious. As regards the majority of the old
electors, the " ten-pound householders," he still declared
that their political notions, " if they had been cross-exam-
ined upon them, would have been found always most
confused and often most foolish." Of what kind of ignorance, then, did he fear that the *new* voters would make a
dangerous or terrifying exhibition ? He explained himself
thus :—

" I cannot expect that the new class of voters will be at all more
able to form sound opinions on complex questions than the old
voters. There was, indeed, an idea—a very prevalent idea when the
first edition of this book was published—that there was an unrepre-
sented class of skilled artisans who could form superior opinions on
national matters. . . . But the Reform Act of 1867 did not stop at
skilled labour ; it enfranchised unskilled labour too. And no one
will contend that the ordinary working man, who has no special skill,
and who is only rated because he has a house, can judge much of
intellectual matters." [4]

[1] Review of James Mill's *Essay on Government*, near end.
[2] Sixth ed., pp. 163-4.
[3] *English Constitution*, 6th ed., p. 211.   [4] *Id.*, p. 15.

But the critic had himself insisted that no other class in politics was qualified to " judge much of intellectual matters." Then there was no new danger. Bagehot's fears and hopes were summarily expressed in the sentence : " Will they [the new voters] . . . defer in the same way [as the old] to wealth and rank, and to the higher qualities of which they are the rough symbols and the common accompaniments ? "[1] The man who so wrote had almost ceased to be a Liberal ; his mind had partly gone out of action. Again and again he had previously averred that wealth and rank were not commonly accompanied by the high political or intellectual qualities which he was now assigning to them. Protectionism, by his own account, had been an evil and hurtful policy, however backed by rank and wealth and culture. The rule of rank and wealth and ostensible culture in England, he did not deny, had meant immense social misery, a brutal criminal code, a war policy which had laid on the back of industry a vast national debt. After the admission of the middle class to representation in 1832 there had occurred the Crimean War, as foolish, as futile, and as ill-managed a war as England ever waged. What new evils were to be apprehended from the enfranchisement of the working class ? More or worse wars, more poverty, more ignorance, more barbarous laws, or a reversion to the Corn Laws ?

Bagehot had himself written before 1867 that " the House of Commons, representing only mind coupled with property, is not equal in mind to a legislature chosen for mind only, and whether accompanied by wealth or not. But," he added, " I do not for a moment wish to see representation of pure mind : it would be contrary to the main thesis of this essay. I maintain that Parliament ought to embody the public opinion of the English nation, and certainly that opinion is much more fixed by its property than by its mind "[2]—a virtual cancelling of his later formula about higher qualities being symbolized and accompanied by wealth and rank.

His fundamental conceptions of politics were in fact entirely confused even before 1867. Of " public opinion "

[1] *English Constitution*, 6th ed., p. 16.
[2] *Id.*, p. 171.

he had no steady idea. " The working classes," he wrote,
" contribute almost nothing to our *corporate* public opinion,
and therefore the fact of their want of influence in Parliament does not impair the coincidence of Parliament with
public opinion "[1]—a mere argument-in-a-circle. A few
pages later he wrote that " A great many ideas, a great
many feelings have gathered among the town artisans—
a peculiar intellectual life has sprung up among them. They
believe that they have interests which are misconceived
or neglected ; that they know something which others do
not know ; that the thoughts of Parliament are not as
their thoughts. *They ought to be allowed to try to convince
Parliament ; their notions ought to be stated as those of other
classes are stated ; their advocates should be heard as other
people's advocates are heard.*"[2]

Thus we arrive at this pleasing paralogism : 1. Parliament ought to represent public opinion, that and nothing
else ; 2. Public opinion is mainly fixed by property ;
3. The working classes, lacking property, contribute almost
nothing to our " corporate " public opinion ; therefore they
ought not, or do not need, to be represented in Parliament ;
4. The working classes, nevertheless, have their opinions
like other classes ; therefore, though their opinions are not
" corporate " public opinion, they *ought* to be represented
in Parliament like other classes ; 5. All the same, their
enfranchisement is " to be exceedingly feared."

It is safe to say that none of the working-class agitators
of 1867 ever put forth so frankly self-contradictory a theory
of representation. Bagehot's entire performance is a
sufficient confutation of the assumption on which he fell
back in 1867. His writings plainly proceed upon a consciousness of special political wisdom, and they betray a
failure to reach coherence of thought upon elementary or
primary political problems. They thus entitle us to recur
to the presumption that, inasmuch as the business of practical politics consists largely in the working out of the conflict of the interests of the working mass with the interests
and prejudices of the Conservative sections of the propertied
classes, the working mass are likely to exhibit no worse

[1] *English Constitution*, 6th ed., p. 166.
[2] *Id.*, pp. 173-4.

or less sense than do others in seeking their interests—interests which, in the terms of the case, are those of the bulk of the nation.

If we apply the test of results, Bagehot's "exceeding fear" finds no justification. English politics grew better and not worse after 1867. Bagehot in 1872 could not deny that under the new franchise important reforms had been carried out to which even in 1872 he could not object. He could not condemn the Disestablishment of the Irish Church in 1869, or the Education Act of 1870. All he could say was that it was a "complete mistake" to ascribe the new life in politics to the Reform Act of 1867. There has been a "change of generations." Since then there has been at least one more "change of generations," and England is happier, in some ways more contented, richer, stronger, better educated than she was in 1867. Unjustifiable and useless wars have been waged since, as before, but they are not to be specially ascribed to the working classes. Their leaders, if not their ranks, in large numbers opposed the South African War : rank and wealth for the most part have promoted all the wars alike, though perhaps this bias is on the way to change. Rank and wealth are now largely concerned in trying to bring about a return in this country to Protection : the working classes in the main thus far resist it. The political sagacity of the enfranchised working classes will bear comparison with that of rank and wealth to-day, by the tests of Bagehot's own administrative code. His "exceeding fear" has been discredited by facts, no less than his reasoning has been by logic.

If a cultured man of Bagehot's training and gifts could thus discount his own claim to special political sagacity in virtue of education and knowledge, it can hardly be maintained that the ruck of less gifted men are made wise or just politicians in virtue of a similar culture and class associations, or even of a more specialized culture. No one who knows academic life will assert that dons and professors are, as a rule, less concerned for the main chance, more magnanimous, more self-forgetting, than the men of an industrial community, though they may be more cautious and more refined in their methods of conflict. Knowledge of Greek and mathematics does not more often confer

saintliness than does craftsmanship or the pursuit of commerce. If then in any academic community a majority are
found to take a Conservative view of licensing laws and
plural voting, education and hereditary legislatorship, it
does not in the least follow that such views are the outcome
of careful study of the needs of nations or the conditions of
public weal.

At no stage of our history have academic men in the
mass been in general zealous about either popular education
or enfranchisement. Then they themselves did not in
general believe that " culture " is good for men in general ;
and if they had had their way there would have been no
enfranchisement of the masses. If they so leant because
of their knowledge of the downward course of ancient
democracies, they simply showed how inadequate was their
political culture ; for while the past does present instances
of progress in civilization under democratic conditions, it
nowhere shows such progress to have been attained or
preserved by keeping a populace in subjection and ignorance against its will. If, in short, the academic man often
coincides in his political preferences with the fox-hunting
squire and the publican, the reasonable inference is that he
has been swayed by the simple interests or class-prejudices
which sway them, not by his culture, which in general is
superficial as regards political science.

It will doubtless be retorted that the academic man is
as well entitled to his class interests and sympathies as is
the working man to his ; and that in the terms of the case
the latter must have even less political science than the
collegian. That is true. But in the terms of the case he is
also as likely to look to and safeguard his own interests ;
and in his case the safeguarding of interests tends to mean
the difference between well-being and hardship for the great
majority of the population. The vital difference between
the aspirations of " haves " and those of " have-nots " is
that the latter make for the expansion of the field of " good
life," and that the former tend to the narrowing of it—in so
far, that is, as the Conservative still pursues limitary ideals.

Of course, when he in turn pushes a policy of change,
whether in home or foreign affairs, the issue is different.
A University man ought to be at least as good a judge as a
working man of fiscal policy, of armaments, and of the

necessity or avoidability of a given war. In these matters the crux is not ostensibly a competition of claims or interests ; and where the issue is thus impersonal, the working-man's instinct or first thought is not likelier than the other's to make for general betterment, save in so far as the working man promptly reflects that the mass of the combatants and sufferers on both sides in an average war are the poor folk, who have no quarrel with each other, and that military expenditure is a constant bar to expenditure on social needs. But here again, when we are estimating the effect of culture on political judgment, the first question must be as to the relevancy of the culture to the problem. Of men who have studied political economy, the majority in this country are unquestionably free-traders ; and in this connection we have had an interesting revelation of the store set upon expert judgment by the Conservative party where expert authority is mainly against it.

In the case, on the other hand, of University men who have not studied political economy—if we may take doctors in general as coming under that description—a · college training seems to give no better preparation for right judgment than is set up by the life experience and self-regarding reasoning of a working man. We see men of college training committing themselves to a policy of which any detailed statement yields a tissue of self-contradictions ; and the explanation, it would seem, must be either that behind the policy are motives of class-interest—*i.e.* interest of, class as distinguished from profession—which are not avowed, or that the simple appetite to retaliation suffices in fiscal matters to shape the opinions of men academically trained, as it does those of so many other people. Supposing the workman to have similar impulses and motives, we are once more facing the simple conflict of self-seeking ideals ; and the presumption is again in favour of the larger class.

To say this, is not to say that the majority is always likely to be right and the minority wrong. In matters of pure judgment, where pecuniary and class interests and prejudices are not determinants, the fact is likely to be the other way, for obvious reasons. It is in respect of class interests only that there is a justifiable democratic presumption. Inasmuch as in these matters selfishness sways all, and in class questions selfishness tends to escape all

discipline, social or culture status gives no security for
political insight. Mistakes as to one's own interests, in the
circumstances, are likely to be common to all. But inasmuch as a certain perception of its own interest is implied
in the prosperity or progress of any class, we remain at the
presumption that, where no special discipline has been
undergone by either side, each is concerned for its own,
save in so far as its members may actually have changed
sides out of sympathy with those to whom they transfer
their support. A given trade or interest, fighting for its
own hand, lies under the normal suspicion of sheer self-
seeking. A combination of the mass of the " not-haves,"
similarly, is to be presumed to be consulting the interest
of the mass. That that interest in turn may be selfishly
and blindly pushed is obviously arguable. But it is not
on any score *more* likely to be so pushed than is that of any
class or of the " classes "—the " haves " as against the
" have-nots." And so we come back to the tests of reason,
of logic, of comparative political science, with a new sense
of obligation to apply them.

CHAPTER II

THEORY AND PRACTICE

§ I

AS a matter of fact, while the initial or root difference between Liberalism and Conservatism is, as we have seen, a matter of moral temperament and intellectual sympathy, it is found that in every dispute between them, every conflict between new political claims and the Conservative resistance, there is resort to moral and other logic, to some working philosophy of right and wrong. And in such debate, to this day, there is a normal failure to reach a well-stated logical question. The true point of conflict is nearly always enveloped in a moving dust of verbal confusion. It seems possible, however, to reach a definite issue, in the light of the inconclusive logical controversy of the past.

So long as men's political conflicts are over the effectual application or interpretation of laws not in dispute, their strifes may be either well or ill motived, but they raise no fundamental moral problem. It is when new laws are demanded that such problems emerge, and almost invariably the first result is inconclusive reasoning on both sides. If a law is proposed in terms of public expediency, it is likely to be opposed in terms of a doctrine of " right " ; and *vice versa*. When Ireton, Cromwell's son-in-law, found the Levellers calling for a drastic redistribution of land on the score of men's natural right to till the ground, he promptly and confidently replied that no such right existed, the only arguable and tenable basis for any claim of right being the law of the land. Ireton was himself concerned in a revolution which at many points destroyed and reconstructed the law of the land : so that his answer to the Levellers tacitly carried the rider that if they could forcibly establish a legislating authority which would enact their wishes, these would be " legitimated " like any other legalized ideals of property.

All political discussion worthy of the name, however, is as between men who wish not to fight but to prove and persuade ; and under parliamentary government men profess to resort even to the peace-keeping expedient of counting heads only when persuasion by argument is found impossible.   Ireton's answer, therefore, was a poor one even for his own day : it was the answer of a lawyer who would not or could not think as a politician.   The true answer to the Levellers would have been (1) that on their own principles they could claim only the right to cultivate land not already cultivated by other men—else the next comer could claim to oust them in turn, thus precipitating at once the appeal to mere force ; (2) that on their own principles men making a simultaneous claim for the best piece of uncultivated land of any given size available to them would have equal rights, yet only one could have it ; and that (3) there were thus left to them only the alternatives of (a) communal ownership and working of the land, and (b) the existing system of purchase, with or without a rectifying system of taxation.   And as to communal ownership it could easily be shown, independently of the actual breakdown of such systems in the past, (1) that they must involve irremediable friction in respect of the different degrees of men's diligence and energy ; and (2) that in respect of the children born to the initial group of cultivators, the problem would be reopened with the rise of each new generation. As no man can claim a " right " to force his fellows to undertake a demonstrated impossibility, the Levellers' claim of right thus fell to the ground.

In this case the Conservative (for such was Ireton in relation to the Levellers) did not know the strength of his own case, and fell back on law where he might have relied on reason.   But the Levellers, even if non-suited by reason as well as by law, retained their " right " to political consideration.   Wherever a community agrees to admit of increase of its numbers, and does not simply propose to expel or destroy all of its units who are found to lack means of subsistence, it tacitly concedes their " right " to be somehow provided for, or permitted to provide for themselves.

In so far as this right is denied by any individuals, they are merely repudiating their part in the tacitly admitted responsibility of the community. The community as a whole can repudiate it only by a law of expulsion, and this no modern community has ever contemplated doing. Anciently the problem, always being reopened by increase of population, was solved by a kind of chronic expulsion-by-consent of the superfluous members—the *ver sacrum* of the Romans. In that case the outgoers normally attempted conquest of the land of other people, whom; if successful, they enslaved thus merely substituting one evil for another. In a world wholly occupied by constituted States or Protectorates, such a course is simply overt war, and is no longer matter for discussion.

It was thus demonstrably the duty of Ireton's party in the Commonwealth either to attempt some method of legally alloting uncultivated land to landless men willing to work, or to demonstrate that that difficult operation was unnecessary in respect of the availability, under the existing system, of other means of subsistence which involved no injurious lowering of the standards of life. The failure of the Commonwealth-men to offer either the scheme or the demonstration of its needlessness was thus one of the proofs of their failure as politicians. Either the community as such was committed to securing a possibility of subsistence for all its units, or it was not. If not, these were simply outside the community, and the straightforward course would be to say so. But such avowal of an absolute limitation of the community was never made, and presumably never will be. The Elizabethan Poor Law Settlement, made urgent by the *sequelæ* of the suppression of the monasteries, is for England the definitive and epoch-marking declaration that the community accepts and somehow provides for the existence of all of its members. The Act of 1834 merely altered machinery and controlled procedure, leaving the principle of responsibility untouched.

But the claim of the Levellers to have access to the land is only the first random voicing of an inevitable demand for something better than a Poor Law solution. Thrust aside in the seventeenth century and obviated in the eighteenth by new industrial and imperial expansions, the chronic craving of the masses for less precarious conditions of life underlay all the agitations for franchise and other reform throughout the nineteenth century. And over every new political demand there is enacted the same drama of resistance, defeat of that resistance, and subsequent acceptance of defeat. Conservatism is seen at its worst in its refusal of parliamentary reform. The " law of the land " argument was at its naked worst in the championship of rotten boroughs, where every principle of representation was farcically defied, and in the dogged refusal to give any representation to the new industrial cities. Doubtless there was on the side of the refusal a fear correlative to one of the hopes on the side of the demand. Even as many of the seekers for the vote, typified among the Chartists, hoped to make it yield better life conditions for the mass, so the opponents of the claim, mindful of the French Revolution, feared at once mob law and confiscation of property. Here was one of the natural points of cleavage between the Liberal and the Conservative, and, by consequence, one of the points whereafter Conservatism itself is modified by surrender or enforced acceptance.

At such a juncture, the Liberal is the man who realizes that the growing demand of the mass for equity of treatment ought not to be refused on grounds of mere apprehension ; the modifying Conservative is he who recognizes that it cannot be refused with safety. The Liberal primarily assents to the claim of political right : putting himself in the place of the voteless proletary, he sees that the simple principle of reciprocity, fundamental to all morals, dictates the concession. To the plea of inexpediency, put by the cooler Conservative, he replies that the inexpediency is the other way ; that the demand, rooted in human nature, is insuppressible, and that to grant the vote is to prevent resort to the weapon. When argument has done what it can, heads are counted, the change is made ; and Conservatism, after fighting to restrict the new franchise as much as may be, accepts the new political basis and henceforth fights on that.

All such extensions of the franchise mean that the community now recognizes not only the membership of all its units but, in an increasing degree, the fitness and the necessity of admitting the unpropertied units to that common deliberation on the governmental machinery by which all claims and " rights " are settled, and problems of poverty are handled. After the first great parliamentary reform, the first great legislative act is the reconstruction of the old machinery for dealing with poverty in general. And it is significant of the sure sequence of the spirit of practical expediency upon every new extension of sympathy, every new recognition of a " right " deduced from the principle of reciprocity, that the new Poor Law Settlement of 1834 is marked by concern rather for regulating and limiting the principle of sympathy than for expanding it further.

The old application of it had in fact become a force of social disintegration, for sheer lack of intelligent adaptation. Poor relief had become irrational and demoralizing under the stresses and perplexities of new social developments ; and men burdened by an effete system which, mechanically worked, fostered idle poverty, tended to be the more hostile to the claims of " the poor " in general to political equality. To make a sound basis for political equality there had to be such regulation of public charity as should preserve the real citizenship of the unpropertied multitude. Unsympathetic in aspect the new adjustment was.; but it none the less secured firmer ground for new political aspiration and progress. If the Poor Law Settlement of 1834, as its framers claimed, " depauperized " the lower multitude, it made so much the more irresistible their claims to be treated as deliberative units in the community, as voting members of a State in which they were admittedly acting and wealth-producing units, not parasites.

§ 2

At this stage, it might have been supposed, the verbal dispute over " natural rights " should have been disposed of. On the contrary, however, it became further embroiled ; remaining so till our own day. Conservatives and " intellectual " Socialists alike have endorsed the dictum of the Liberal Bentham (who was probably thinking of Godwin) that the doctrine of " natural rights " is an " anarchic sophism." They fail to see that Bentham, in working out his own system of utilitarian reciprocity, was only formulating a better and clearer notion of " natural right." In all statements of natural right there was implicit the true conception of *deducible* rights—rights deducible from the simple law of reciprocity, the principle of doing as you would be done by, which all men professed to accept. This was " natural " right, or *Recht*, if there was any standing notion of " right " at all. Had Bentham recognized this, and proceeded to the task of defining or limiting the practical application of the principle of reciprocity, much sophistry and many heavy books would have been saved. The ideal of " right " and " rights," as apart from mere law, is indestructible, and happily so, else there could be no reform of law.

The early utilitarians are responsible for the prolongation of misconception on this head, in respect of the formal fallacies into which they fell in their fear of countenancing the resort to violence which marked the French Revolution. John Stuart Mill, who, in 1851 was a rather heedless defender of the principle of revolution, was dislodged from that attitude by the *coup d'etat* of Louis Napoleon. Thereafter, trying to improve on the attitude of Ireton, he laid it down that " law is the mother-idea of justice " ; but this is certainly untrue. Justice is much more nearly the mother-idea of law, else law could never have begun save as the fiat of the despot : the idea of law as the measure and expression of justice is secondary ; and the spirit of justice asserts its growth by the impeachment of law, which impeachment is to be met, if at all, not by crying " anarchy " but by showing that the law is juster than the proposed change, or simply that the change cannot be wrought. The formulated claim of " natural right " to means of subsistence or anything else is an " anarchic sophism " only in the sense in which the mere blank denial of all but legal right is an anarchic sophism.

All political doctrine, indeed, may broadly be termed " anarchic " in tendency which, if acted on, would lead to anarchy : sheer Conservatism no less so than the sheer despair or ignorant zeal which demands impossible courses. The function of Liberalism is to recognize the element of " right " which is established by the universal moral law of reciprocity—the generally avowed duty of doing as we would be done by—and to find the feasible means of satisfying the eternal and indestructible aspiration towards "liberty, equality, fraternity." The ideal " Anarch Old " would find his account less in fostering that aspiration than in inspiring the men in possession to flout it, to resist it, to drive it back on itself. That way lies perdurable hate, social degeneration, national decadence, inveterate social strife avertible only by social paralysis, as in imperial Rome.

The political limits and definitions of the law of reciprocity are obvious enough. Inasmuch as political action takes the form of law, compulsory on all, it cannot give such scope to the principle of self-sacrifice as the " law of love " may dictate to the individual in his private action. One man may freely give his blood to be transfused into the veins of another ; the State can never dictate the act. Parents may make heavy sacrifices for their children : the State in its laws must aim at equality of sacrifice, in so far as it commands any ; and where it imposes sacrifice on all the "haves" for the relief of the "have-nots" it must justify its action—or those who propose the given action must justify their proposal—in terms of the good of all.

But this very principle, to begin with, involves the duty of enfranchisement of all contributors, all working, wealth-creating, service-rendering units. To exclude any such is to belie the very principle of " community," to refuse the first step towards doing as we would be done by in public life. If it be argued that certain working units are too ignorant to be capable of good counsel, the obvious answer is that some education should be at once placed within the reach of all. When the State has established a universal and compulsory system of schooling, the plea is at an end : the system is either adequate to the political need or intentionally inadequate, and as such a fraudulent expedient. Given education for all, franchise for all valid units follows. This much is now substantially accepted even by Conservatism ; and the business of Liberalism from that point onwards is to guide and inspire the sequent forms of the aspiration towards the " liberty, equality, fraternity " which, being already the accepted ideal of *every class or group within itself*, in virtue of the fundamental law of reciprocity, is inevitably the ideal for the community as a whole. This is, in a word, the formula of democracy.

§ 3

Without any further schematic elaboration, the whole task of Liberalism, which is the cause of progress in politics, may be thus envisaged. To that task there is no end. Men want the vote because they are, and feel as, men ; and the man already in possession sympathizes with the desire in the degree of his power of imaginative sympathy. If, possessing such power of sympathy, he still refuses, his refusal is intelligible only as a doctrine of despair, a result of the conviction or fear that the whole drift of human aspiration is fatally wrong. Some indeed who profess fears of a downward evolution of democracy as such may deny being pessimists, and claim only to seek safeguards against a headlong application of democratic principles. To the latter the answer is that every step is to be discussed on its merits, and that the safeguarded steps of our fathers have been followed by better and not worse life than that of the past. To the former the answer is that all the communities of the past which suppressed democracy either went straight to national perdition in visible consequence or sank into permanent or protracted stagnation, involving general worsening of life. Democracy is not advocated as the realization of perfection or the reign of perfect wisdom, but as the one feasible way *towards* social perfection, the one set of conditions which give a fair chance to what wisdom there is.

As men want votes because they are men, irrepressibly bent on betterment, so do they want better conditions of life for themselves in the mass, better distribution of wealth, comfort and culture. That they will often propose unsound courses to that end is quite certain : political education consists in learning to understand what are the better or the feasible courses ; and there is no conceivable way of leaping straight from bad into quite good conditions for an entire society. The divergence between Liberalism and Conservatism is, primarily, in terms of desire that the progress or transmutation should go on or desire that it should not. And if any Conservative deny this, contending that they too want better distribution of wealth, comfort and culture, more and more liberty, equality, fraternity, the answer is, first, that from their side and theirs only, to-day, come the doctrines (*a*) that " what is wanted is to make the rich richer, to enable them to employ the poor," and (*b*) what comes to the same thing, that social well-being is for ever a matter of accumulated wealth in one class or in " the classes," and dependence and subordination on the part of the masses.   The Conservative who repudiates that ideal is at least the colleague of those who profess it.   And if he claims that their policy promotes the contrary ideal, he will have to do so with a clearness proportionate to the improbability.

To this issue we now come.   Either present-day Conservatism means the old resistance to the common aspiration for betterment, or it does not.   Either it is bent on checking the movement of popular betterment at the point we have reached, or it is concerned to further that movement, adding to political enfranchisement social elevation.   Either it is moved by the old dislike of " upstart " democracy and the old fear that the rise of the masses means the fall of the classes, or it has learned the whole lesson of the past, and sees in the ascent towards " liberty, equality, fraternity," the way to higher civilization.   Of the learning of such a lesson, what leading Conservative makes any avowal ?   Of such reversal of ideals, who gives any hint ?   Of such a change of tendency where shall we find proof in deeds ? We have been told, it is true, that British Conservatism is now " progressive," and Liberalism retrograde.   But this claim is based, and based solely or mainly, on the reversion of the Conservative party to its own policy of from seventy to a hundred years ago.

That reversion constitutes its sole " constructive " policy, apart from (*a*) *naval* construction, involving a vast addition to the national debt ; and (*b*) a doctrine of peasant proprietorship to be carried out by way of a system of State purchase, which will further add vastly to the national debt and inevitably raise greatly the price of land.   And these great additions to the nation's burdens, the old mortgage on the labour of posterity, are to be met—how ?   By a fiscal system which shall so " broaden the basis of taxation " that the poorest will contribute in respect of the price of every mouthful they eat, every garment they wear, every dish and every implement they use.   If this is the way to a better life for the multitude, Liberalism is certainly now, and as certainly has been for a hundred years, on the wrong road, undoing with one hand what it has done with the other.

Regarding the Conservative proposals on the other hand as the transparent devices of wealth-seekers to broaden and strengthen their position of economic advantage, the Liberal sees himself committed in terms of his tradition and policy of sympathy, his recognized law of reciprocity, to providing rather new safeguards for the disadvantaged class. He is revising the whole State provision for poverty : is he not called upon further to aim at preventing the plunges into temporary poverty entailed upon multitudes of the working mass by sickness and unemployment ? The admission is irresistible. In past years Liberalism has imposed upon the employer, even at some risk of hardship to him, the duty of compensating the workman injured while in his employ. But sickness and unemployment are commoner causes of distress than accident : *they* cannot be relegated to the care of the employer ; and if State provision be not made for them, there remains a ghastly gap in the social machinery of betterment. A measure of such provision is the last achievement of Liberalism ; and on the Conservative side we have seen, along with a profession of desire to aid, an eager concern to exploit to the utmost all forms of resistance to the enactment.

§ 4

The measure of the extent to which the lesson of Liberalism has been learned will be found in the degree of readiness with which new needs and duties are recognized. At every such new departure, however, the old dispute over " natural right " tends to be reopened ; and in this case it has been precipitated by the form of the demand put forward in the name of " labour," the so-called " Right to Work Bill." This inevitably elicits the " Benthamite " reply ; and in this and other connections we find both educated Conservatives and a few Liberals making that reply. The former in particular habitually profess to regard the claim of " natural right " as obsolete, and to substitute for it the conception of " public utility." The old logomachy must here be clearly solved ; and this is the more easy when we note the flagrant inconsistency of the Conservative resort to it.

The repudiation of " natural right," it will be found, is
always made by way of a negative to some claim on the part
of the proletariate or the unenfranchised, and then only.
At other times the plea of natural right is confidently put
forth by the deniers themselves, on their own behalf. While
Old Age Pensions were commonly resisted on the plea that
they do not tend to the welfare of the community as a
whole, there has occurred even in that connection a return
to the plea of " natural right " on the part of the very
politicians who profess to regard it as obsolete when it is
urged from the side of the democracy. It is over the
question of revenue-raising that the somersault takes place.
One day a Conservative may be heard in the House of
Commons averring that the idea of " natural right " is as
dead as Rousseau ; on the next, the same thinker may be
heard denouncing new taxes on the score that they offend
against that very principle.[1] It is as a matter of fact
impossible to debate any project of law whatever without
raising questions of " justice " that are quite independent
of the conception of " legality." And when we come to
discuss principles and methods of taxation, Conservative
leaders and led alike propound theories of " natural right "
beside which those of Rousseau become plausible.

When labour leaders put forward a claim of " right to
work," and a project of law to enact it, the valid answer to
them is simple. A community whose captains of industry
are at a given moment unable to employ their workmen in
their own business without loss, cannot rationally be
supposed capable of organizing economic employment for
the unemployed in general. It can at best set on foot
" relief works," which the promoters of " Right to Work "
Bills expressly repudiate as bad forms of charity. That
which is impossible to society as at present constituted
cannot rationally be claimed by any man as a right. What
the unemployed have a " right " to claim is an earnest consideration of their case, and an earnest effort by the legislature to find the best way of succouring them. To refuse to
make this effort is, on the part of any citizen, a repudiation

---

[1] In recent years, Mr. Balfour and the late Professor Butcher thus
repudiated the principle of " natural right." Yet both reasoners,
like Conservatives in general, frequently took " natural right " for
granted in their opposition to Liberal measures.

of the law of reciprocity, and a negation of the real member-ship of the unemployed in the community : to refrain from making the effort is, on the part of the politician or the legislature, a confession of sheer political failure. It is no longer permissible for a Liberal to argue, with a Liberal leader of the last generation, that nothing can be done for the unemployed, because " man is born to trouble as the sparks fly upward." Distressed men so dismissed cannot rationally be expected to be loyal to the principle of com-munity, which for them has ceased to be usefully operative.

The strong point in Cobbett's otherwise ill-argued case for the retention of the unmitigated Old Poor Law in 1834 was that the " haves " were always ready to insist on mili-tary service from the " have-nots," while disposed to deny them so much membership in the community as carried with it the right of maintenance. It may be worth the while of the promoters of " national military service " in our own day to note that they of all people are specially bound in decency to provide for the livelihood of all upon whom they call to defend the nation. In the past, their predecessors in political thought have not been concerned to provide even for the actual fighter who is " paid off." And if the possessed militarist, much more the Liberal, with his leaning rather to constructive than to destructive activities, is committed to an active and not a merely negative recognition of the membership of the valid unit. The maxim of *laissez-faire*, when first put forth, was per-fectly valid in the connection in which it was urged, inas-much as mediaevalist State interference was usually motived by class-interest, and operated to that end. But that justification of *laissez-faire* disappears before a system of State interference which is democratically motived and scientifically planned with an eye not to the enrichment of classes but to the well-being of the entire community.

CHAPTER III

LIBERALISM AND TAXATION

§ I

AS States pass out of the military or " feudal " into the industrial or commercial stage, their political ferment inevitably throws up problems of taxation. The machine of State cannot be worked without it ; and the more organized the State becomes the more pressing is the fiscal problem. In the nature of things, too, it becomes the point of contact or friction of class claims, wealth seeking at this point to retain its acquired advantages, and poverty resenting any further deprivation. In the struggle, principles are developed in the ratio of the degree of socialization attained by the community. Wherever we can follow such evolution in the past—in ancient Athens, in Renaissance Florence, in Republican Holland—we see the problem of taxation grappled with in ways which testify to a more or less clear recognition of the need to secure equality of sacrifice. In Athens, where democracy on the whole went furthest, the resulting revenue was to some small extent applied, more or less badly, to the rectification of financial inequality, the better distribution of wealth : in the other instances named, that ideal was scarcely dreamt of, and the problem of approaching it was never reached. Florence and the Dutch Republic lost their freedom before such an ideal could well emerge ; though Republican Holland was noted for its systematic way of grappling with poor relief, and indeed gave England the lead in dealing with that persistent problem.

Already in England we have reached the stage of a thorough reconsideration of the system of poor relief, both of the great parties being so far committed, for very different reasons. For a certain time, Mr. Chamberlain's strategy forced upon a largely unwilling Conservative party

45

a propaganda of Old Age Pensions, many votes and seats being thereby won in 1892 and 1895. It was in a time of Liberal division and discouragement. Under the ill-starred leadership of Lord Rosebery, defeat on the question of Home Rule had been followed by a helpless and hopeless policy of " masterly inactivity," the beaten leader preaching distrust of " long programmes " and propounding a grotesque plan of starving out Conservatism as Leslie planned to starve out Cromwell at Dunbar. Lack of political instinct and insight never yielded a worse sample of impolicy : the pseudo-science of political tactics never a stranger instance of spurious analogy between physical and moral force. The astute tactician who had crossed to the other side saw the opportunity to take the wind which the Liberal sails were losing, and steered accordingly. It was what he described in the language of his pseudo-science, as a " flank attack " ; and for the moment he succeeded ; but inevitably, as we can now see, it all came to nothing.

A Conservative Government, even when leavened with Liberal " Unionism "—a mainly negative force—could not be brought to grapple with such a task. A large number of Unionist Members of Parliament, honourably concerned to redeem their pledges, presented to their Government a signed petition, praying to be enabled to do so, but the prayer was not granted. The circumstances were memorable. There had been fought in Egypt a successful campaign ; the battle of Omdurman was won ; military glory irradiated the air ; Liberal journals joined in the national self-felicitations, and it was officially felt to be safe to break the pledges which had put the Conservative party in power. Military glory and social betterment " are of two houses " : a people sated with one must be content—and is in the mood to be content—without the other. From that moment the apparent chance of a transformation of Conservative policy by the working of an imported Liberal principle was at an end. It was left to Liberalism, after another and more protracted episode of imperialist militarism, and of signally expensive glory, to return to its tasks, to recover its mission, to renew its inspiration, and to establish Old Age Pensions.

In so doing it set up a historical landmark similar in

significance to that constituted by the Elizabethan system of poor relief. A higher plane had been reached in the ascent to the ideal implicit in the conception of a community. The pressure of sympathy, lowered in 1834 before an urgent danger of social demoralization, had been more than recovered. For a system of severe State charity, stigmatizing its recipient as pauper and disfranchised, the State began the substitution of a system of rational and considered sympathy, providing to start with stipends given as a Civil right to all of its poor at a certain point of age. The age point was high, and the stipend small; but it meant no small total outlay, and the financial undertaking was onerous enough to perturb some Liberals as well as most Conservatives. The financing of the undertaking, in fact, precipitated the due conflict between Liberalism and Conservatism in the matter of taxation.

§ 2

It is needless now to dwell on the equivocal attitude of Conservatism towards Old Age Pensions at the time of the passing of the measure. Whatever be the strength of surviving Conservative antagonism to the principle, it is professedly accepted by Conservative statesmen. But all the more acute becomes for them the stress of the problem of combining such acceptance of democratic finance on the side of expenditure with a contrary ideal of finance on the side of revenue-raising. The aged poor are pensioned; who are to pay the pensions? The less aged proletariate or the recipents of super incomes and unearned increment? To the latter sources of revenue the Liberal party has at length turned, after two generations of academic and other discussion on the economics and ethics of taxation, carried on with little regard to the teaching of historical experience, and perhaps no more regard to the teaching of economic science.

Here are two elements of the problem—on the one hand, the accepted duty of paying Old Age Pensions, with the prospect of an early demand for a lowering of the age limit and a later demand for a raising of the pension; on the other hand, the need for financing such expenditure by new taxation. When these aspects are considered together, the issue can be seen by any thoughtful student of politics to be of high importance. If any intelligent Conservative were to argue that the present progression points to a crisis like that which evoked the new Poor Law of 1834, though he would be wrong, he would have to be reckoned with and answered. But no official Conservative so argues. Thanks to its past acceptance of Mr. Chamberlain, the Conservative party is formally committed to Old Age Pensions. While its leaders and its rank and file alike absurdly denounce as Socialistic the further graduation of the Income Tax and the new taxes on unearned increment in land values—as if Socialism recognized taxes of any kind—they have latterly vied with each other in claiming Conservative paternity for the one modern measure which so far advances on all previous State treatment of the problem of poverty as to savour of conscious Socialism, in the sense, that is, of a new and wider recognition of the membership of all in the community.

Such a step, had it been proposed solely from the Liberal side, could not have been taken without the most determined resistance from the forces of natural Conservatism. As it was, these were recalcitrant. But Mr. Chamberlain's strategy had done its work, and his party, *as* a party, could not oppose the principle, though it strove vainly in the House of Lords to reduce the measure to an experiment with a time limit, and though its leader in that House signalized its surrender by predicting the worst social results for a policy, the promulgation of which had once actually helped to place his colleagues in power. The dilemma for the " new Conservatism " was never more dramatically set forth. In the very act of accepting a Liberal development which had been imposed on it by a dangerous ally from the outside, the accredited spokesman revealed the persistence of the fundamental Conservative temper.

§ 3

Sooth to say, the economic soundness of the step taken was not realized by all the Liberals concerned in taking it. In the case of many, the Liberal attitude and temper counted for more than political or economic theory. On one thing all were agreed—that those of the proletariate who had reached old age without contriving an adequate provision for their own maintenance were to be treated rather as worn-out servants of the community than as wrecks or wastrels entitled to mere charity. No man of affairs could dispute that for multitudes an adequate provision by saving and investment had been impossible, and that for many more the average chances of loss on investments were fatal. Intelligent sympathy made all this clear, and when Conservative opponents, reckless of repudiating what had once been a Conservative pledge, argued that the pensions would discourage " thrift," common sense answered that no person capable of having his conduct influenced by forethought could conceivably be led to be wasteful through a long lifetime on the chance of getting five shillings a week at the age of seventy. But perhaps sympathy and common sense did not reveal to many that Old Age Pensions constitute a great stabilising measure, securing, *pro tanto*, the maintenance of productive industry.

One of the maladies of competitive industrialism is the chronic tendency of manufacturing production to outrun demand, and the consequent reaction, which involves more or less protracted unemployment and distress. The common notion has been that the natural precaution of saving in time of prosperity to meet the " rainy day " is the last word of political as of personal wisdom in the matter. But it will become clear, when the economic process is thought out, that largely increased saving throughout the community, however advisable for any individual as against the rest, and however absolutely expedient as against foolish and wasteful expenditure, must, in other regards, tend (1) on the one hand to check production, since it is a lessening of demand ; and (2) on the other hand to provide superfluous credit capital for an extra production which, in the terms of the case, is not called for by demand for products.

If the saved credit could be really turned to other kinds of production, the dilemma would be solved. Where industry has reached the limits of demand for goods easily produced, mechanically or otherwise, in any quantity, there lie open indefinite possibilities of new demand for products and services giving employment to higher forms of labour—

intellectual and artistic. But the individual need to provide for old age and sickness by saving and investment closes or limits this outlet for labour no less than it limits the expansion of simple manufactures. Thus the very instinct of thrift, taking the dictated economic form of credit-saving for investment, necessarily tends, beyond a certain point, to curtail potential industry and total wealth ; and saving must become either a matter of competition between credit-savers for the limited field of investment that is safe, or a speculative seeking for investments that will yield higher return. The result is an immense amount of unsuccessful enterprise, often exploited by professional promoters.

In so far as this evil is at any time reduced for existing industrial countries, it is (thus far) commonly by reason of expansions of world-trade, which means adequate demand from outside for industrial products. Such expansion in recent years, concurring with other causes, has reduced the demand for State debt stock, with its low rate of interest ; and continued expansion promises to keep interest chronically high for a long time to come. But at every depression in international trade the trouble recurs ; and the shrinking in the field of profitable investment always tends to double the depression by intensifying the shrinkage of demand for products. It is thus eminently desirable on economic grounds that the consuming power of the most easily depressed sections of the population should be maintained ; and Old Age Pensions and national insurance against invalidity and unemployment are alike advisable on this score, no less than on that of prevention of distress.

Humanity and economic science here join hands : it is the panic-mongers who bewail discouragement of thrift and cry " pauperization " that are economically astray. They habitually confuse " thrift " with saving for investment. It takes a tolerably thrifty person to get much satisfaction out of five shillings a week ; and myriads of poor folk are thrifty perforce all their lives long without being able to save money enough to yield them £13 a year of interest or annuity. If such citizens, and some who *can* contrive so much, being secured that stipend in old age, scrape and pinch a little less throughout life in order to purchase to that extent " better life," they have so far helped to maintain decent life conditions for the industrial mass as well as for themselves. Their expenditure makes easier the saving done by others.

This fact furnishes a valid answer to all those who repudiate the conception of " natural right " and substitute for it that of " public utility." A sound citizen, it might be supposed, would accept the real content of the concept of " natural right," to wit, the ideal of reciprocity, to the extent of agreeing to do for the aged poor in general something of what he would desire to have done for himself were he in the same case. Such sympathy was in fact professed by the Conservative advocates of Old Age Pensions in the past. But even if we put the principle of reciprocity wholly in suspense on the score of the danger of an uncalculating altruism, we find that the policy of direct help is at this point justified both positively and negatively—positively in respect of the accruing furtherance of industry ; negatively in respect of the lessening of the misery which the pensions are established to avert. The welfare of the State is not safeguarded but depressed by leaving masses of unrelieved aged indigence to blot the spectacle of industrial civilization.

" Laissez-faire," indeed, is not done-with as a principle of rational limitation of State interference, but it is quite done-with as a pretext for leaving uncured deadly social evils which admit of curative treatment by State action.

§ 4

So much is admitted on all sides, in fact, in respect of such an institution as the Labour Exchanges. These are run at the State's cost. But effectual provision against misery from unemployment will obviously not be attained until there is in force a comprehensive system of State Insurance ; and, whatever attitude may be taken up by Conservatism on that head when the recent measure comes to be extended, there is no dubiety as to its attitude on the taxation which is to yield the required revenue for new social expenditure. Already the two parties have joined battle over the provision of the revenue required to pay

Old Age Pensions ; and the ground has been taken on both sides in full consistency with their general inspirations and ideals, their historic bias and their general commitments.

Tariffism, that is to say, is the counter move to Liberalism in national finance. Whatever were the immediate tactical motives of the Conservative resort to Protectionism in 1903, the tariffist movement inevitably tended to become a revenue policy as against the revenue policy adopted by the party of Free Trade. Whatever were its pretences as regarded the " binding together " of the Empire, the prevention of unemployment, and the checking of emigration, it of necessity became avowedly a plan for " broadening the basis of taxation " ; and the nominal leader of the tariffist party in 1908 actually took his ground on the claim that such a fiscal policy would yield the revenue required for Old Age Pensions, and that " Free Trade finance " could not do so. " The dregs of Free Trade finance " was the description given beforehand of the Budget of 1909 by the tariffist side. In other words, the tariff was pitted as a mode of taxation against any extension of direct taxes or any new taxation on the basis of land values.

Under such circumstances, nothing could be more obvious than the insincerity of the pretence of keeping out foreign goods by means of import duties, and so " making work " for the unemployed. Either the manufactures to be taxed were to come in as before in order to yield the required revenue, or the whole extra revenue was to be yielded by the new taxes on food ; and the latter development was expressly excluded in the pledges of the leaders of the movement. Yet not even the flagrancy of the contradiction between the two promises of revenue from manufactured imports and exclusion of such imports could lead to a withdrawal of the former. Promises to " make work " were necessary to win working-class votes, and the promises of a new basis of taxation were no less necessary to win votes from the middle and upper classes.

Many manufacturers and most landlords, of course, were at once captured by the prospect of raised prices and raised rents ; but the large sections of the well-to-do classes who were not in trade, and not landowners, had to be gained by other lures. It was done by holding out the hope of partial

relief from Income Tax and other direct imposts on wealth
by means of a fiscal system which burdened the mass. [1]

Tariffism, then, is essentially a system of taxation framed
in the interest of the well-to-do and wealthy classes. As
things stand, the workers are actually taxed by the subsisting duties on tea, coffee, sugar, tobacco and liquors, out
of proportion to their incomes, tea and sugar and tobacco,
in particular, being taxed by quantity and not by quality.
Taking all of these taxes into account, we find that the
share of an average workman's wage absorbed by the State
is relatively larger than the share taken from the rich by
those taxes and Income Tax together.   Indeed, if we make
any reservation of the income needed to sustain life, the
pressure of the " breakfast-table " taxes on proletarian
incomes is noticeably heavy in proportion to the pressure
of all taxes together on large incomes.   Upon all the
principles that make for Liberalism, then, it is the business
of Liberal politicians to aim at relieving the incomes of the
poor, and transferring the pressure to the shoulders of
wealth.

§ 5

It is well to put this proposition as directly as possible.
Those who resent as " plunder " adjustment of taxation
which relieves the poor " at the expense of the rich," as
the phrase goes, are merely applying a theory of taxation
which has never been thought out, in the light of a theory
of society which has been still less considered, At what,
let us ask, is taxation supposed to aim ?   Merely at obtain-
ing anyhow so much revenue for the State ?   Obviously
not : no civilized State avowedly plunders or fleeces its

---

[1] Thus Mr Balfour, speaking at York on 12th January, 1910, said :
" I have long thought that there are immense advantages in what is
called broadening the basis of taxation, in raising the necessary
revenue for national purposes so far as possible from indirect taxation
and as little as possible from other taxation. (Cheers.) I do not
believe I shall live to see the time when Mr Gladstone's ideal will be
carried out, and the Income Tax will be abolished. I should like to
see that time—(laughter)—but I do not think I shall." It need
hardly be remarked that Gladstone's idea of abolishing the Income
Tax has long been abandoned by all Liberals, and was never held
even by Gladstone as involving new indirect taxation.

subjects at random. All profess to set up, in some sense, equality of pressure : all profess to seek justice. Even the theoretic deniers of " natural rights " normally stipulate for " fairness " in new imposts, apparently affirming here some " natural ought." But what then is, in effect, fairness in taxation ? Not absolute equality of payment : an absolute poll-tax is nowhere now imposed by a civilized State. It is recognized that any given poll-tax, to be worth the trouble of levying, would be relatively crushing to the poor and relatively light for the rich, and that a national poll-tax must therefore not be imposed. This is either a principle of right or a rule of expediency : for our present purpose it matters not which. On either view, riches and poverty are to be taxed at different rates.

If we apply the rule of reciprocity or " natural right," given the primary rule that inequality of burden or pressure is wrong, we must soon arrive at the Smith-Mill formula of " equality of sacrifice " ; and upon any reasonable interpretation of that rule we should be led to an adjustment of taxation which would tax " the poor " far more lightly and the rich by consequence more heavily than they ever have been taxed. The late Sir Louis Mallet, in his pamphlet on *The National Income and Taxation* (Cobden Club, 1886), uses as an argument against the principle the fact that it might be made to lead to a tax of £80,000 on a man with an income of £100,000. But the fact that " no line or limit is possible " is not a valid argument against the use of the principle as a guide to direction *when no better principle can be formulated*. And none has been, within the limits of practical politics. In point of indirect taxation, the workman is obviously more pinched by the taxes on his drink, tobacco, tea and sugar than is the rich man. For the one, the tax is a very small fraction of income ; for the other a large one. As regards direct taxation, probably every Income Tax ever imposed has recognized the necessity of some discrimination or gradation ;[1] and very few British politicians now deny either the rightness or the expediency of reserving a " living income " which shall be entirely

[1] The point is discussed in some detail in the present writer's pamphlet, *The Great Budget*. (Liberal Publication Department.)

untaxed.[1] On that principle, if on any, the poor are
" relieved at the expense of the rich "—taking " expense "
in the empirical or monetary sense ordinarily given to it.

If, in disregard of all the fore-cited considerations, upon
which all civilized fiscal systems do actually in some measure
proceed, the term " expense " be persisted in by way of
begging the question, it will be found that the opponent of
so-called " democratic " taxation has again raised issues
the solution of which cannot tell in his favour. What, at
bottom, is " expense " in relation to the maintenance of the
entire social machine? Obviously, money payment is
merely a mediate or secondary adjustment : what ultimately
maintains the State either as a political or as a social whole
is the sum of the activities of its members ; and of these
the fundamental and essential activity is production, in
the full sense of the term—that is, the producing of the
given thing where it is wanted. Production is the formula
of all services. Expense, then, is the last analysis, is
expense of labour, of service : the State is maintained by
those who render necessary service. And even if we define
the lending of capital or credit as a service in the more
general sense, we shall still be forced to discriminate, for
fiscal purposes, either by a test of right or by a text of
expediency.

If by the former, we begin again at the problem of
" natural right." Does the opponent of discriminate
taxation (who normally flouts, as we have seen, any idea of
" natural right ") himself revert now to just such a formula,
making it mean that every man has a natural right to keep
all he has got ? If so, the formula has put it in the most
plainly untenable sense. So to delimit the right of *keeping*
as to exclude the right of each to take all he can get, it is
necessary to call in the right of possession given by law ;
and inasmuch as law always sanctions taxation, the alleged
right to keep all falls at once to the ground. The only
further application of the idea of right that the case admits
of is the raising of the test of the mode of acquisition of
property or income ; and here we come again to the con-

[1] Mr. Harold Cox is the only exception I can recall. [It is, however, noteworthy that in Germany taxation, both before and since
the War, falls on incomes far below the British line of exemption.]

sideration of the " expense of labour," the degree of vital
importance in public service.

Of the three requisites to wealth production—land,
capital, and labour—the last (understood as including
control or organization) is clearly the social determinant,
inasmuch as it is the source of the capital, which is the
source of the command of land.   The land and the capital
are, abstractly speaking, appropriations, made primarily
by force and secondarily through acquisition of the second.
The most loosely extended application of the theory of right,
then—in the sense of what might be termed " non-natural
right," as being the contrary of what is meant by natural
right—does but lead us once more to the conclusion that
taxation is fitly to be discriminated so as to press less
heavily upon the poor than the rich, and thus to keep
their sacrifice proportionate.

And if it be urged that a man may grow rich through
sheer wages or direct reward for services, as in the case
of the famous actor, the famous artist or singer, the jockey,
or the physician, we are again led to the principle of discrimination by the test of the general or primary importance
of the service rendered, taking the kinds of service as wholes
or totals.   The services of any one great surgeon or artist
are on any broad view more important than those of any
one labourer ; but when we have regard to the sheer
maintenance of the State, the total services of any one
of the well-rewarded *classes* are clearly less vital than those
of the producing classes commonly so-called.   The labourers
collectively, and the community as such, can exist without
the services of the artist, the jockey, or even the surgeon :
these classes in turn cannot exist without the services of the
labouring class commonly so-called.   So that, as regards
the classes under notice, the argument from conventional or
non-natural right leaves our principle of controlled and
discriminated taxation still undisturbed.

Less simple, perhaps, is the case of that section of the
community which renders the great services of organizing
labour, inventing methods of production, and " finding
markets "—a class which we have above included, for
purposes of social analysis, under the head of " labour "
itself.   Here, if anywhere, the principle of conventional
right may be urged with some plausibility as against that of

equality of sacrifice or the adjustment of taxation to
capacity. The organizer, the inventor, and the market-
finder are clearly to be reckoned as no less indispensable
to the " labouring class " than the latter is to them. Numbers of labouring men could of course subsist primitively
by their own tilling of the soil, with unpatented implements,
and by simple barter with other producers of necessities,
independently of organizers, inventors, and market-finders.
But the *number* of workers who could so exist would certainly be much smaller than the number now subsisting.
Tho whole class of industrial " heads," then, is to be
reckoned a vital part of the existing organism of the State,
a part without which, indeed, the State would disintegrate.
How then, upon any principle of natural or non-natural
right, shall we tax its members, as compared with " hands "
or labourers ?

In all likelihood, they will be collectively ready either
to stand by the simple test of reciprocity (recognizing a
natural right of the labouring unit to be subjected only to
proportional sacrifice) or to apply the test of expediency.
It could not be pretended that the class of " heads " under-
goes a greater expense of labour, a greater drain on life,
than the class of " hands." Service for service, theirs is
in general rewarded out of all proportion to its stress, as
compared with the case of the labourers. And as between
the two orders, there can be no absolute claim of superiority
of importance for the heads, inasmuch as they could not as
such exist without the hands. " Right," then, cannot be
urged for them as against the principle of discriminate
taxation save by reversion to positions already overturned ;
and if there is to be any further discussion of that principle
it must be on those grounds of expediency on which Conservative politicians profess normally to stand.

§ 6

We have here, in fact, by way of closing loopholes, carried
the discussion of conventional or non-natural right in
regard to taxation further than most practical politicians
would think of doing, on either side. Candidates for
Parliament are not wont to repudiate the law of reciprocity.

It is only the extremists of the arm-chair who discuss the claims of labour with a disavowal of sympathy, or a refusal to put themselves, for purposes of political ethics, in the place of the toiler. Still, the extremist has to be met ; and, having met him, we may now fitly turn to the other line of test. That is to say, we have to ask whether or not it is to the interest of the State or community to adjust taxes expressly to the burden-bearing power of classes and individuals, or, in other words, to apply in taxation the principle of equality of sacrifice. The problem of expediency is here that of the maintenance or promotion of the total prosperity and efficiency of the State. Do we, by taxing capital or incomes, or super-taxing large incomes, or specially taxing unearned incomes or unearned gains from land-values, tend in any way to impair the efficiency or welbeing of the community ?

If we do, in any reasonable sense of the terms, we are at once barred. Here the two ideals will coincide. No doctrine of right can countervail a demonstration that its application will injure society, as a whole. Concerning any possible tax, indeed, it is possible to argue that it works " injury " to some one, not merely in the sense of taking from him some of his income, but of putting him to inconvenience and moving him to indemnify himself by means which to some extent disturb industry or commerce. " Every tax," said J. S. Mill, " produces a great deal of incidental mischief, and the problem is to find which are those that produce the least."[1] The same verdict is embodied in the German saying that " Every old tax is good : every new tax is bad." Mill, admitting the harmfulness of indirect taxes, brought a " very serious " indictment against the Income Tax. " One who knew city people very well predicted, when the Income Tax was first laid on by Sir Robert Peel, that the consequence of it would be a great deterioration of commercial morality. Since then, we have always been hearing complaints of the growth of commercial dishonesty. . . I have never doubted that the tax has greatly contributed to it. A false return of Income Tax has probably been in innumerable instances the first dereliction of pecuniary integrity." Most city men

Letters of J. S. Mill, 1910, ii. p. 316.

probably, would now smile at the " since then," and the whole theorem. Commerce was sufficiently complicated by dishonesty before there was any Income Tax ; and it is not commonly claimed that either in the United States or in the Levant, where Income Tax is not levied, commerce is perceptibly more honest than in England.

To such a problem we must apply a simple rule of common sense. Since indirect taxes promote smuggling, even as direct taxes give rise to false returns, we must treat the moral difficulties as balancing each other, and try the two methods of taxation by the tests of (1) equity in respect of incidence or sacrifice ; (2) good or bad effect on total production and distribution ; and (3) proportion of yield to cost of collection. This is what is meant by effect on society as a whole. If a tax not merely irritates payers and affects prices but clashes with all canons of fairness, yields badly, and positively diminishes production, it is plainly inexpedient. Conversely, a proof that a given course thoroughly defensible as right is also expedient, must be held conclusive. If indeed any State could be proved capable of advancing its total wealth and well-being by a social system which recognized only labour rights to property, no arguments against Socialism which admitted such proof would be valid against the system, save by a reversion to a theory of " right " which ignores expediency. It is precisely the lack of such proof that keeps Socialism at the status of a Utopia, an ideal.

But inasmuch as no one can rationally dispute the fundamentally essential character of labour, it is the duty of all who profess to make social well-being their first political principle to safeguard, in fiscal as in other matters, the well-being of the " labour class." The only relevant counter-argument would be a thesis to the effect that labour abounds and will abound sufficiently without any lightening of its lot. And to this thesis we can offer a confident negative. To argue that labour is sure to be forthcoming under any conditions, and that there is no more need to intervene socially in its interest than in that of wealth or capital, would be not only to exclude ethics once for all from politics, but to refuse to apply science to the fiscal problem.

It would indeed be unjust to impute to tariffists in general

any such avowed attitude of moral indifferentism. They
profess to have the interests of labour, the welfare of the
mass, especially at heart. A raised standard of comfort
for the workers is their most commonly professed object.
Obviously, if the improvement of the workers' lot by a
tariff system would justify that as a fiscal policy, such
improvement by other fiscal methods would be justifiable
if such methods involved no countervailing evils. On this
head, however, we have the usual sinister and significant
conflict of voices on the Conservative side. The very
leaders who declare that tariffism is above all things a movement—a fiscal movement—to benefit labour, and who
repeatedly plan fiscally for the benefit of the " agricultural "
class, expressly contend that the object of benefiting labour,
or bettering the lot of any class, is not a licit fiscal motive. [1]
Finance Bills, they contend, should aim solely at the raising
of revenue. [2] Such a position obviously leaves open, and
indeed points to, the further contention that fiscal relief
to the working class in particular is either unnecessary
in the national interest or positively inexpedient.

§ 7

It is necessary, then, to establish its positive expediency ;
and the proofs are fivefold.

I. Efficiency of production demonstrably depends upon
standard of comfort, including in that term education.
Economists in general are now agreed on the paradox that
" cheap labour is dear labour " : that is to say, that low-paid
labour is relatively inefficient to the point of economic loss. [3]
Labour in India, and even in Japan, is excessively cheap ;
but even with this relative advantage, textile production
in India and Japan cannot compete with that of the far more

---

[1] On 18th April 1911, Mr. Balfour and other leading Conservatives
expressly argued in the House of Commons, in Committee on the
Parliament Bill, that the explicit aim of class betterment ought to
take a Finance Bill out of the class of " Money Bills," over which the
House of Lords are to have no control.

[2] This was maintained by Mr. Austen Chamberlain and denied by
Mr. Asquith.

[3] See *The Economy of High Wages*, by J. Schoenhof, 1892 ; and
The Wages Question, by Prof. F. A. Walker, 1884.

highly-paid textile industries of Britain. The same law holds in regard to the competition of low-paid and long-houred textile work in the Southern States of North America with that of the more highly-paid workers of the New England States, working a shorter day. At least a very much longer day was needed in the South to produce on competitive terms a few years ago. British labour, finally, is more highly paid and better-conditioned than that of either France or Germany, and its higher efficiency is practically proved by the resort of both of those countries to protective tariffs against British competition. If then a higher standard of comfort, as secured by trade union organization, legal control, and the play of a system of free imports, produces a higher efficiency of labour, any further raising of the standard of comfort by fiscal relief must be expected to raise efficiency yet higher.

II. Fiscal relief must tend to retain and attract the more efficient labour which, for other reasons, is attracted to the United States.

III. It is not disputed that British labour to-day is more efficient all round than it was in the days of the Corn Laws and dear bread.

IV. A number of judicious employers go out of their way to provide not only ideal ventilation but recreation rooms, pension funds, gratuitous dentistry, etc., for their workers, finding an economic reward in increased efficiency, as well as a higher reward in better human relations with their workers.

V. From the merely military point of view, the physical efficiency of the mass of the people is a highly important end. In the South African War the high percentage of inefficients among recent British recruits was gravely commented on by military experts;[1] and the commonness of defective teeth was assigned as one of the causes of the very high percentage of enteric fever.

It is difficult, in short, to conceive of a more thoughtless fiscal policy than one which repudiates primary concern for the standard of comfort of the mass of the people;

---

[1] It is hardly necessary now to remark on the overwhelming testimony of the same kind evoked by the strain of the World War.

especially when such a policy is bracketed with a professed policy of promoting efficiency all round.

If then there be any valid counter-plea, on lines of expediency, to the doctrine that fiscal policy should aim at the relief of the multitude, it must apparently lie in the direction of the idea that fiscal favouring of the labouring mass will tend somehow to minimize production, whether by setting the workers upon progressively reducing their working time or by " pampering " them to the point of making them ever less industrious. Such fears are not seldom privately expressed, with whatever measure of sincerity ; and indeed a not ungrounded fear of some such results actually moved many people at both the beginning and the end of the eighteenth century. At one time it was possible to say that large numbers of " the poor " were to be moved only by urgent want to work ; and that a little money in hand was sufficient at any time to turn them idle. Such facts are dwelt upon by Mandeville, in his annotations to his *Fable of the Bees*, early in the eighteenth century ; and some generations later the pleasure-loving tendencies of many of the working classes in industrial centres were pointed to as a constant stumbling-block to regular production. Still later, the cult of " Saint Monday " was a real factor in industrial life ; and to this day it has not wholly disappeared. Can it then be seriously argued that new developments of a similar kind might result from a fiscal favouring of the working mass ?

The decisive answer to such a suggestion is that regularity of industry has constantly progressed in the obvious ratio of, and as a plain result of, the rise in the standard of comfort. It is the experience of steady conditions of decent life that has educated the working class in steadiness of application. The more comfort, the less drunkenness ; the more thrift, the more assiduity. The notion of making the hands industrious by keeping them ill-paid has been exploded for all practical employers. In our own colonial politics, it has become a commonplace that the " native " is to be made more industrious by arousing in him new wants. In that sphere, indeed, it is common to hear pleas for hut-taxes or poll-taxes grounded on the same generalization : the argument being that a " want " is to be forced upon the indolent native by compelling him to find so much cash.

Here the psychological truth is irrationally turned to the account of oppression : a forced and artificial need is to be substituted for a genuine want, and is expected to work in the same way. In our own life the true principle emerges from the history of industry : the British workman is more steady with shorter working-time than with long ; with higher wages than with low. Having tasted comfort, he is progressively more willing to work to maintain it. The very formulation by organized labour of " the right to *work*," tells of an increasing loyalty to the law of service.

Types of idler and shirker doubtless remain ; and it may be urged that whereas in the eighteenth century such types tended simply to be killed out by misery and vice, a system of national fostering tends to preserve them. But here again organized labour gives no countenance to any ideal of pampering ; the promoters of the Right to Work Bill expressly demand the coercion of the idler. Even, then, though the scheme be unworkable as it stands, it tells not of a risk of encouraging unproductiveness, but of a real concern to maximize production, howbeit under good life conditions. In short, the fear that fiscal or any other real " protection " of labour will undermine industrial efficiency is chimerical.

It is true that working men, having their share in human perversity and short-sightedness, are at times unreasonable in their disputes with their employers, the younger men in some of the skilled trades being on occasion notably reckless alike of economic possibilities and of the suffering which their strikes inflict upon the worse-paid unskilled workers of the subsidiary kind. But it would be hard to find even an unsuccessful strike in which there was not some element of real grievance on the strikers' side ; masters having *their* share in human perversity and egotism. In the long run, the course of things industrial is determined by permanent economic conditions and factors, and the broad facts of competitive industrial life are always educating the workers in the mass.

We may speculate as to the amount of perversity that might come into play in a state of socialism that is clearly a long way off ; and if we always assume that the workers of a future age will be collectively no wiser than those of to-day, we may make a terrifying fancy-picture. But while industry is a matter of international competition, depending on the maintenance of markets, especially under free-trade conditions, it is impossible that organized labour should be long misdirected to the disadvantage of production. Each country's industry is conditioned by that of the others. Protracted perversity on the part of the workers of any country would bring its condign punishment in the loss of their own livelihood, inasmuch as their function would be taken up by rivals elsewhere. And that risk is safeguard enough.

§ 8

A very real danger, indeed, might be set up on this as on other sides if the workers of Britain were in the mass converted to tariffism : so converted, they would be committed to a policy of impairing the springs of production. In every backward industry they would be committed to protecting the home producer against the better machinery and organization, or the greater natural advantages, of the foreign competitor ; and only where home competition was keen would industries progress at all.

What would happen may be divined by comparing the actual history of the town of Coventry with the fate which would have been entailed upon it by a systematic policy of protective tariffs. A century ago, and later, it was mainly a place of silk manufacture, languishing as such under the full play of Protection. In the words of Mill : " The mere exclusion of foreigners from a branch of industry open to the free competition of every native has been known, even in England, to render that branch a conspicuous exception to the general industrial energy of the country. The silk manufacture of England remained far behind that of other countries of Europe, so long as the foreign fabrics were prohibited."[1] After Huskisson in 1826 substituted *ad valorem* duties for prohibition there came about a notable revival ; but even in that revival Coventry did not soon participate, through sheer persistence in the use of antiquated machinery.[2] In the day of Free Trade, again, other

[1] *Princ. of Pol. Econ.*, bk. v. ch. x. § 4.
[2] H. Martineau, *Hist. of the Thirty Years' Peace*, i. p. 480

textile industries necessarily flourished more than one for which France had natural and acquired advantages ; and Coventry did not keep pace with the growth of the cotton and woollen centres. But gradually other industries emerged : to trades of dyeing and the weaving of ribbons and trimmings, woollens, carpets and elastic webs, were added watch-making, bicycle-making, art metal-work, motor car-making and the manufacture of sewing-machines ; so that the population, which in 1841 was 30,000, and in 1871 only 37,000, had in 1907 risen to 91,000. Nowhere in France has the silk industry shown itself capable in the same period of sustaining such an increase of population.

As against such healthy discoveries and revivals, Coventry under a tariff system would have remained a place of vale-tudinarian industry, sustaining a small, discontented and unprogressive population. But, in the terms of the case, it is from Conservative and not from Liberal fiscal policy that such a truly fatal form of " pampering " is to be apprehended. Organized labour, thus far, repudiates the method. It would be strange, indeed, if it did not. The tariffist policy, in its relation to industry, really aims, as we have seen, not at raising wages but at raising prices, merely claiming that this will lead to that. Workers who have to make a fight for every rise in wages they obtain can well gauge the amount of effort they will require to make to secure the double rise in wages to which, on the theory, they would be entitled—the rise in proportion to the employer's extra profits, and the further rise to counter-balance the rise all round in cost of living. It is intelligible that in countries like the United States and Australia, where the main productive bases are the primary ones, and where the burden of artificially increased prices of manufactures falls mainly upon agricultural and other primary producers, the artisan minority may see its interest in a tariffist policy. In Britain, which earns its living mainly by manufactures and by such a form of primary production as coal-mining, which is insusceptible of pro-tection, the interests of the working mass coincide against tariffism. It must mean taxation of the labouring many as against the landowners and the manufacturers.

§ 9

Thus, on a full survey, the Liberal policy of fiscally relieving the working mass is seen to involve no risk of minimizing production, where the contrary policy precisely does. Does the Liberal fiscal policy, then, let us next ask, menace productivity or efficiency on the side of its taxation of wealth ? Such a risk is theoretically possible : fiscal exaction has admittedly been the main factor in the impoverishment of the once rich lands under the Ottoman Empire ; and in the struggle over the Budget of 1909, vaticinations were thrown out as to evils which were to flow from the " taxation of capital " as well as of income. They may be reduced to five positions : (1) Increasing taxation of wealth, by way of extra rates on super-incomes and death duties, will discourage the accumulation of capital, and so disadvantage industry. (2) It will further force rich men to curtail (a) charities, (b) their pleasures, (c) the non-economic employment they give on their estates to aged and other labourers, and (d) the pensions they voluntarily bestow on their aged and disabled employees. (3) Death duties tend to cripple industrial concerns by withdrawing capital necessary for working them. (4) The taxation complained of will further have the effect of driving capital abroad for investment. (5) In general, too, it will provoke evasion.

As usual, the Conservative objections are found to be reciprocally contradictory. If extra taxation of large incomes and large estates will discourage the saving of capital, it must be either (a) by inducing men to spend instead of saving, or (b) by disinclining them to carry on their wealth-earning activities. But if they spend more freely in order to escape super-taxation, their charitable and other non-economic outlays need not be affected, and will not be, save on the unpleasant hypothesis that they resolve to make poor folk suffer for the policy of a Liberal Government. If, on the other hand, they spend more in general consumption, on travel, on luxuries, or on art, they will be increasing the demand for labour, goods, and services. Outlay in foreign travel involves the export of British goods to make good the necessary letters of credit, or to redeem the gold or bank-notes taken from the country.

The argument as to the injury done to commercial concerns by the death duties seems a little more serious than the foregoing ; but that also is quite fallacious. Death duties are levied on admitted capital values. The inheritor of a commercial concern is called upon to pay a sum in proportion to its capital value, and, let us suppose, has to borrow the money. But, the concern being of the said value, he can borrow upon it like any other business man ; and the tax simply means a curtailment of his income. The doctrine that there is a fundamental economic difference between a tax on capital and a tax on income is in fact a superstition of the amateur economist.[1] The fiscal minister, faced by the problem of finding revenue, has to resort to different methods ; but all taxation in the end must work out as a deduction from incomes. And in this case it involves nothing more. It in no way checks or minimizes production. The taxed capitalist is stimulated to fresh efforts to increase his income.

It has accordingly been argued that, instead of concerning itself to secure mere equality of sacrifice—which is of course very difficult to measure—the State should simply tax alike the capitalist and the high earner up to the point at which the tax would prove unfruitful or repressive by causing limitation of effort. To this the Conservative, with his professed repudiation of " natural right," could offer no consistent objection. In point of fact the direct taxation

---

[1] It must be admitted that Mill objected to any tax upon savings as if it were fundamentally different from a tax upon income. (*Letters*, as cited, ii. p. 317.) But though he speaks of expediency, he is mainly thinking of justice. " No income-tax," he writes, " is really just, from which savings are not exempted " (*Princ. of Pol. Econ.*, bk. v. ch. iii § 4). Immediately, however, he recognizes the difficulty that the exemption could be " taken fraudulent advantage of, by saving with one hand and getting into debt with the other, or by spending in the following year what had been passed tax-free as saving in the year preceding." Further (§ 7), in discussing the general rule, sometimes laid down, " that taxation should fall on income, not on capial," he writes : " To provide that taxation shall fall entirely on income, and not at all on capital, is beyond the power of any system of fiscal arrangements. *There is no tax which is not partly paid from what would otherwise have been saved.*" Finally, he denies that in a wealthy country taxation of capital is injurious. " To take from capital by taxation what emigration would remove or a commercial crisis destroy, is only to do what either of those causes would have done, namely, to make a clear space for further saving."

thus far imposed by any of the more advanced countries on capitalists and high earners falls far short of causing limitation of effort, and may confidently be held to stimulate it. But if ever the principle of taxing to the limit of will-for-exertion should be adopted, it would be found that that limit also is very difficult to fix, inasmuch as individuals vary in response to pressures.

The argument from risk of evasion, again, employed by Mr Balfour against the super-tax of 1909, has obviously no more force against that than against Income Tax in general. Doubtless many people try, more or less successfully, to evade Income Tax; but no politician now admits that to be a valid argument against the impost. Indirect taxes in turn are evaded so far forth as there is successful smuggling. And on a survey of the circumstances, evasion of super-tax by the wealthy must be more and not less difficult than evasion by those who pay on profits and fees below the super-tax limit.

Mr Balfour's argument may have been, in intention, a variant on the thesis of "export of capital." It is argued by tariffists that such export takes place from this country on a dangerous scale in virtue of free trade; and it is further contended that the super-tax and the increase in death duties reinforce the impulse to seek foreign investments. Again the theory fails to bear the slightest scrutiny. If capitalists in large numbers should sell commercial concerns at home in order to invest the proceeds in foreign stock or estate, they would simply stimulate home industry (1) by enabling the purchasers of those concerns to produce more cheaply, inasmuch as forced sales mean low prices; and (2) by promoting the export of British produce to make good the money drafts conveying the capital abroad. The income from the foreign investments would of course arrive in the form of goods, mainly food and raw material, thus tending to keep the prices of these low for the home consumer; and upon this income the receiver would pay Income Tax as before, unless indeed he found it easier to conceal income from foreign than from home sources. There is a possibility of that kind. But it is to be guarded against, like other risks of evasion, by increased vigilance in the Revenue service. All the while, the concerns sold at home will continue to yield at least the old income, which will pay the tax as before. Thus the total revenue from Income Tax will be increased.

On the old view of capital interwoven with the wage-fund theory, this of course could not take place. There was " only so much capital in existence," and if any went abroad there must be less at home. But that again is a complete fallacy. Credit-capital is an economic quantity which expands and contracts in terms of productive activity. A concern which is worth a given sum while trade is good is " worth " much less, or it may be nothing, in a prolonged depression. And home industry can never be impoverished by the investing of capital abroad.

Such investment means one of three processes : (a) The leaving of the price of exported goods, carrying services, etc., to be invested abroad instead of being balanced by imported goods and return services ; (b) the express export of goods to make good drafts ; or (c) the sending of foreign scrip held here to make good the fresh investment. The three processes amount to the same thing, since the balancing of a foreign loan by foreign scrip already held means merely change of source of interest ; and the leaving of interest on foreign investments to accumulate for further foreign investment, is only a delaying of the receipt of the interest, unless, of course, the owner ultimately goes out to his capital. The latter event—expatriation—might conceivably result from resentment of home taxation ; but inasmuch as taxation of wealth is on the increase in all civilized countries, and increased cost of living results in all of them from tariff policy, it is hardly worth serious consideration.

As for simple investment of British capital abroad, it can mean, in terms of the foregoing analysis, no curtailment of home production. The notion that sound concerns languish here for lack of the capital invested abroad is a chimera. Money might indeed at times be cheaper if loan credit-capital were forced to accumulate at home for lack of foreign openings ; but inasmuch as foreign investment means for us either the fresh export of British goods or a temporarily lessened import of foreign goods, the lack of some of which means further home demand, the total result is increase of production. Labour is needed to make the export possible, and any concern actually producing or manufacturing to meet demand can always either borrow what capital it needs or produce on credit. Credit expands on simple expansion of demand. On the other hand, a refusal to lend credit-capital abroad would be a refusal to undertake increased production, of which the result would be actual shrinkage in the market value of the withheld capital. Capital can be profitably employed in production only to meet demand ; and no accumulation of it can be nationally useful unless demand for products is proportionally increased.

If, in the face of these considerations, any politician should remain sincerely concerned about export of capital, he may be either reassured or otherwise consoled to learn that in France and Germany, under protectionist fiscal systems, the outcry against such export is increasingly loud—much louder than in Britain—and takes the shape of impassioned demands for legislative prohibition. Seeing that such prohibition, to be effective, must involve either lessened export of goods or increased imports, the outcry in question is a specially notable sample of the economic incoherence of tariffist thinking. In point of fact, tariffs on imports must tend to increase foreign investments by putting difficulties in the way of the return of goods for goods. If there be added a direct (and effective) veto on foreign loans, either more imports must arrive in direct exchange for exports, or less goods will be exported.

A hardly less dramatic illustration of intellectual incoherence, indeed, is supplied by the successive dicta of the nominal leader of the tariffist party in Britain on this same problem of export of capital. In 1903 Mr Balfour expressly argued that export of capital and the consequent receipt of interest from abroad was a national advantage inasmuch as it secured for us cheap imports of food and raw material.[1] His fear was that the export of capital was coming to an end, and many of his followers averred that we were in point of fact exporting our foreign scrip to pay for the food and goods we required. It is a memorable fact that the same leader in 1908 cried shame on his antagonist for expressing satisfaction in the continuance of the investment of British capital abroad.

[1] Speech in the House of Commons on May 28, 1903, rep. in *Fiscal Reform*, 1906, p. 33.

§ 10

While the fiscal policy actually associated with Liberalism is thus seen to be economically and socially sound, as well as morally vindicated by the law of reciprocity, the antagonistic policy is demonstrably the reverse. As a mere means of raising revenue for the United Kingdom at the present time, a tariff system is open to every kind of objection. On the pretext of " binding the Empire together," it is proposed to tax corn, meat, and dairy produce, thus making the successful continuance of " the Empire " a matter of specific hardship to the mass of the people. Such hardship might perhaps be reluctantly accepted, even for the purpose of guarding against a vague and utterly unauthorized menace of " separation," if the mass of the people were satisfied that the burden was adjusted to capacity all round. But when the method proposed is obviously framed in the interests of a single rich class, to wit, the landholders, the policy in question can be relieved from the charge of iniquity only by being convicted of folly.

Ignorance of economic history may perhaps make possible for some the belief that a tax on corn and other foods will benefit the " agricultural " class in general.; but such ignorance on the part of professed statesmen would be criminal. It is past dispute that in the first half of the nineteenth century, when " agriculture " in Britain was rigidly protected by the Corn Laws, there was more agricultural distress than has ever existed since.[1] Five parliamentary inquiries were made on the subject between 1816 and 1836, and appeals for relief were chronic. The fact was that the landlords alone profited steadily by the restriction of imports. In every time of scarcity, indeed, high prices temporarily benefited the farmers : but inasmuch as the high prices invariably led to extended cultivation, at raised rents, a few years of plenty were sufficient to reduce most of them to the verge of bankruptcy. And throughout the entire period, the economic position of the agricultural labourer was probably worse than it had ever been since the Black Death.

---

[1] Details are given in the author's *Trade and Tariffs*, pp. 75, 76, 82-83.

It would be difficult to imagine a more undesirable system than one under which the prosperity of the farmer class is artificially made to depend upon dearth. Under Free Trade, agricultural depression did indeed set in when, in the late 'seventies, the United States policy of granting new land to farmers for a term of years without rent, on the sole condition of cultivating, led to an abnormal and " non-economic " production of American wheat. But the agricultural loss caused in this country by the importation of that cheap wheat was rapidly passed on to the class best able to bear it, namely, the landowners ; and the returning prosperity of farming remains specially associated, as always under Free Trade, not with dearth but with plenty. Had the Corn Laws been re-established a generation ago, the farmers would have been temporarily relieved by the hardship of the multitude, whereafter the whole gain would have gone to the landowners, a state of things incompatible with any pretence of fiscal justice.

The plea that a " small " duty on imported corn would not appreciably raise the price of bread, can hardly be regarded as otherwise than frivolous. If the price of bread is not to be appreciably raised, the plea for encouraging agriculture, constantly put forward by food-taxers, is purely fraudulent. It is, further, a matter of invariable fiscal experience that protective duties begin at a low figure, and are soon progressively raised to a high one. The existing corn duties in France and Germany are six times as high as that now proposed by British tariffists, but they began at almost exactly the latter figure. Their present effect, as has been repeatedly shown, is to raise enormously the incomes of the large landowners ; the great mass of the small holders raising little more than the corn needed for their own consumption. Land in Germany, in particular, has risen to a price at which the latest buyer can make no more profit than does the British farmer under Free Trade. The gain has gone " unto him that hath."

Discussion on the proposed food duties, further, has duly ignored the effect of the proposed duties on meat and dairy produce. If any considerable revenue is to be raised from food duties, and the tax on corn is to remain inconsiderable, those on other foods must be serious. We are invited to " build up the Empire " by a policy of stinting the food of the mass of the people, at a time when the degeneration of the town population is declared by leading personages of the tariffist class to be a serious national danger. And the flagrant folly of the entire tariffist scheme is enhanced by the further proposal to reduce the duty on tobacco. National stamina is to be built up by making narcotics cheap and food dear.

If, as seems possible, the proposal to tax food be abandoned by the tariffist school—despite their primary declaration that their object is to bind the Empire together by Colonial Preference, which can be given only by taxing food or raw materials—the tariff policy will remain open to the same class of fatal objections. Either the tariff is to yield a considerable revenue or it is not. The extra revenue provided by the Liberal Budget of 1909 was some sixteen millions ; and the tariffist party professed to contemplate raising the full sum by its special methods. An average duty of 10 per cent. on all imported " manufactures" was the proposal before the country ; and it was proclaimed that upon imported manufactures alone this would yield some £15,000,000. All the while, the same politicians were assuring the working classes that the primary object of a tariff upon manufactures was to exclude foreign goods, and so " make work " for the unemployed at home. The goods were to be kept out for the sake of the workers, and at the same time were to come in for the sake of the revenue they would yield. Never before in the political history of any nation has there been witnessed, on any similar scale, such a combination of imbecility and effrontery in the programme of a powerful party.

If, putting the fraud and folly aside, we assume that the goods in question are to continue to come in, the working class being thus thrown over as soon as their votes are obtained, the policy incurs no less fatal objections. Of the £150,000,000 worth of " manufactured goods " imported in an average of recent years, only £50,000,000 worth, roughly speaking, are completely manufactured goods, ready for the final consumer. The rest are articles destined for further manufacture ; in other words, they are the virtual raw material of great industries. Leather, paper, chemicals, dyes, steel, pig-iron, copper and other metals are the principal types. Taxes on such articles are open to exactly the objections which the leaders of tariffism have all along admitted to be decisive against taxation of raw materials commonly so-called. If it be harmful to industry to tax wool, it must be harmful to tax leather. If it be expedient to protect tanners, as tariffists have actually promised to do if returned to power, it is expedient to protect sheep-breeders.

Particularly gross is the confusion of principle in the tariffist camp on the subject of the effect of a tax on semi-manufactures as regards primary production. It has been repeatedly argued[1] that the decline of Britain from the first to the third place among the nations as a producer of iron is due to the adoption of a tariff policy by our rivals, and to our persistence in a policy of free imports. On the very face of the case the inference is false, since only two countries of the many under a tariff system have exceeded our output of iron. The very simple facts which explain the situation are that the United States possess an enormously greater store of iron-ore than we, and that since the invention of the Gilchrist-Thomas process for working phosphoric iron Germany in turn has come into possession of greater iron resources than ours, her formerly unworkable ores being now as useful as others. Under any possible fiscal system, her iron output would now exceed ours.[2]

The argument that a tax on iron imports would raise our output of iron to its old proportional level obviously implies a tax on iron-ore ; and this is expressly justified on the score that a forced production of native iron-ore means more work for the labouring class. Yet the same school, seeking another class of votes, are found promising shipowners that a tax on pig-iron and steel will benefit them by forcing the importation of raw ore instead of semi-manufactured metals. So that iron-ore is to be excluded for the sake of the iron miners, while it is to be imported in increased quantities for the sake of the shipowners and the smelters. Thus does fraud continue to mark the propaganda, step by step.

Again ignoring the fraud for the argument's sake, we have to ask what would be the effect of excluding either (a) pig-iron or (b) steel bars. In the first case, we are told,

[1] Notably by Mr. Bonar Law.
[2] This pre-war proposition is of course profoundly affected by territorial changes. The fundamental argument is unchanged.

it would be an increased import of ore, the smelting of which would be a means of livelihood to many. But the iron thus produced would be required for advanced manufactures which we now export in large quantities, and which we *can* successfully export because our iron is cheaper than that of our rivals. Pig-iron is imported only when and because it is cheaper than would be home-manufactured pig-iron. The resulting rise in price would thus mean instant difficulty in our competition in foreign markets, in the ratio of the amount of ore imported. Exactly the same thing would happen in respect of import duties on steel. Upon that our ship-building and machine-making industries largely depend. A relative rise in their cost of production would mean arrest of demand, and the throwing idle of many thousands of workers. Thus we should have displaced labour on a great scale in highly skilled industries for the purpose of employing a less quantity of labour in one or two of the least skilled.

Our whole store of iron-ore being relatively small, the total fresh employment possible in the forced production of it would be little, and would be of a low grade. But, such as it was, it would simply mean the rapid exhaustion of the supply at a national loss. Exports of manufactures of metal being checked, the producers of ore would be in a position to do what has been chronically done by the German producers since 1879, namely, to export iron to their industrial rivals at a lower price than they charge to their fellow-countrymen..

This, the exact reverse of " making the foreigner pay," is the invariable result of the protection of raw or semi-raw materials, as well as of manufactures. The protected producer exacts the full market price at home, and disposes of any excess of his product at lower rates abroad. Thus the German iron-mining industry has repeatedly been kept going in times of depression by wholesale exports of iron at the lowest possible prices—a virtual enrichment of the foreigner at the cost of a depletion of the irreplaceable national stock of ore. Our own tariffists frequently profess to regard our export of coal, from this very point of view, as a national calamity. Yet the same men avowedly aim at the rapid reduction of our iron-ore, though it takes two tons of coal to smelt one of iron.

In the United States, where cities are now in large parts being built or rebuilt with steel, the depletion proceeds so rapidly as to alarm all thoughtful economists ; and it has there been urgently pleaded that the tariffs on iron and steel should be removed for the express purpose of securing foreign imports. Even the vast iron stores of the States, it has been calculated, will at the present rate of increase of exploitation be exhausted in some seventy years. And it is at this very time that the tariffist school in England proposes to adopt the policy which in the States is being recognized as ruinous.

When we turn to the effect of import duties upon manufactures in general, the weight of the economic objection becomes even greater. It is not certain, to begin with, that any raw material would escape taxation under a protectionist system. A tax on wool actually exists in the United States : it is one of the few possible forms of protection to the American farmer ; and its effect is to make the price of clothing in the States at least double the British price. Expert testimony avows that in much of the " woollen cloth " in the American market there is only 10 per cent. of wool. But even a tax on raw cotton is contemplated by some British tariffists as part of a system of the preferential promotion of cotton-growing within the Empire. There is no theoretic limit to the policy in question.

Assuming, however, that raw cotton were allowed under a tariffist system to remain on the free list, the great staple industry of cotton manufacture would still incur fatal burdens. Tariffists propose to tax chemicals, which would raise the cost of bleaching. They propose to tax dyes and colours, which would raise the cost of dyeing and printing. They propose to tax leather and non-illuminant oils, which would raise the cost of lubricants and driving-bands. Their tax on corn would raise the price of the flour used in cotton-dressing ; and their taxes alike on metals and on machinery would raise the cost of all machines. Unless the workers were to be plundered without the slightest compensation, their increased cost of living would further force up wages. Thus the relative economic advantage which makes possible the vast export of British cottons would be impaired or destroyed at every point.

It has been expressly argued, by Mr. Balfour for instance, that under Free Trade we run the risk of having to export our primary products—as coal—to pay for the raw materials and the food we require to import. But the effect of a tariff is precisely to force such an export, where Free Trade conditions leave it unforced. The United States, from which we take our largest import of foods and raw materials, do not want our coal in return, and cannot be so paid. If they do not take our manufactures in full, the account must be balanced by their import of the primary products of other countries which by exporting to the States balance their accounts with us. Our exports to those " neutral " markets are thus our typical means of purchasing food and raw material ; and it is precisely these exports that would be struck down by a tariff policy.

The industries, on the other hand, that could conceivably be expanded or newly built up by protecting them in the home market are as nothing in comparison with those which export more than the home market can absorb. In the terms of the case, such newly expanded or created industries, further, must represent wasteful application of capital and labour, so that on its constructive as well as on its destructive side a tariff policy would for this country be one of relative impoverishment. Those politicians who are wont to point to the expansion of German industry as a result of tariff policy may perhaps be at least made to pause by a perusal of the verdict of a high economic authority in Germany :

" As a matter of fact, it is to be feared, and unfortunately it has been also demonstrated, that the State in Germany is very ill-suited to be the guardian of the people in the departments of commerce, industry and agriculture. It cannot be denied that error after error is made. The organs of the State, majorities in the Bundesrat and the Reichstag, as well as the Government authorities, are not as capable as are private individuals of guiding the thousand and one threads of national production ; they do not possess sufficient technical knowledge, or the adaptability suitable for the constant and often rapid change in economic conditions. The organs of the State are not directly interested in the movements of production which they have brought about. The profits of practical undertakings do not accrue to them ; when mistakes occur they do not bear the loss. They easily fall into the temptation of encouraging a weak and unprofitable branch of industry because it happens to be failing and requires assistance, without first carefully examining whether it possesses any real vitality ; and in this way they waste the productive strength of the nation, which could be well used in other healthy branches of industry.

Through the State's interference with production it also happens that the average productiveness of many branches of industry is reduced, since the artificial raising of prices brings in its train the exploitation of less favourable productive conditions.   The artificial raising of profit means here a reduction of real productiveness, and so a social-economic loss results.   Mistakes which private enterprise has made are quickly corrected in open competition.   But when the State makes a mistake in guiding production on to the wrong path, the evil consequences easily become permanent.   Like paupers, the false foundations laid by the State receive dole after dole, and so lay a lasting burden on economic growth." [1]

The truth is that, in Germany as in other protected countries, the laying of a tariff is a matter of concession to the more powerful as against the less powerful interests. Even as in Britain, in 1846, the repeal of the Corn Laws was a result of the combination of the interests of the manufacturers with those of the general consumer and the labouring mass, under the auspices of a statesman concerned for the good of the majority, so in Germany in 1879 the imposition of a new tariff was a result of the combination of the interests of the landowners and manufacturers against the mass, under the auspices of a statesman concerned to create a new source of imperial revenue for military purposes.

Once imposed, a tariff is maintained or modified in respect of the influence of the interests concerned.   As another German economist has put it, it is not even industries that are protected, it is always firms.   Thus, though in countries like Australia the artisan class may hope to gain by a protective tariff of which the burden falls on the primary producers who cannot be protected, in the predominantly industrial countries a tariff is always a reversion to anti-democratic ideals of taxation.   The simple fact that in Britain the common monetary and working-time standard of comfort (questions of domestic economy apart) remains higher than in Germany, is a proof that it has the more democratic and the more economic fiscal system.

Thus, after scrutiny from every side, the strife between the Free-Trade and the tariffist systems is seen to be, in

[1] Prof. Arndt, *Deutschlands Stellung in der Weltwirthschaft*, 1911, pp. 103-4.

this country, the fresh extension into finance of the continuous and as it were fundamental struggle between democratic and anti-democratic ideals, the effort of the "haves" to keep and to accumulate at the expense of the "have-nots." And this effort is seen once more to be not only the negation of the greatest happiness of the greatest number, but in total tendency a minimization of national wealth. From the feudal system to the tariff system there is a long evolution; but the two have in common the purpose of a class domination and the effect of materially retarding civilization.

CHAPTER IV

LIBERALISM AND POLITICAL MACHINERY

§ 1.—*Theoretic Issues* [1]

THE simple principle of reciprocity, we have seen, obviously dictates equality of franchise rights. Either a given adult is a valid unit of the community, or he is not. If not, he is conceived to be disqualified mentally, morally, or physically ; and on any of these grounds he ought in consistency to be either under restraint or under probation. Where he is admittedly a working, valid, and law-abiding unit, his non-enfranchisement is sheer inequity. This being granted, the only relevant theoretic ground for the refusal of the vote to women is that they are not in general to be regarded as valid social units ; and as they have already the municipal suffrage on a house-holding basis, the refusal to extend to them the parliamentary franchise involves in consistency the proposal to withdraw the other.

Notably enough, the Society expressly organised to resist the demand for Woman Suffrage, instead of proposing such a withdrawal, made a point of stressing the importance of women's sharing in municipal work. Thus once more we are facing the chronic instinctive aversion to the consistent extension of an accepted principle which has marked all previous progress in political enfranchisement. Even among those who accept the principle of female enfranchisement, about a half refuse to let it apply to married women as such, offering it only to female property-holders or householders in their own right. Thus the more con-

---

[1] [It has seemed fitter to leave the sections on Woman Suffrage and Home Rule to stand as they did in the first edition, thus expounding the Liberal principles involved, than to put them retrospectively. It is involved in the argument that the solution actually reached in Ireland, under stress of evil post-war conditions, is not the best.]

servative can retort the charge of inconsistency upon many
of the less conservative, who include many women opposed
to adult suffrage for men no less than for women.

While inconsistency thus prevails in regard to the simple
problem of the franchise, it is not to be expected that there
will be general consistency or agreement on the problem
of legislative machinery. Thus we are still in the stage
of strife as to provincial government and as to the constitution of Parliament ; and in these cases too the
explanation is found to lie in the imperfect acceptance of
the principles ostensibly founded-on in all constitutional
government. You shall find one and the same Conservative
arguing in one and the same speech that while women are
competent to vote on municipal affairs they are incompetent to vote on national affairs ; and again that while
Irishmen should continue to vote on imperial affairs they
are not to be trusted with any management of strictly
Irish affairs. The argument as to the women is that they
lack either the training or the kind of judgment which
qualifies for the right handling of imperial affairs, while
they can judge very well upon local problems. Irishmen,
again, are pronounced dangerously unfitted to deal with
their home problems, while it is proposed to leave them
their full voting and representative power on issues concerning all the rest of the United Kingdom.

Before such anomalies of attitude and incongruities of
doctrine, it is impossible to doubt that we are in the
presence of infirmity of judgment on the part of those who
thus dogmatize as to the judgment of other people. All
round, evidently, there is at work the old fear that the
extension of political power or status will work harm ; and
so inveterate is this fear in some form that a generation
or more may well pass before we reach a solution of all
the problems implicated. Supposing either of the main
issues of 1912—Home Rule and Adult Suffrage—to be
more or less completely solved within the lifetime of the
existing Parliament, there will still remain the vexed
question of the Second Chamber, as to which the old
fear of the play of democratic principles is ostensibly most
prevalent. But as any solution of either of the two former
will have to run the gauntlet of two years of political
suspension before becoming law, it may be well to discuss

all alike, in so far as such discussion can be supposed to
count for anything in modifying opinion.

On the theme of Woman Suffrage, as on that of the
Second Chamber, there is notably diversity of view among
Liberals as well as between them and Conservatives ;
and the two issues are thus the likelier to be protracted
in comparison with that of Home Rule, on which professed
Liberals are now nearly all substantially agreed, though
the men who broke with Liberalism on that score a generation ago are still to be reckoned with. That their withdrawal was in many cases a result of imperfect affinities
for Liberalism is to be inferred from the completeness with
which they assimilated the creed and practice of their
Conservative allies. But an old fear, even if it could
impel so far, may conceivably be overcome in time ; and
as regards the theory and the usage of Second Chambers,
discussion must clearly persist for the present in the
Liberal ranks.

§ 2.—*Woman Suffrage*

It is not to be denied that the volume of opinion against
this extension of the franchise is very great ; and few
doubt that a strict referendum on the point would elicit
an overwhelming veto whether or not the women themselves were polled. Yet there can be no valid theoretic
answer to the claim.[1] Those who hold the opinion that
women as such are not valid units of the community ought
in consistency to condemn the municipal franchise for
women on that score ; but this no one now seems to do.
The argument that " the balance of voting power should
be with those who possess the balance of fighting power "
is clearly untenable ; for no one can tell how the balance
of fighting power really lies. It finally lay with Cromwell
on the Parliamentary side in the Great Rebellion : in the
absence of Cromwell it would have lain on the other side.
No one to-day, outside of Ulster, dreams of applying the

---

[1] The fact that woman suffrage is most loudly urged in connection
with methods of unexampled violence and uproar by women may be
urged against any concession upon that particular claim, but not
against claims of law-abiding women.

fighting test ; and a Home Ruler who uses the physical-force argument is encouraging Ulster to resort to rebellion. The argument is, in fact, a deliberate negation of the higher principle of rational appeal which in every constitutional State has now supplanted the physical-force theory of government. Yet some Liberals who use it are found to be champions of backward nationalities, to whom that theory would hold out no hope. The old argument that women should not have votes because they " cannot fight " in defence of the State is a still more patent sophism. Honestly applied, it would disfranchise not only the chaplains and doctors in an army, as well as the women nurses, but the multitude of males pronounced physically unfit for military service, and indeed all who, in any war, are sure to remain non-combatants. Among these would be most of the legislators. All the while, the men of the fighting forces are actually disfranchised [1912] as the law stands ; and no party proposes to enfranchise them.

Much more respectable in this case is the plea of social danger. In its strongest form, that plea dwells on the unprecedented multitude of indifferent voters whom woman suffrage would at present enfranchise, and whose votes would in a high proportion be likely to be saleable, by reason of their indifference. To this plea it can but be replied that the indifference or objection of seven women out of ten does not justify the refusal of the vote to the three who want it, and who, it may be, pay taxes. The weaker plea of women's ignorance need hardly be discussed; for multitudes of ignorant men are deliberately enfranchised, while multitudes of highly-educated women are kept voteless. Obviously, there is always a risk that ignorant voters will be corrupt ; but in the case of men the risk is now accepted by all Liberals. Manhood suffrage is accepted by the party.

Equally untenable is the plea, urged by Gladstone, that the suffrage would " contaminate " women by leading them to touch the " pitch " of politics. To say nothing of the paralogism of thus describing one's own chosen pursuit, and thus aspersing what is treated by the reasoner himself as a sacred birthright in the case of men, the fact is notorious that both parties, and all leaders, Gladstone included, have freely used women's services in precisely that kind of political work which is least unlikely to be demoralizing, namely, canvassing.   Such pleas tell of a weak case.

A much stronger plea, not often made, might be framed on another ground.   Politics, unquestionably, involves bitter and acrimonious public strife ;   and there can be few politicians who have not at times used language of severe denunciation against opponents.   Charges of mendacity are common.   If women are to play in general politics any such part as some have played in the franchise struggle, aspersing men with violence, it may be difficult for the men assailed to refrain from language of harsh aspersion in reply ;   and this will mean, it may be argued, a frequent occurrence of a kind of hostile relation between the sexes, which will be painfully unseemly.   Men who shrink from it will be in the position, it may be said, of choosing between silence under calumny and the resort to a kind of duel which they would detest.   Such an apprehension, though seldom formulated, is perhaps present to the minds of many opponents of woman suffrage ;   and it could not well be disputed that if it were realized the results would amount to an element of retrogression in civilization.

But the apprehension is speculative only ;   it has not thus far been realized in any of the countries where woman suffrage has been conceded ;   and there is equally good ground for a contrary anticipation.   Men who resorted to violence when persistently refused enfranchisement, are not found to do so when, the franchise being granted, they have failed to obtain through it the measures they desired. A continuance of disorderly conduct on the part of enfranchised women is the more unlikely, because it would wholly discredit them with all other voters.   On the other hand, it may be argued at least as confidently that, even as general discussion between the sexes is marked by more and not less amenity than obtains in discussion among men, the full entrance of women into public life will inevitably tend to the softening and not to the further exacerbation of political warfare.   It has certainly not worked ill as regards municipal politics.   Women in the mass cannot conceivably be " unsexed " by the mere opportunity for harsh polemic ;   and the certain bias of the great majority may be trusted to set the key for the sex in general.   In short, precisely because the normal instinct

of the male in the human as in other species is to
avoid battle with the female, it is not on reflection to
be feared that the simple concession to women of the
power to vote will reverse the whole natural trend of
things.

It is doubtful whether much weight is attached by any
to the common plea that if once women are entitled to
vote, they cannot be denied the right to sit in the legislature.
Perhaps it would be a sufficient answer to say that while
our legislature resorts to all-night-sittings it may very
fitly veto the admission of women, even as it vetoes night
employment for them save as hospital nurses.   But if that
objection were to cease to apply, the consideration would
remain that in the terms of the anti-suffrage argument
the majority of women would certainly not vote for a
woman candidate ; and if such a candidate be unfitting, it
would simply lie with the men to give effect to that conviction.   If the anti-suffrage argument from the hostility
of women has any foundation, the woman candidate can
never be elected.   And, when all is said, even her occasional
election could hardly mean " the end of all things."

What inspires most of the resistance on the part of
Liberals to woman suffrage is probably a fear upon which
they cannot well take their stand—the fear, namely, that
women voters would be Conservative and " clerical " in a
proportion disastrous to Liberalism.   The fact that a
majority of Anglican bishops are understood to favour
woman suffrage gives colour to such a fear, while, on the
other hand, it surely should give pause to some of those
who insist on the tendency of female enfranchisement to
lower women's moral influence.   But if fear of the way
a vote might be cast is to be a ground for refusing to grant
it, all Conservative opposition to extensions of the franchise
is so justifiable.   On the simple point of probability,
however, it may suffice to say that if the vote be given,
in terms of Liberal first principles, to all women, wives
included, the plain chances are that the balance of voting
power will stand very much as it does at present.   Workmen's wives will in general vote with their husbands, the
variants cancelling each other ; and the domestic-servant
class, being in general the daughters, sisters, and sweet-
hearts of the proletariate, are likely to vote in the same

fashion.   The equitable form of woman suffrage is at the same time the " safest " form for Liberalism.

Conservative opponents of woman suffrage, seeing this, naturally appeal to Conservative supporters of a limited suffrage to abandon it, on the score that, given a partial enfranchisement, a complete one is sure to follow.   To this we need but add, once more, that the thin end of the wedge is in already in the shape of the municipal franchise. In short, woman suffrage is visibly " a question of time."

§ 3.—*Home Rule*

Twenty-five years of " practical " debate have brought the issue of Home Rule to the point of settlement.   It is in fact simply one of constitutional readjustment, in the light of a multitude of precedents.   As Mr. Balfour agreed in his House of Commons speech in support of Woman Suffrage in 1910, " government by consent " has become the accepted principle for all the self-governing portions of the British Empire ;   and the measure meted to the former colonies has now to be meted—with the necessary differences in respect of the maintenance of the United Kingdom—to Ireland.   It was the inspiration of the Home Rule schemes of 1886 and 1893.

To the Home Rule Bills of Mr Gladstone there lay objections on the score of (1) the alarms of property in Ireland ;   (2) sectarian fears ;   (3) fear of national " disintegration " ;   and (4) inconsistency in the schemes proposed.   The first objection is cancelled by the simple fact that a " Unionist " Government has done what Unionists would not let Gladstone do—buy out the Irish landlords and establish peasant proprietorship.   The fourth objection can and must be met by a fresh scheme.   Before indicating it, let us consider the second and third.   They are hardly stated before it becomes apparent that they validate, by their very nature, the plea for Home Rule itself.   It is in order to substitute in Ireland national contentment and consent for disaffection and distrust that Home Rule has been proposed by English statesmen.   If it be argued that they did so in order to secure for other purposes the support of Irish Nationalist politicians, the answer is that on their

LIBERALISM AND POLITICAL MACHINERY 87

own principles they were bound, sooner or later, to try to give effect to the Nationalist demand. To say that they were unwilling to do as much is to say they were unwilling to act as Liberals. There was only one way in which the Irish demand could ever have been turned aside without disloyalty to the Liberal creed ; and that would have been by the systematic treating of Ireland as an integral part of the United Kingdom under the existing parliamentary system. That is to say, Irishmen should have been invited to the Cabinet ; and Irish needs should have been faced as part of the common task of the organized State. But the time for this was really past when the fitness of the course began to be recognized. On the one hand, the entire Nationalist party declined to enter into the party system of England and Scotland : on the other hand, the party which styled itself Unionist was of all parties the most destitute of the spirit of free union.

And, as the Irish claim grew more and more compulsive, it became more and more clear that after all this was the way to a better political machinery for the whole State. A main cause of the perpetual postponement of Irish problems was the sheer incapacity of the House of Commons to achieve its five-fold task of conducting the national fiscal and financial system and the control of all administration concurrently with the separate special legislations chronically needed for the four sections of the United Kingdom. No other advanced constitutional State lies under such a burden. Germany, Austria-Hungary, Switzerland, the United States, Canada, and latterly Brazil, Australia and South Africa, all deal with sectional issues by sectional Pariiaments, leaving collective needs to be dealt with by the central or collective Parliament. France, unified by her history, and especially by the unitary equalitarian system set up at the Revolution—though she once had a dozen separate " Parlements "—has no ostensible need for sectional legislation : one law serves for all France. Italy, unified by the national need for independence, is in the same case, as are Belgium and Holland. This country alone has to do endless sectional legislation alongside of collective administration in one legislature. Thus the demand of the Irish majority for a sectional legislature coincides with the consensus of practice in the most progressive States of the world. All legislation for Ireland is sectional now, as it has been in the past. Do what we will, we must treat her as a province with special and separate needs. To give her a legislature for her own needs is then emphatically the course of common sense, inasmuch as it not merely provides the only means by which the special work can be properly done, but relieves the central legislature of a burden which it cannot bear.

To this reasoning it has been objected that whereas all the other great States are tending from heterogeneity to homogeneity, setting up central legislatures to unify federated States, it is a reactionary and retrogressive course to revert in our own case to subdivision. But this is a flagrant paralogism. The political unification of the States in question is seen to be valid and satisfying precisely because it rests on the basis of consent, which is secured only by the continuance of their sectional legislatures. British union is thus far invalid and unsatisfying precisely because that condition is not present. To insert the condition of stability in a prematurely and oppressively unified system is no more a reactionary step than it would be to remedy a demonstrated omission in any other constructive or synthetic process.

But the nullity of the plea under notice becomes doubly clear when we collate it with the actual doctrine of the small recalcitrant section in Ireland. In that there is no pretence of an ideal homogeneity. The motive of resistance of one bitterly prejudiced section of the Protestant population of some counties in Ulster is avowedly one of detestation and fear, a clinging to old hatreds, a demand that the spirit of separateness in that minority as against the Irish majority shall override the reasoned and practical political need for sectional treatment on the part of that majority as against the incompatible sectional needs of the rest of the United Kingdom. If indeed the recalcitrant Orangemen propose a sectional Parliament for themselves on all fours with that demanded by the Nationalist majority, they would have a presentable moral case. But when that very solution was proposed to them in the past, they flouted it as a suggestion that they should " abandon " their fellow-Protestants in the rest of Ireland, a course to which they declared they would never consent. In point of fact, a line of demarcation for a Protestant Ulster canton would be so difficult that they might well decline to make the attempt. Their refusal, however, was put not upon that ground, but upon that of sheer angry aversion to any change. Thus their attitude is not one of claim to equal rights, but one of claim to veto any reconstruction of the legislative system of the United Kingdom in the interests of all its sections alike. The will of a small group is to be imposed on the whole State, simply because that group will consent to only one form of constitution. *Stat pro ratione voluntas.*

Apart from this purely froward resistance, the argument against Home Rule for Ireland resolves itself into a series of fallacious theses to the effect that the establishment of sectional legislatures is a " disintegration of the Empire." It is always " the Empire " that is specified in these formulas ; though the proposition is at once reduced to nullity on simple confrontation with the imperial facts. The " Empire " means the collocation of either the self-governing or the non-self-governing dominions of the Crown with the Mother Country, or that of both. If the stress is on the former, the contention falls at once. Every one of the self-governing dominions of the Crown is for all purposes far more detached from the Mother Country than Ireland would be from England under Home Rule. Is the Empire then " disintegrated " by the substantial independence of those dominions ? On that view it has ceased to exist *qua* the self-governing dominions. If on the other hand the stress of the term is on the non-self-governing dominions, as India, the argument implies that the ideal imperial management of Ireland would be one of sheer Crown control without any representative system. The " disintegration " formula is thus a mere counter-sense.

There might indeed be a substantial disintegration of the United Kingdom, as distinct from the Empire, if, as some propose, Ireland under Home Rule were to have absolute fiscal autonomy, establishing her own system of customs and excise as well as all her other taxes. In that case the United Kingdom would be divested of that fiscal unity which marks all the other federated States above named. Ireland would be on the footing of a self-governing " dominion," joined to the Mother Country only by the tie of the Crown, and free to set up import duties against her. But that has

never been the Liberal plan of Home Rule. A truly states-
man-like plan must substantially conserve fiscal unity—
though not necessarily absolute uniformity—as it is expressly conserved by all the States of the world which rest
on the Home Rule principle.

The true lines of Home Rule reveal themselves as soon as
we come to the fourth of the grounds of resistance to it,
namely, the inconsistencies of the Gladstonian scheme in
both its forms. That scheme fixedly evaded the federal
solution, though Gladstone's utterances on the subject
before 1885 expressly recognized the feasibility of a Home
Rule system, provided that it put England and Scotland
on the same footing as Ireland.[1] The main flaw in his later
schemes was that they did not co-ordinate Ireland with
England and Scotland. Given a Home Rule Parliament
at Dublin, the British system must be readjusted to permit
of Irish representatives sharing in the collective national
administration without also sharing in that sectional
British legislation which corresponds to what Irishmen are
doing at home. Where Irishmen settle points of Irish
education, for instance, in their own Parliament, their
representatives must not be empowered to vote also on
English education at Westminster. Discussion of the
problem and of proposed solutions revealed that the only
course by which the intolerable anomaly can be permanently
averted is that of establishing either for Britain *minus*
Ireland, or for each of two or three British sections—
England and Wales together, and Scotland separately—or
for each of the three separately—a Home Rule Parliament
subsidiary, like the Irish, to the central or imperial Parliament. Under such a plan, all anomaly disappears ; and
whatever be the first step, such a plan is finally inevitable
if we are to be consistent. The official objection in Gladstone's time was understood to be that we cannot have all
of the constitution in the melting-pot at once ; and it is
true that business must be " carried on during the reconstruction of the premises," as the shopkeepers say. But
what was lacking was the avowal that the constitution must
in the end be consistently readjusted ; and that avowal is
now called for by every consideration of expediency.

[1] See Lord Morley's *Life of Gladstone,* iii. 58.

Home Rule, in short, is simply a business-like application
to the parliamentary machine as a whole of the principles
of sympathy and reciprocity which are the essence of
Liberalism. The interests of Ireland require it, because at so
many points they differ from those of England, cannot be
concurrently provided for, and are in simple fact not understood by Englishmen. In the transference of these specifically Irish interests to Irish management, no shadow of
wrong is done to anyone in Ireland, inasmuch as the funda-
mentals of union are not only retained but newly secured
by an arrangement which turns most Irishmen from unwilling to willing members of the subsisting State, while
absolutely no disability is inflicted upon any inhabitant
of Ireland. The Orangeman who denounces Home Rule,
if he goes beyond the mere blatant plea that he hates or is
afraid of the Catholics, is committed to one of two lines
of political argument. Either he maintains that all the
special concerns of Ireland can be better managed from
England, at the hands of a majority of Englishmen and
Scotchmen and a minority of Irish legislators, than by
Irishmen on the spot—a proposition the contrary of which
has been many a time maintained by Ulster Unionists
themselves—or he is contending for a continuance of his
present power of interfering in specifically English and
Scotch affairs ; a claim which multitudes of Englishmen
and Scotchmen will meet by denying *his* competence to
legislate for them ; while at the same time they diasvow
competence to legislate for him. He is thus pretty completely out of court in the character of a reasoning politician.

Apart from this divestiture of powers of interference
in specifically English concerns, the Irish Orangeman loses
under Home Rule no tittle of political right which he
possesses, and he acquires powers of control over Irish
affairs which he does not now possess. As represented in
the central or imperial Parliament, he will retain his share
in the determination of national financial and fiscal policy,
national armaments, and foreign relations. At home, he
will be safeguarded against all the forms of interference
which he professed to fear, even including some which at
present lie in the competence of the imperial Parliament.
If, as he sometimes alleges, Catholic Ireland is specially
backward and mismanaged—a circumstance which, if it

exist, must be to his own detriment—he will henceforth have power with his Catholic fellow-citizen to plan for better things. And if, instead of contenting himself with professing an abstract enthusiasm for the Empire, he will consult the opinion of the peoples of the self-governing dominions thereof, he will learn that in over-whelming majorities they prescribe to him the acceptance of the Home Rule solution, and a brotherly co-operation with his fellow-Irishmen towards a better life for all. That he does not take this course is due to no political calculation of means and ends. It is the result of the hypnotism of an evil tradition, which has ceased to govern political life in any other part of Christendom. Not by such an obsession can a civilized State allow its constitution to be determined.

§ 4.—*The Second Chamber*

Hypnotism by other kinds of tradition, however, is not unknown in other fields of politics ; and it constitutes one of the chief difficulties in the way of settling the question of a Second Chamber. As in this case the traditional attitude is still very widely prevalent, it may be that the immediate solution will have to be made under its sway. None the less it is fitting that Liberals should try to contemplate the problem under dry light, if that be possible.

It will hardly be denied that there is nothing in the conception of representative government which involves the principle of two legislative chambers. That principle was never really acted on by the Greeks and Romans, though the Athenian and Roman constitutions in certain periods presented the spectacle of separate Councils or assemblies. It emerges quite fortuitously in the growth of the English Parliament, as an outcome of the feudal division of classes into nobles and commons. At one time the classes certainly sat together : the date of their first severance cannot even be fixed, so little trace is there of principled provision in the evolution. In the old Parliament of Scotland, though there were three " Estates," no such severance took place. " The Estates were not divided into two Houses, like the English Parliament, but transacted their business in one place of meeting."[1] In the

---

[1] Burton, *History of Scotland*, iii, p 389.

Parliament of Sicily, from which Simon de Montfort seems to have drawn his inspiration, there was no severance of classes. So, in the old États Généraux of France, though the three orders sat in their respective places, they were in one room, the king presiding.[1] Neither did severance take place in the old *curia regis* of France of which the Paris Parlement, later duplicated in eleven provincial Parlements, was a continuation. In the old Spanish Cortes (never developed to the point of a truly elective assembly) it was not even obligatory that nobles and clergy should be summoned by the king.

It was simply the successful survival of the British bicameral system, after nearly all other self-governing systems in Europe had disappeared, that moved Montesquieu to give it the endorsement which established it as a kind of ideal model for other States concerned to be constitutionally governed ; and the external imitation of it in the constitution of the United States sufficed to establish the convention, in the teeth of all criticism. The fact that the British system had " answered " served to discredit all opposition. But, though the fact is now commonly forgotten, the Second Chamber principle has been continuously impeached on its merits from at least the time of Bentham onward. Mill, in his *Representative Government*, opens his chapter " Of a Second Chamber " with the remark that " of all topics relating to the theory of representative government, none has been the subject of more discussion, especially on the Continent, than what is known as the question of the Two Chambers." That question must necessarily be reopened before a new Upper House can be established in the United Kingdom, though the present balance of opinion dictates the establishment of one in the Home Rule Parliament to be set up in Ireland.

As the controversy at present stands in England, the demand for a reconstituted Second Chamber necessarily involves a re-establishment of the power of absolute veto, the withdrawal of which from the House of Lords is said to have left the country under " Single Chamber government." Seeing then that the First Chamber is a strictly representative body, albeit not selected by scientifically

[1] Hervieu, *Recherches sur les premiers états généraux*, 1879, p. 57.

exact methods, such advocacy of a Second Chamber implies distrust if not dislike of the very principle of representative government. And this in fact underlies to some extent the principle of Second Chambers everywhere, save, perhaps, in so far as the Second Chambers in federal systems are avowedly established to guard the State rights of the federating bodies. First Chambers stand for the acceptance of the will of the people as an indefeasible principle : Second Chambers stand for partial disbelief in the principle. This is so obvious that it is usually taken for granted, and the discussion turns on the particular expediencies alleged to operate.

Three reasons have commonly been given for demanding a " check " on the legislative action of representative bodies : the first being that by their means the " have nots " are not unlikely to plunder the " haves " by way of taxation ; the second, that in General Elections the majority may vote for one party on special grounds, whereafter the party in question may proceed to carry legislation for which it had no " mandate " ; the third, that legislation by debate tends to be hasty, and that against that danger provision should be made by way of a Second Chamber.

The last appears to be the ground now chiefly founded on by Liberals who advocate an Upper House. Power of delay is now the specialty of the House of Lords as controlled by the Parliament Act of 1911 ; and it appears to be generally agreed that no further power should be conferred on the Chamber which it is proposed ultimately to substitute for the historic House. In this connection we may note the pronouncement of Mill :—

" I attach little weight to the argument oftenest urged for having Two Chambers—to prevent precipitancy and compel a second deliberation ; for it must be a very ill-constituted rerpresentative assembly in which the established forms of business do not require many more than two deliberations."[1]

Under the Parliament Act, as it happens, amendment of a delayed measure is positively interdicted, save on agreement of the two Houses, by way of giving full effect to the power of delaying for two years any provision in any

[1] *Representative Government*, ch. xiii. par. 3.

measure ; so that the principle of repeated deliberation is secured only on the broad issues on which change of view is most unlikely to arise. Obviously, a fuller sceurity, if required, could be obtained either by the method of the Norwegian constitution, in which the legislature chooses a second revising body within itself, consisting of one-fourth of its members, or by enacting a rule as to the size of the majorities requisite to carry a Bill without delay.

If, however, the principle of a Second Chamber be adhered to, under the limitation that the Second House shall only have power of delay, the debate reverts to the question of its constitution. Liberals are now more or less agreed that it must be a purely elective body, chosen on the same franchise with the first ; in which case the Second Chamber will be a body with merely deliberate and delaying functions, either substantially the same as the First in composition, or differing from it in virtue of having been elected at a different date. Such a system would at least have the merit, from the proposers' stand-point, of potentially subjecting each party in turn of tenure of power to the resistance of a House in which an Opposition predominated ; though on two successive triumphs at the polls the check might disappear. And this is probably the most tolerable form of Second Chamber that can be proposed, from the point of view of Liberalism.

It will of course fail to satisfy those who consider the system now in force to be in effect one of Single-Chamber government, and who demand an Upper House with veto powers. On that issue, however, it may be presumed that Liberals will not recede.

Returning to the first and second of the grounds of expediency urged for the retention of a Second Chamber, we at once note that the first—fear of plunder of the rich by taxation—has virtually disappeared from the discussion. The express historic claim of the Commons to hold the power of the purse, the desperate repudiation of which by the Upper House forced the crisis which ended in the Parliament Act of 1911, was promptly conceded by the latter House in its appeal for a reconstitution agreeable to itself. The question then cannot now be revised ; and there remains to be considered only the plea that a party elected on one issue or set of issues may use its power to pass unforeseen measures of another kind.

That may undoubtedly happen : it notoriously took place in the British Parliament of 1900-1905, when a party returned to power on the promise that the support given to it should be used only " to end the war," proceeded to pass measures for which its leaders knew they would not have the same support had those measures been proposed to the electorate. In that case the Upper House made no attempt to resist the breach of faith ; and we return to the conclusion that an elective Upper House would not resist in a similar emergency save when, through the over-lapping of periods, its majority chanced to be constituted of the party opposed to that in power. This, however, might frequently happen ; and we may for the present rest in the conclusion that if the legislative action of a fully representative body needs to be checked by that of another, this is the best way of doing it.

Before that conclusion is carried into effect, however, Liberals are bound to ask themselves, as aforesaid, whether the true course is not the thorough acceptance of the democratic principle, and the throwing upon the electorate of the wholesome responsibility of choosing representatives with some of that deliberation which all profess to require in the legislative work of the representatives themselves. The plan of a Referendum, so suddenly imposed on the programme of the Conservative party in the Second Election of 1910, encouraged the maximum of irreflection in the election of representatives and the maximum of turmoil and uncertainty in public life. The special pecuniary burden of propaganda set up at each Referendum would throw a new advantage on the side of wealth ; and the hostile candidate would have the new advantage of being on the scene of election while the sitting Member was confined to his legislative duties—unless before each Referendum the business of Parliament was to be suspended for a considerable period. The Referendum, in short, though plausibly defensible on theoretic grounds, is but one more expression of unfaith in the system of government by representation ; and a Second Chamber would seem to be a quite sufficient indulgence in that direction. Of the two, the Referendum is the more direct invitation to the people to be precipitate and capricious on its own account ; whereas the heightening of the standard of caution among the electorate is the most obvious way of guarding against all the dangers said to arise under either a Single or a Double Chamber system.

The latter, even in its safest form, seems rather likely to involve repetition of the friction which has forced the radical curtailment of the powers of the House of Lords. Either the elective Second Chamber will be substantially the same in composition as the first, or it will not. If it be, it will in the terms of the case supply no check. If it be not, it will tend to set up, by constant resistance, delays in the carrying of all important non-financial measures, however urgent, while it will have no power whatever to control finance, which must on any view be as much in need of checking as any other form of policy. For a factious policy of delay, it may be said, power of punishment lies in the hands of the electorate. But the proposition holds equally in regard to the errors of a First or of a Single Chamber. And as no one suggests that Single Chambers have been found to work ill in the cases of Norway, Greece, Bulgaria and Montenegro, or in any of the forty-four federated States or provinces in which they are in actual operation, there is a clear ground for deliberation before we are committed in this country to another Upper House.

The problem, it will perhaps now be seen, is much more far-reaching than the popular discussion on the subject. For that reason, it is not to be lightly grappled with. It was a wise decision which, on the passing of the Parliament Act, postponed the planning of something to be put in the place of the fettered House of Lords ; and when that institution is playing its part in delaying certain measures for two years while passing others which it declares to be fraught with disaster, the cause of Liberalism suffers little more than it is likely to do at a pinch from any substitute which may be set up. And, as we have seen, the expediency of a substitute is likely to become more and more problematical as time passes and legislative reconstruction proceeds.

§ 5.—*The Situation in* 1925

The proceedings of the Conference of members of both Houses of Parliament during the War, under the able presidency of the late Lord Bryce, on the matter of a reformed Upper House, supplied a remarkable proof of the unripeness of opinion on the subject.

A majority of the members, of both parties, had apparently set out with the confident assumption that an elected Second Chamber would meet their sense of need for an Upper House that could be trusted to resist " dangerous " tendencies in the Lower. No one, I think, sought to revive the luckless Rosebery-Dunraven scheme of 1888-89, under which a large part of the reformed Upper House was to be elected by the local authorities for the time being. Speedily, though not without debate, a further agreement was reached on the inexpediency of making the Second Chamber as large as the First. The generally avowed ideal being to secure a body of tried, experienced, and politically competent men, it was apparently felt to be somewhat fantastic to pretend that such specially competent men could be secured in numbers equivalent to the members of the Commons.[1] Members, accordingly, were soon content to have the reformed House elected by areas in general double the size of the electorates of the new Reform Bill.

It was thereupon pointed out by the present writer, among other members of the Conference, that such a system was wholly incompatible with the avowed ideal. The men desiderated for the ideal Upper House had been conceived and described as for the most part elderly, and on that account no longer disposed or qualified to fight the wearing battles of our electoral system. The new scheme, however, it was pointed out, actually subjected the candidates for the Second Chamber to a far greater strain of platform contention than that faced by a candidate for a seat in the House of Commons. Their struggles, in point of fact, would be twice as hard.

This sufficiently obvious fact, previously unrecognized

---

[1] Some romantic members of the Conference had contemplated a still larger body than the Commons. The present writer remembers that he had to call attention to the primary difficulty that the proposed aggregate could meet only in Westminster Hall.

by the advocates of the new scheme, was by them speedily and candidly admitted to be fatal to their plan. They were, however, unshaken in their conviction that their intuitions could still yield a way out ; and there was reached (with startling rapidity, considering the " revolutionary " nature of the theorising) an edifying agreement between Liberals and Conservatives to substitute for the plan of election by constituencies, of the efficacy of which they had been previously quite convinced, a system of election of a Second Chamber by the members of the first, voting in regional groups—a system of which, it is perhaps safe to say, no one had previously dreamt, and which would before have been flouted by all the members who now so readily adopted it.

That this scheme in turn, was as unsatisfactory as any other from the point of view of principle, seemed to the present writer obvious. It would evidently tend to result, if set up, in a mere election by the Lower House for the time being of an Upper House of its own political complexion ; thought it might be possible so to gerrymander the regional groups of the Lower House as to bring about in those groups differences of party predominance not identical with the general balance of forces. In any case, all that could be claimed for the scheme was that in this fashion elderly members of an Upper House could be elected by their colleagues of the Lower without subjecting them to the strain of a contested election.

The first practical question was : In what fashion was it to be secured that the candidates for the Upper House should be made known to their distinguished constituents ? Were they to have a hustings of any kind ? Were they simply to be taken for granted in respect of their " record " ? The second question was : Should the candidates for the Upper House be named in advance at each General Election, thereby enabling the electorate to pronounce on their merits, and to secure from Commons candidates pledges to elect this or that " Lord "? In that event, would not the composition of the Upper Chamber be simply settled in advance by the electors who returned the Lower ?

Such problems elicited various devices to give the Upper House a tenure of office overlapping that of the Lower. They so conspicuously failed to satisfy either the test of principle or the test of fitness, as means to given ends, that it was not surprising to find the majority taking refuge later in a compromise by which the elected Upper Chamber was somehow to retain a goodly proportion of hereditary peers—and bishops. The acceptance of the latter element was a bitter pill to the late Sir Thomas Whittaker, who combined a vigorous Nonconformitarianism with a still more compulsive concern for a Second Chamber of some kind. That overmastering predilection really determined the findings of the Conference. The representative of the Labour party, formerly a professed believer in a Single Chamber, tolerantly fell in with the prevailing view.

To the present writer, the findings of the Bryce Conference have always seemed to be hopelessly vitiated by refusal to face the fact that they would be substantially unacceptable to the electorate. This attitude strengthened as the debates went on.[1]

At the outset, even the Conservatives seemed prepared to admit that the Upper House control of finance, claimed by the House of Lords in respect of the Budget of 1909 in defiance of two centuries of usage, must be abandoned. It was that very claim that had precipitated the crisis. When, however, it was pointed out to them that the professed ideal of a controlling Second Chamber was negatived where the Second Chamber had no control of finance, the most vital of all modes of political innovation, many promptly reverted, with the assent of most of the Liberal members, to the claim to control Money Bills.

---

[1] I gather from the speech of Lord Haldane in the House of Lords on 25th March, 1925, that there was so much dissent over the question of how the non-elected peers were to be " appointed " that in the end Lord Bryce was unable to make any Report to the Prime Minister and had to content himself with writing a letter. It may then be worth while to record that Lord Bryce did prepare a long and careful Report ; and that the present writer had a long private interview with him on the question of an insertion to the bare effect that among other views put forward had been those of a Single Chamber and, alternatively, of an Upper House with only advisory powers. Lord Bryce was so unwilling to make even a bare mention of this, without names, that I drew the inference that he was successfully securing assents all round—as, indeed, I understood him to say. Only my reluctant declaration that, if he would make no mention of the *fact* of the advocacy of a Single Chamber, I must make a separate protest, induced him to give a reluctant assent.

The argument put by the present writer was that inasmuch as control of Money Bills *could not* be given to the Second Chamber, the fitting course for the adherents of that institution, seeing that it could not realise their ideal, was to agree to maintain it as an Advisory Body pure and simple. On that footing it might do really useful work. The existing system of peer-making sends to the Upper House a considerable number of men of wide experience and real ability ; and if life peerages were substituted for hereditary peerages the proportion might be kept high. In any case, an Advisory Body of some such composition as the present might exercise a real influence on opinion. Its considered criticism of Commons Bills, when sound, would receive a degree of attention such as is never given to arguments bracketed with a veto on a Bill passed by the elected Chamber. But though one distinguished Conservative member argued that the really " honorific " function of the Upper House is not voting but advising, neither he nor any other Conservative would listen to the theory of an Advisory Chamber. The result was a scheme for an Upper House only partly elected by the Lower, yet vested with control of all Money Bills—a proposal which it was plainly useless to recommend to the nation.

Yet the Conference was largely composed of men of ability of both of the then prominent parties. The present writer, at least, while dissenting from most of its conclusions, found its debates to compare favourably in point of relevance, temper, and brevity with those of either House. One of the unexpected pleasures it yielded to him was a recognition of the practical good sense of the Archbishop of Canterbury. Heat never entered, save momentarily, into the debates. Theory apart, good sense and good temper prevailed ; and, as has been noted above, the readiness to abandon one unworkable scheme for another, though it was startling on the part of men alarmed about revolutionary proceedings, was morally creditable in itself. But there remained the fundamental drawback that nobody *with a plan* seemed to have thought out the problem—though the unfailing sagacity with which Lord Crewe, for instance, handled all issues, excluded the possibility that *he* could have overlooked any beforehand.

This general display of lack of practical forethought on

the part of so many intelligent politicians, with plans for an ideal Second Chamber, raised in the mind of at least one member of the Conference the question whether it did not invalidate their primary assumption. The need for a Second Chamber seemed to them, so to say, axiomatic. The House of Commons, they took for granted, sets up grave risks, which must be guarded against. It is apt to be " hasty," and it might be at a pinch " revolutionary." Then we must set up a body which shall be incapable of undue haste or of any leaning to revolution. But the plans suggested were one and all " hasty," and might themselves, without extravagance, be termed revolutionary. Then many of the selected champions of a Second Chamber are themselves (to speak it profanely) hasty and revolutionary! Any House of Commons Committee, probably, would have irrefutably ground their plans to powder—with less amenity of procedure, doubtless, than marked the temperate and unhurried discussions under the calm presidency of Lord Bryce. Then what became of the Second Chamber theory?

No one, perhaps, who has sat for a dozen years in the House of Commons, will seriously dispute that it can at times do hasty things, though good Conservative and Liberal statesmen have been known to agree that it is enormously difficult there to make any serious innovation at all. Descriptions of some actually achieved modern legislation as " revolutionary " belong rather to the plane of rhetoric than to that of history. But the broad answer to the vague and general language usually employed to make a Second Chamber seem a practical necessity, is that we have never had a House of Lords which was incapable of acts as hasty as any of those of the Commons ; that the House of Lords just before the War *did* act in a provocatively " revolutionary " manner ; and that in these matters there is really nothing to choose between First and Second Chambers, as hitherto known. On what ground then are we to believe that hasty new plans will yield the infallible ideal House?

The strangest feature in the deliberations of the Conference was that, while a conviction of the absolute necessity and the absolute rightness of Second Chambers seemed to be generally held as axiomatic, nobody appeared to face the disturbing issue it raised, namely, whether it can plausibly be proposed to give one Chamber power of control over another without thereby lowering the qualification standards for the Lower House ? If the Second Chamber is to have veto control over the First, what politician will want to be in the latter if he can hope to be in the other ?

The obvious outcome of such a system would be a progressive exclusion of experience from the Lower House. The men of experience, declared *ex definitione* to be the proper material for the Upper House, will not care to spend their labour over legislation which is always liable to rejection by the higher body. They will leave the Lower House to the inexperienced men ; in other words, the House of Commons will, *ex hypothesi*, be more than ever given to crude and hasty legislation. For even the younger men of real ability, who might conceivably make up by critical thought for lack of experience, will not care to seek election to a body always in tutelage, always subject to the over-ruling of another.

Such *would be*, that is to say, the operation of the Two Chamber system in terms of the ideal entertained by the majority of the Bryce Conference. The plan of an Upper House wholly elected by the Lower in every Parliament, as we have seen, would stultify the ideal by making the Upper House a mere expression of the preferences of the Lower. For that very reason, the original plan was speedily mutilated, and a compromise was arrived at which would yield the result now set forth, to wit, the stultification of the House of Commons.

Thus we have the problem in a nutshell : We cannot have two *equipollent* Chambers. What thoughtful Liberal, then, can after reflection assent to a scheme which makes the House of Commons systematically subservient to the House of Lords ?

For, a House of Lords the reformed Second Chamber was still to be. Its members were to be *ex facto* Lords. As usual, the Conservatives had no thought of giving the elected Lords salaries. They took for granted, that is to say, that the possession of a good income, whether by inheritance, by marriage, or by success in business, is in itself a merit, and as such indispensable in the case of a member of the Upper House. This view, of course, was never crudely put; nor was it vindicated when assailed; but it was taken for granted. The Reformed Upper House was thus to be chosen from the monied class. That was in fact taken to be one of its special claims to acceptance. It is difficult now to recall how those who professed readiness to welcome Lords from the ranks of Labour proposed to meet the difficulty of adequate income. The writer has however a fairly clear recollection that there was small readiness to provide any.

All the foregoing reasons for diffidence over schemes for a Reformed Upper House appear to be in effect supported by the remarkable debate on the subect which took place in the House of Lords on 25th March and 2nd April, 1925, on a motion ably and temperately introduced by the Duke of Sutherland. That debate fully proved at once the high debating power of the existing House of Lords, the unfitness of it, as a body, to control legislation, and the hopeless difficulty of framing any reconstructive scheme which will win general acceptance and at the same time be worth framing.

Distinguished speakers, as the Earl of Birkenhead and the Marquis of Lansdowne, agreed that nearly everybody has a scheme, and that no two schemers agree. One remarkable fact emerges : the representative Conservative speakers, the two last named in particular, are agreed that the Parliament Act of 1911 *must not be repealed*, though it may be amended in the matter of the machinery for deciding what really constitutes a money Bill. The wisdom and necessity of the Parliament Act are thus, at least, " historically " vindicated ; and the practical supremacy of the House of Commons is thus ostensibly accepted.

On the other hand, speakers of all parties (the Labour Party included) appear to be agreed that a Second Chamber is still " indispensable " ; and when that opinion is voiced by a statesman so eminently practical and so conspicuously sagacious as the Earl of Oxford and Asquith, few politicians will dispute that the continued existence of the Upper House cannot be regarded as for the present in question. Nothing in the debate, indeed, elicited more comment than the emphatic counsel of Viscount Haldane, given as from the Labour Party to the Conservative Government, to " leave well alone," in other words, to leave the House of Lords just as it stands, with the Parliament Act in substantially full force.

This last pronouncement might be taken to express gratitude for the facilities which the Labour Ministry found in that House during its short tenure of office. It was free to appoint new peers ; and it found some already appointed who were ready to serve it. The heads of the party are thus apparently prepared to " carry on " with the existing Upper House, despite the sub-acid pleasantries of Lord Birkenhead as to the improbability of their finding again a " Christian Socialist " Lord Parmoor, a Lord Chelmsford, and a Lord Haldane. They appear, indeed, to rely on a general disposition of their Lordships to make things comfortable for a moderate Labour Ministry as against a Liberal one.

Lord Haldane, however, had indicated that in the event of the Conservative Government introducing *any* measure of reconstruction the Labour Party will bring forward proposals of its own. And whereas Mr. Ramsay Macdonald before the War expressly advocated a merely Advisory Upper House (a position which, as aforesaid, was abandoned by the Labour Party's representative in the Bryce Conference), Earl de la Warr, speaking with spirit on behalf of the present Labour Party, declared that " We are against the reform of the House of Lords, but we are in favour of a new Second Chamber " ; and, again, that he was personally " in favour of setting up a *real democratic Chamber.*"

Thus, then, the situation latterly stands. Representative Conservatives believe in curtailing the numbers of the Upper House, but (so far) reject the electoral schemes favoured by the majority of the Bryce Conference. These schemes, they declare, " nobody wants " ; and they omit to add proof that " anybody " wants the schemes they now outline. Those schemes would in effect set up a House of Lords of about 300 members, partly chosen by its own members among themselves, partly by automatic retention of those peers " who have occupied either high political or high administrative, or high military or naval situations in the service of the State." Such is, broadly, the scheme of Lord Birkenhead, who disclaims speaking in this matter for the Government, but who obviously, as Secretary for India, may be held to be in its confidence. Some such scheme, then, is presumably to be looked for as a result of the Cabinet Committee appointed by the Baldwin Ministry, with an express abstention from any serious interference with the Parliament Act.

On the other hand, the Labour Party declares, through its Peers, that any such scheme will be met on its part with a counter scheme for a " really democratic " Second Chamber—that is, presumably, an electoral body. And this, it would seem to follow, must be an Upper House with Suspensory Power. For, while the House sketched by Lord Birkenhead could be a really useful Advisory Chamber, the House indicated by Lord De la Warr would not be so. It could be plausibly advocated only as a Suspensory Chamber, with power to overrule measures of the House of Commons. Competent men would not fight contested elections merely to become members of an Advisory Body. If, on the other hand, an elected Second Chamber is to have Suspensory Power, the result, as aforesaid, must be to lower the status and consequently the competence of the First Chamber.

Any compromise made to escape this dilemma—by way, say, of giving the Second Chamber power over all ordinary Bills, while leaving the House of Commons supreme in finance—would only set up an illogical and anomalous conflict of motives. An elected Chamber which is really competent to control non-financial legislation is surely in theory as competent as the House of Commons to control finance. And no intelligible reason can be given why an elected body fit to control legislation in general should be pronounced disqualified to control the most important form of legislation.

Liberals may now, perhaps, begin to see that whereas the Liberal Parliament Act has secured the democratic position, and the Conservative scheme (*so far as it has been disclosed by the speeches above cited*) will at most effect a formal reconstruction of the Upper House that will leave it at least no more potent than at present, the threatened Labour Scheme will only raise new and insoluble difficulties of principle. The proper course for Liberals, then, unless they can agree on a new Second Chamber scheme of their own which shall escape the condemnation earned in advance by the Labour scheme, is simply to take precautions to ensure that the Conservative scheme shall introduce no new dangers. And to frame a new Liberal scheme might be confidently pronounced a formidably difficult task, even if we had not Lord Oxford's express avowal to that effect. Indeed, the difficulties of all reconstruction schemes are so great that it will not be very surprising if the Conservative scheme should come to nothing. Lord Birkenhead does not appear to deny that he was previously much disposed to let the matter alone.

It is only a strong sense of the unripeness of opinion in general on the subject that induces the present writer to acquiesce in the situation thus outlined. While the overbalance of opinion in favour of Second Chambers is so great as it is, that very fact is an argument in favour of substantially leaving the House of Lords alone. In the nature of things, no good scheme is framable ; but not till this is widely realised can the fact be usefully made a ground for advocacy of the resort to a Single Chamber—which of course is what we should have if the Lords became a purely advisory body. It is clearly better that the House of Lords should slowly pass away by euthanasia than that it should be abolished while the majority of people are blindly craving for "something in its place." In the meantime it is fitting that Liberals should be invited to reconsider quietly the problem of a Single Chamber system, with or without an advisory body. On that subject they are apt to hear little save mystification. As is pointed out by Mr. Harold W. V. Temperley (himself an advocate of a Suspensory Second Chamber) in his really valuable work on "Senates and Upper Chambers,"[1] the usual references to the Single Chamber principle by prominent politicians reveal a discreditable ignorance. For instance :—

" In opening an epoch-making discussion Lord Rosebery—the life-long apostle of reform of the Upper Chamber, to whom at least

[1] Chapman & Hall, 1910.

we might look for accuracy—spoke thus :—' There are two exceptions to the general protest of all civilized communities against being
governed by a Single Chamber. I will name them. They are
Greece and Costa Rica.' Now no one has made more reckless
reference to Federation than Lord Rosebery, and, if we were to
imitate him, we could discover not two, but fifty-three ' exceptions to
the general protest of all civilized communities.' " [1]

It may be worth while to indicate the list in question,
setting forth the facts as before the War :—

" Sixteen of the Swiss Cantons have only a Single (representative)
Chamber, six have a single direct Assembly of all citizens ; all of
these had Single Chambers before the Federation existed in any real
form.   Sixteen of the German States have Single Chambers, six of
which existed before Federation was a reality.   Six provinces of the
Dominion of Canada have Single Chambers.   Of Latin-American
States, Costa Rica, Panama, Honduras, Salvador and San Domingo,
have Single Chambers ; in Europe, besides Greece, are Bulgaria,
Montenegro and Norway." [2]

But as regards the customary " Costa Rica " gambit
there is a further answer, put by the same impartial writer :

The Report presented to the House of Commons in 1907, which
describes the Constitution of Norway, begins as follows :—" In the
Norwegian Parliament there is, strictly speaking, no Upper House ;
the so-called Upper House is merely a committee elected out of the
Lower.   Yet in spite of the ' general protest of civilized communities,' Norway enjoys an internal peace and stability which any
bicameral country might envy. . . . Mr. Balfour . . . . thinks
it sufficient to condemn the Resolutions for limiting the power
of the Upper Chamber by saying that in case they pass, we should
be governed for the first two years of a Parliament like Costa
Rica.   If for ' Costa Rica ' we read ' Norway ' we should be giving
a literal and not a rhetorical example of what would happen ;
but no one would be alarmed by England's Constitution resembling
Norway's ; everyone is by its resembling Costa Rica's.   Yet when
this deceptive example is invoked, no single member of the Commons
challenges the facts or the accuracy of the deduction therefrom,
though the material for refutation lies to hand in the Paper which
they themselves ordered to be printed." [3]

It may suffice to sum up the Single Chamber principle
in the words of J. S. Mill : " The really moderating power
in a democratic constitution must act in and through the
democratic House."[4]   Mill did not indeed proceed in any

[1] Work cited, pp. 8-9.
[2] *Id.* p. 9, *Note.*
[3] *Id.*, p. 10.
[4] *On Representative Government*, ed. 1865, p. 98.

strict consistency with that sound proposition, since he went on to argue that " were the place vacant in England " for a new Second Chamber, it might be fitly filled by a Senate after (of all models !) the Roman form, a " Chamber of Statesmen " made up of specially trained legislators, ex-judges, ex-ministers of State, ex-commanders-in-chief, experienced ex-diplomatists, ex-members of the highest grades of the Civil Service, and so on. The very list is a warning against " fancy Chambers," and a reminder to Liberals that where one eminent Liberal teacher missed consistency in his teaching, they will do well to be on their guard for their own part.

It need but be added that no valid argument against a Single Chamber system is conveyed by Mr. Temperley's objection[1] that such a Chamber does not safeguard the rights of minorities. The rights of minorities are not safe-guarded at present, nor would they be under the anomalous system preferred by Mr. Temperley, save through some such machinery as is understood under the title of Proportional Representation ; and that safeguard is as feasible under a Single Chamber system as under any other. When, then, it is remembered that, as Mr. Temperley also reminds us,[2] " Whigs and Radicals of the '32-'67 period—like Macaulay, the third Earl Grey, Cobden, and Bright—practically advo-cated a Single Chamber," the thoughtful Liberal may see a new reason for reconsidering the whole matter. But, once more, the issue is not ripe.

[1] Work cited, p. 151.
[2] *Id.* p. 158.

CHAPTER V

LIBERALISM AND FOREIGN POLICY

§ 1.—*Diplomatic Relations*

[The following chapter stands as it did in the edition of 1912.   The
World War, in which the Liberal and Conservative parties stood
together on a firm moral ground, was regarded by earnest
Liberals in general as " a war to end war."   And the cause of
the League of Nations, broadly speaking, is whole-heartedly
embraced by all Liberals.   The great services rendered to the
League by Viscount Cecil (to name no others) are a standing
proof that on this ground there may be further co-operation
between the parties ; and the Labour Party is in this regard to
be reckoned as a force for peace.   But until the mass of the
Conservative Party takes up the same ground, it is necessary
to keep in view its former contrary tendencies ; and the following statement of the case as in 1912 may still serve a useful
purpose.]

IT is customary in recent Conservative polemics to
assert or imply that there is a standing difference
between Conservative and Liberal policy in respect
of readiness to maintain the national dignity and the
national safety.   The claim, whatever be its professed
basis, is quite modern.   Hallam, in outlining the substantial divergences of Whigs and Tories at the beginning
of the eighteenth century, says nothing of proclivities in
foreign policy.   Cromwell maintained a strong navy where
Charles II. did not, and was tolerably aggressive in his
foreign policy ; the Tories under William III. resisted the
European adventures of that monarch ;   the Whigs
were more than the Tories identified with the wars of
Marlborough, which the extremer Tories opposed ;   and
the advantageous terms of peace granted to France by
Bolingbroke excited the indignation of the Whig, Shaftes-
bury, on his death-bed, as they did that of Hallam in
retrospect.   Walpole, it is true, long preserved peace ; but
Walpole was " no reformer," save in fiscal matters ; and

Chatham, who opened the era of imperialism, was no Tory, being " the first to sound the note of parliamentary reform."[1]

It is with the revolt of the Colonies and the French Revolution that a measure of differentiation begins in the attitude of the two parties on military policy.   The Whigs opposed and the Tories conducted the war with the Colonies; and Burke, who had been for peace and accommodation as a Whig, became as a Tory a furious instigator of the war with France, which Fox opposed.   Yet Pitt had set out as a reformer, and had in some regards more faculty of that kind than Fox ; and after 1802 the parties were very much at one on foreign policy.

In a later generation the Conservative Peel was notable for his readiness to " run risks," rather than spend increasingly on armaments ; and the Liberal Palmerston was what would to-day be called " Jingo " in his foreign policy. Disraeli turned imperialist only in his latter years ; and Gladstone, after denouncing the wanton Afghan War of 1878, startled many of his followers by his intervention in Egypt.   To this day, there is in the Liberal party much of the temper which made Gladstone willing to go to war with Turkey on behalf of her oppressed Christian subjects. On the other hand, though Lord Rosebery resisted that temper, he was at some points less pacific in his foreign policy than was Lord Salisbury during the greater part of his time of power.   Had a Liberal Minister submitted, as did Salisbury, to the menace of President Cleveland against British interference with Venezuela, he would probably have been more violently denounced by Conservatives than was Gladstone for the Alabama Arbitration.

It is only since the beginning of the twentieth century that a policy of peace and of moderation in armaments has become an outstanding mark of British Liberalism as against Conservatism.   Even in the case of the lamentable South African War, a certain number of Tories strongly, though silently, disapproved, and a number of the Liberal leaders substantially supported the war policy, though the then chief opposed.   But the influence of Sir Henry Campbell-Bannerman largely chimed with the tendency of thought in his party, while the exploitation of the war

[1] Green, *Short History*, p. 731.

on the side of Tory imperialism fixed upon that party the stamp of " Jingoism " which it had taken on under Beaconsfield. It would now be broadly true to say that most Liberals deplore, and many condemn, increasing expenditure upon armaments ; while most Tories obstinately demand and extol it, feeling that they thereby appeal to a still prevalent instinct in the mass of the people. Only partisans, however, affect to believe that Liberal Ministers insufficiently maintain the nation's naval strength ; and though many Tories advocate the insensate policy of universal military service, while insisting that the nation shall also be the supreme naval power, it is noteworthy that the party will not run the risk of taking a vote on the subject in the House of Commons.

Toryism, broadly speaking, voices loudly the animal jealousy felt by the foreigner-hating Briton of the old type, and it is chiefly among Liberals that movements for the promotion of good relations with foreign powers find support. As the attitude of the Labour party· is still more markedly internationalist, it may be safely inferred that the democratic tendency is more and more toward peace. But while both in the Liberal and the Labour ranks there are men ready to make or risk " war to prevent war," and to intervene unwarrantably in the affairs of foreign States on the side of popular rights, it cannot be said that British Liberalism has cast off the ancient British tendency to take part in other people's quarrels. Even as in international morals, so in international politics, reason and equity are of slower growth than in the relations of individuals within a community.

It will be a sufficient vindication of British Liberalism if it shall continue to keep the peace with all the civilized world as its leaders have done since 1905. If they can further bring about such an understanding with the leading naval Powers as shall ensure a reduction all round of the armaments which so heavily weigh upon the resources and hamper the social progress of all, they will have identified their cause with the cause of universal civilization in a degree that will ensure their hold on their own countrymen. For the cultivation of peace with the nations of the world is but the directing to international relations of the principle of sympathy and the concern for human betterment, which are the springs of Liberalism in the life of the Fatherland.

§ 2.—*Relations with Subject Peoples.*

Foreign policy, in respect of the relations of a dominant with a subject State, is something of a touchstone for democratic principles. It might have been forecasted that communities which established popular rule and liberties within themselves would, in the earlier stages of their political consciousness, show small concern to extend their own measure of freedom to other communities over which they had any power. The natural instinct of parent States to retain dominion over their colonies exhibits itself in the history of self-governing Greek cities as in that of modern monarchies, constitutional and autocratic. Hume went so far as to say that " the provinces of absolute monarchies are always better treated than those of free States " ;[1] but this proposition, though borne out by a comparison of English rule in Ireland with French rule over Alsace and Lorraine, will not hold of Turkish or Spanish rule over conquered or colonized provinces in comparison with that of Britain or Holland. Nor has France in Algiers played a better part than Holland in Java or England in India. The element of truth in the charge is that self-governing States are nearly as slow as others to practise reciprocity in their dealings with subjugated races.

But here as in other fields of political debate the growing moral sense is seen at work ; and the formation of a progressive policy in regard to dependencies is a mark of current political thinking in France and Britain. The crucial relation remains that between the dominant and the backward race. As regards communities of the European stock, the principle of self-government has become axiomatic. Since the Report of Lord Durham on the troubles of Canada in 1839, no English Government has long hesitated to grant a self-governing constitution to a colony save on the score of the smallness of the num-

---

[1] Essay *That Politics may be reduced to a Science.*

bers of the settlers relatively to aborigines. Even where
the interests of the aborigines are far from being safe at
the settlers' hands, the concession is made as soon as the
demand is at all powerful. But even as the average
settler everywhere habitually tends to treat natives as
having no rights save those he chooses to confer, so the
home community is collectively slow to conceive that an
" inferior " community can pretend to claim any measure
of self-government.

The problem is unquestionably a delicate and difficult
one. J. S. Mill faced it somewhat hesitatingly in his book
on *Representative Government*. A people, he observed,
" may be unwilling or unable " to fulfil the " conditions "
of free self-government ; and if from any cause they are
" unequal to the exertions necessary for preserving it,"
they are " more or less unfit for liberty."[1] This really
amounts to saying that a people which cannot throw off
oppression ought to be subject—a doctrine which, however, Mill would hardly have maintained in plain terms,
and which no one is now likely to assert. The real justification of English rule in India—which is the great test case
—is of course the certainty that if that rule were withdrawn
there would ensue an anarchy which could end only in
the arbitrary rule either of one of the more warlike native
races or of some other power which seized the opportunity
to invade. And this obvious proposition is habitually
put forward as if it were a ground for doing nothing to
prepare the peoples of India by a collective political
training, involving a gradual bestowal of political powers,
for ultimate self-government.

It is in respect of their employment or rejection of this
evasion that men exhibit in this connection Liberalism
or its contrary ; and the ethical value of Liberalism is
manifested in the amount of progress latterly made in the
direction indicated. Conservatism, which furiously resisted the beneficent bestowal of full self-government on
the two Boer States, though it had been promised in the
Treaty of Vereeniging, is for the most part callously hostile
to all Indian aspirations—here receiving much support
from the Anglo-Indian bureaucracy, which stands to all

---

[1] Work cited, ch. i.

native self-assertion very much as Conservatism has in all ages stood to the demands of the lower classes in all European communities. If, compassionately recognizing the backwardness of Indian evolution, and the complication of the problem by the variety of conflicting racial and religious elements in Indian life, the Anglo-Indian ruling class thoughtfully planned any scheme whatever for the elevation of the native races, they might achieve for their own race a credit never earned by any other in human history. But if that credit is ever to be won, the enduring impulse, it is to be feared, must comes from the Liberalism of the dominant race in its own home.

Whether British Liberalism has risen to its duties in this direction is a question which it behoves every Liberal to put to himself. In the light of history in general, it was not to be expected that the inter-racial duty would be readily accepted; and at this moment it would be accurate to say that most British Liberals are more alive to the responsibilities of other dominant States than to those of their own. Britain is practically paramount in Egypt; and though there, as in India, Liberal statesmen have latterly made beginnings in the preparation of the people for an ultimate self-rule, there is no such party pressure behind them as tends to arise when, as in the case of Russian ingerence in Persia, a foreign power checks the effort of a backward people towards self-government, advancing the pretext of their inefficiency, but using the opportunity supplied by their weakness. When the British Liberal is as keen a critic in his own country's case as in that of the foreigner, he will speak with more weight to the latter.

We can but trust that as he grapples ever more thoroughly with the evolving problems of domestic politics, more and more cultivating alike the scientific and the ethical sides of his nature as a " political animal," he will be increasingly alive to the claims of the less fortunate races. Self-criticism will reveal to him the anomaly of a self-felicitation which claims honour and gratitude for a rule over alien races that denies to them all hope of the freedom which for himself he sets above all other forms of well-being. Only by their progressive advancement in the scale of

nations will he be justified as more than a self-seeker in his
capacity as member of a ruling race.[1]

On the problem before us, it is to be noted as significant
that in parliamentary discussions on the management of
India it is invariably from Liberal or Labour Members
that there come appeals for progress in the direction of
self-government, demands for the direction of Indian
expenditure less towards military and more towards
social ends, protests against every semblance of arbitrary
or cruel treatment of recalcitrant native politicians. The
protests may or may not be at times inspired by imperfect
information : the fact remains that they never come from
Conservatives, any more than the appeals for betterment.

In home affairs, many Conservatives profess concern
for social reform—especially when Liberals are in power :
in regard to India they criticize nothing save frontier
policy and measures for enlisting the people in some little
degree in the conduct of their own affairs. The Conservative test for an Indian politician or publicist is the simple
one of " loyalty " ; if he criticizes British administration
he is " seditious " : if he proclaims his devotion to the
British Crown he is to be cherished. Conservative policy
in these matters, in so far as it is to be gathered from the
press, the platform, and parliamentary oratory, is but an
unscrupulous insistence on British domination, with an
implicit denial that our administration in India can be
fitly subjected to any criticism whatever from the native
point of view—save, indeed, when Moslems protest that
they, as " loyalists," need to be safeguarded against Hindu
ascendancy. Conservative politics in regard to India,
in short, is a distillation of the simple dialectic of Mr.
Rudyard Kipling.

In so far as Liberals lean to that primeval policy, they
have reason for searching of heart. The current journalistic
rhetoric about British rule in India will bear no critical
scrutiny : it is, as Arnold would say, " idolatrous work."
According to the conventional view, which is whole-
heartedly professed by Conservatism, India is the country
where Englishmen become infallible. At home, being

[1] The author would refer to his paper on " The Rationale of
Autonomy " in the *Transactions* of the International Congress of
Races, 1911, for a fuller discussion of the problem of subject races.

divided into Liberals and Tories, they are open to each other's reciprocal vituperation as traitors, blunderers, tricksters, cheats, fools. Neither side can govern the Mother Country for a day without incurring fierce or contemptuous imputation of improbity or imbecility. We have seen Liberal statesmen, the sons of Liberal statesmen, accused by sons of Conservative statesmen of unscrupulously shielding an incompetent or dishonest police in its persecution of an innocent female.[1] In such a case, the Conservative English press will back up any Conservative politician. But when a charge, however circumspect, of arbitrary action is brought by any one against an Anglo-Indian *qua* official, no Conservative will for an instant admit that there can be anything in it. It is not a matter of calculated attitude, of the maintenance of a certain traditional pose : the denial of the criticism is as spontaneous as the snap of an animal at its assailant. The Conservative in these matters has not begun to think.

Unreason can in the nature of things be no safer a master in foreign than in home affairs, and it is solely in virtue of some higher political creed and guidance than that of Mr. Kipling that the British Empire in India has endured thus far. But Liberalism is concerned with something more than the mere maintenance of the State in any of its relations. The spirit of Liberalism in home affairs can never long subsist prosperously if in any foreign relation the bulk of men professing the Liberal creed are not concerned to do by aliens as they would be done by. It would be an ill omen for their cause if there were not for ever found among them men zealous to plead the cause of backward peoples—and more zealous to safeguard those for whom their own country is accountable than for those dominated by other rulers. Whatsoever be the accuracy or the success with which such chamipons of " natural rights " conduct their pleas in given cases, there is a perpetual presumption, for the true Liberal, that they may " lean to virtue's side." For they prove themselves at least potentially capable of that moral and mental

[1] The D'Angely case, in which Lord Robert Cecil and others attacked Mr Herbert (now Viscount) Gladstone, in his capacity as Home Secretary, imputing to him gross inequity.

temper which we have seen to be vital to Liberalism—
the temper which we have named that of intellectual sympathy.   And in the cultivation of the same temper will
lie the best safeguard against that proclivity to self-righteous
intervention in the affairs of foreign States which is perhaps
the outstanding snare of democracy in matters of international politics.

PART II
LIBERALISM AND SOCIALISM

CHAPTER I

THE FEAR OF SOCIALISM

A T the Church Congress of 1907, one rev. gentleman gave his brethren the sound counsel not to talk about Socialism if they were afraid of it, for in that case they were pretty sure to talk nonsense. Nothing wiser was said in the discussion. Fear and hate are not only the worst distorters of moral vision in the subjects ; they morally tend to set up a corresponding perversity in the objects. After a certain age, indeed, men are apt to grow unsanguine about persuading anybody who strongly differs from them ; but in so doing they are likely to recognise the advantage of being on speaking terms, which is, that opposition does not then become infuriated and demoralizing. And there is always the consideration that while weak people may be made to take sides by mere declamation, they will less easily be led to change by it, while stronger brains will be simply set in stronger antagonism.

To those who have studied Socialism sympathetically, further, there is apt to be a ludicrous aspect in the attitude of fear towards it. Fear of what may happen in a visionary or a violent attempt to realize the ideal is indeed intelligible, and is as justifiable as fear of any other outbreak of violence, or miscarriage of wild experiment. But that is not the kind of fear now most commonly professed. It is the realization of the ideal that is presented as a horror of great darkness. It is as if men should go about in fear of the millennium ; which is, perhaps, rather more absurd than the attitude of those who go about propounding the enactment of the millennium as a policy at elections, to be given effect to by votes in the House of Commons. One type proposes to establish the millennium by vote ; another is afraid that he will do it !

One fact in particular should be a warning to any Liberals

who are concerned in denouncing Socialism, not as a visionary scheme, but as a dreadful ideal. In so doing they are joining hands with their natural antagonists, the out-and-out Tories ; and when that happens there is nearly always something wrong. For years past, Tory journalists have been hard at work seeking to excite the people of Britain by rhetoric about " The Socialist menace," a cry which has not been unsuccessful in London municipal elections. For joining in this movement stray Liberals will not get even the thanks meted out to Liberal Unionism by Toryism in the past. They are being daily told in the Tory Press that Liberalism has " shown itself powerless to stem the tide of Socialism," and that only Toryism will avail. If any Liberals think to fight such a tactic by crying still more loudly against Socialism, they are sorely mistaken. They will only help to create an atmosphere of passion and panic, such as is always far more helpful to Toryism than to Liberalism, which in the mass and in the long-run must depend upon reason, reflection and goodwill. The voting at the London County Council election of 1906 was an object lesson as to what such an atmosphere generates—in so far, that is, as the polling represented panic and prejudice, and not financial forces. And the vote of the majority in that election, be it remembered, was really directed against practical Liberalism, denounced as Socialism. The fact that so much of practical Liberalism is Socialism for the Tory should give the critical Liberal pause.

Even as regards the electioneering opposition of so-called Socialism to Liberalism, there has been much wild inference from very slight data. Socialist candidatures are not new in English politics. Not to name the many attempts of less prominent Socialists, Mr. Hyndman has repeatedly stood, without success. At the General Election of 1906 quite a number of known Socialists, including Mr. Keir Hardie, were elected. What has happened since is that here and there a Socialist has been temporarily elected ; and that in some three-cornered contests one has been elected by a minority vote ; and even in one of those cases the successful candidate, though a Socialist in opinion, did not stand as such. In the 1907 bye-election in Liverpool, the " Socialist " candidate, in a square fight with a Tory, was badly beaten.   The " wave " theory is slenderly founded.

Such recent success as Socialist doctrine has lately had, further, whether at elections or in point of mere growing popularity, is visibly the result of hard work.   Had the Tariff Reformers worked as long and as hard, and run as capable candidates, they would probably have polled quite as many votes ; unless there had been a proportionate propaganda on the Liberal side,   A turn of events which thus arouses Liberals to think out their creed anew and justify the faith that is in them is not a serious disaster, provided only that it does not breed that temper of fear and malice which, no doubt, some Socialist polemic is only too well fitted to set up.

A moderately careful analysis of the theory and pro-gramme of Socialism will soon show that anything in the nature of revolutionary legislation—revolutionary, that is, from a Liberal as distinct from a Tory point of view—is not rationally to be apprehended.   All that is con-ceivably workable in the proposals of British Socialists, while society remains broadly what it is, is only a further development of plans already laid down by Liberalism. With all the Tory outcry against Socialism, the fact remains that the plans of Old Age Pensions and of National In-surance were accepted unanimously in the House of Commons.   To both of these measures might fairly be applied the description so uncritically attached by Mr. Balfour to the Budget of 1909—" Not Social*ism* but Social*istic*."   For a scheme of taxation, either term is a pure misnomer, inasmuch as theoretic Socialism excludes all taxation ; but to the scheme of Old Age Pensions, which newly affirms the solidarity of the body social, the adjective might justifiably be applied by an opponent. Nothing more radically Socialistic can well be attempted in our day.   Nationalization of railways, which has long been mooted by Liberals, and to which Mr. Lloyd George has indicated a decided inclination,[1] is only an extension of the principle already applied nationally in the case of the telegraphs, and municipally, on all hands, in the matter of tramways.

[1] Written in 1912.   Mr. Winston Churchill, it will be remembered, proposed such a measure in 1919 as part of a Coalition policy.

The notion that any legislation going much further than this will be carried in our generation can be harboured only by those heads which cannot distinguish between ideals and programmes, between absolute conceptions and living adjustments. And those who fear that such enthusiasts may, in our day, achieve a Socialistic organization of all society, controlling all life on collectivist lines, are themselves victims, for the moment, of the same fallacy, and are unwittingly encouraging the others in their delusion. Socialists who talk of collective ownership of all the means of production as a parliamentary programme for their own time, are thus extravagantly sanguine because they have never critcally tested their hopes or analysed their proposals. It is for Liberals to supply the tests and the analysis.

Too much of Socialist propaganda, unfortunately, is bad-blooded as well as visionary ; the profoundly anti-social doctrine of " class war " being a large part of its inspiration. But mere spite and envy will never create an important political party ; and in the terms of the case, what is best in the Socialist movement is there in virtue of nobler ideals and aspirations than those of malice. Some of the most unselfish men in the world have been and are political visionaries ; they are to be seen even now in the Anarchist movement, alongside of some men not worthy to black their shoes. Liberals who cannot reason patiently and sympathetically with visionaries of the better type have something yet to learn of the spirit of Liberalism.

As for the preachers of hate, they are the surest frustrators of even the more moderate types among their sweeter-minded colleagues. Of what are called the ironies of life there is none, I think more grotesque than the spectacle of an undertaking to build up by the forces of malevolence a society which shall be the consummation of fraternity. To this insane conception of social progress, too many ill-instructed men have been led by the pseudo-scientific doctrine of catastrophic evolution, laid down originally by Marx and Engels, and strangely reproduced by William Morris in his forecast of a beautiful world arising out of an age of desperate civil war—an evil aspiration, of which, I have heard, and would fain believe, he repented. What pass current as the ideals or ultimates of Socialism are attainable, on the face of the case, only by the widest and deepest development of the spirit of brotherhood—a development far in advance of the present moral capacity of most Socialists, as of most other people. The notion of a violent triumph of one class over another, a setting of the foot of poverty on the neck of wealth, is so far from being compatible with either the economic or the moral stability of Socialism that it might pass as a hostile statement of the first stage of the catastrophe in which its professed enemies say Socialism is doomed to end. Few men, indeed, have better reason to resent and repudiate the doctrine of " class war " than those who look to Socialism to regenerate mankind.

To fear that humanity will be Socialized by compulsion, on the other hand, is to be, in a negative way, as visionary as the fanatics themselves. There is a story of a lady who approached a liberal-minded clergyman with an avowal of her fear of being forced to associate in Heaven with Christians of the lower orders. " Have no fear, madam," was the reply ; " you will never get there while you feel like that." To those who propose to build a heaven on earth on the basis of the " broken bottles " of class hatreds, we may say with a more modest confidence : Take no trouble over the plan of campaign of your " class war." You are marching away from Socialism when you propose to regiment yourselves for it.

CHAPTER II

THE theoretical economic case for Socialism, one may venture to say, is stronger than the majority of Socialists themselves realize. Had they been more bent upon a scientific study of human affairs, and less upon framing an indictment against capital and capitalists, politicians and bourgeoisie, they might have framed a much more persuasive ideal than that they commonly present. It is not merely that indictments against classes evoke counter-indictments, but that the argument is so much stronger when the assumption of " a double dose of original sin " in the middle class is abandoned. To this day the average Socialist, though he probably does not read Marx, follows Marx's tactic in representing capitalist production as a process of exploitation in which the employer (who is usually, but erroneously, identified with the capitalist to whom he pays interest) gets an iniquitously large share of the total product. To those who know how much of individual capital is lost by the chances of trade and invention, this attack is not impressive. A far more serious evil, economically speaking, is that of chronic loss of capital on the one hand, and the constant waste or non-utilization of labour power on the other, under the system of competitive production.

The Miscarriages of Competition

One of the most painful chapters in a systematic history of industry, were such a book written, would be that which told of the misery inflicted by the successive expansions of machinery. In the past, the facts have been recited sometimes with pitying comment on the folly of those workers who sought to destroy new machines, sometimes with cold censure of their futile violence, rarely (save by Socialists) with sympathetic avowal of the desperate position in which the workers found themselves, with starvation staring them in the face. When any of the vested interests of the more fortunate classes have been put in jeopardy by social and political reforms, they have left no stone unturned in the way of furious social and political resistance. Workmen whose very livelihood was for the time being destroyed by the introduction of new machinery were in a far more terrible plight than these ; and their violence was as that of men fighting for their lives. Long ago, Mill justly declared that no class of men had a better claim for State aid than those so situated. But no such State aid, other than " poor relief " or " distress relief," has ever been given them ; the problem being in truth a terribly difficult one.

Not merely labour, however, but capital, is chronically sacrificed by new invention. The admirable and costly machine of to-day may be superseded by the still more ingenious machine of to-morrow ; and the competitive manufacturer has often no choice but to take the newest and send the other to the scrap heap. In the theoretic Socialist State, an exact calculation could be made whereby the total quantity of labour power involved would be made the guide to action ; and the old machinery would be superseded at that rate which yielded the minimum of total sacrifice. At present, the possibility of gain to the competing individual is unavoidably the sole test of action all round.

The Waste of Labour

Still more serious, however, is the periodic paralysis of labour which seems inseparable from competitive production on a large scale. When Robert Owen came to the front in the first quarter of the nineteenth century, the long spells of unemployment for the workers in the great new factories were already so dis-quieting a feature in the national life that men of all classes gave a ready ear to proposals which promised to cure the evil. One of Owen's great deeds was to pay his men full wages during four months of enforced idleness.   But what we are chiefly concerned to note is that all suspension of industry, all restriction of work to half-time, is a minimizing of the annual product of labour, and therefore of the total wealth.   Strikes alone have counted for a vast amount of economic loss.

On the other hand, competition in production, and still more competition in distribution, involve an enormous waste of labour power.   Long ago a calculation was made showing how ordinary shopkeeping means the employment of perhaps from two to three times the number of persons who would be required to accomplish on organized lines the whole work actually done.   In every street of shops, hundreds of men and women are more or less idle during several hours of an unduly long working day.   And every establishment of any size unavoidably wastes much labour power in competition, however well it may be organized. Two firms in an east-end street may have to send two vans, requiring two horses, two men, and two boys, right across a town to deliver two parcels in a west-end street, it may be at the same house.   The possibility of reducing this waste in the case of composite stores has already been the cause of much superseding of small establishments by large, but to eliminate it is impossible while competition lasts.

Limits of Competitive Production

The most serious and fundamental drawback of all, however, is the inevitable limitation of production by the abstention from consumption which is forced upon all who are concerned to provide for their families and for their own old age by saving for investment.   The only really fruitful basis for investment—as distinguished from national debts, which are mere grounds for taxation— is fresh production.   A., accordingly, abstains from consumption to the extent of saving money which can be usefully employed as productive capital only in the event of an increase of consumption.   (For simplicity's sake, I put aside the cases in which saved capital is successfully employed to supersede, and in effect annihilate, previous capital.)   But if B., C., and the rest, all abstain and save in the same way, consumption in the terms of the case does not increase, and fresh production cannot be profitable. It is plainly impossible for all to save and invest successfully to the point of providing for the old age of all. The need to abstain and save and invest is perpetually clashing with the demand of the saved capital for productive employment. In other words, under competitive conditions the theoretic maximum of production can never be attained.

What is worse, the kind of production that best thrives is not the best. There is a fatal propulsion to the multiplication of the cheap and the common, but not of the good and the beautiful. The ideal would be that the available labour power in excess of what is needed to produce the necessary should be set to work to produce the beautiful— to add handicraft to machine work, and art to manufacture. But the economic compulsion narrows such higher production to the demand made by the wealthy and the devotees of beauty. Thus the theoretic optimum and the theoretic maximum alike are impossible in the competitive society, and are conceivably attainable only in the ideal Socialized State.

The Practical Dilemma

Such, broadly speaking, is the outline of the theoretic economic case for Socialism, as distinguished from the moral case, and from the gospel of " class war," which is alien alike to economic and to moral science. I have heard many Socialistic addresses, and read many Socialistic writings, which fell far short of recognizing these theoretic facts. Less than ten years ago [1] I heard a lecture by a leading Socialistic propagandist on the theme " Socialism Inevitable and Necessary," in which practically no attempt was made to prove that thesis. The sole proposition sustained was the expediency of systematically taxing land values—a proposition long before maintained on most Liberal platforms, and now in part translated into action by a Liberal Government. Perhaps the lecturer realized in the act of speaking how much more profitable it is to expound to an ordinary audience a practicable reform than to demonstrate the

---

[1] Written in 1912. The lecturer was Mr. Snowden.

necessity of a complete transmutation of the entire structure of society, a thing thinkable only by way of setting aside the entire problem of the immediate policy to be pursued. To that attitude, indeed, all reasonable Socialists must come ; and we shall be established in it after the fullest survey of the case for Socialism and the possibilities of joint action at the given moment.   But it is well that those who are concerned to comprehend the theory as such should realize its basis, its scope and its rationality *as* theory.

CHAPTER III

THE CASE FOR SOCIALISM (MORAL)

IF the Marxian Socialist fails to put the economic side of his case at its best, no less does he fail to set forth aright the moral side of the theory of Socialism. Preoccupied with his vendetta against the employer-capitalist, who is primarily an organizer and not an idler, he brings only a secondary indictment against the typically idle class of wealth-consumers. It is the Georgians, in this country, rather than the Marxians, who lay supreme stress on the fact of the absorption of economic rent by idlers as such; and the Socialists who give out the same doctrine are following rather Henry George than Karl Marx, though Marx, assimilating previous arguments, did propose to make the appropriation of rent the first act in his predicted " revolution."

But the Georgians in turn are ready to assent to idle living on the part of all who can live idly on investments apart from land; and neither school presents us with a satisfactory code of civic morals. The basis of such a code was indicated for Liberals by Mill when in his *Political Economy*, speaking of the surplus which goes to unproductive consumption, he remarked on " the prodigious inequality with which this surplus is distributed, the little worth of the objects to which the greater part of it is devoted, and the large share which falls to the lot of persons who render no equivalent service in return." There lies our moral problem.

The Employer Captain of Industry

The one-sidedness of the Marxian ethic is at first sight puzzling. One would have thought that even resentment of the employer's profits could blind no friend of the worker to the fact that the employer, as captain of industry,

renders service as does the worker himself, whatever
doubt may be cast on the justness of his reward. Obviously, too, the employer is often only a borrower of
capital on which he pays interest ; and the difference
between his personal income and that of his workers,
were it divided among them, would, as a rule, make but
little difference in their wages. Behind the working
employer, whether capitalist or borrower, stand the class
whose sole claim to their large incomes rests in their
ownership of land or invested credits. Yet it is always the
employer rather than the idle capitalist who is assailed
by the Marxian polemic ; and to this day Marxian writers
are found directing a constant fire of unscientific odium
against, not the idle rent-drawers and interest-drawers as
such, but the bourgeoisie, the class which, though it saves
and invests for its old age, is in the main an occupied
class, playing its part in production, distribution, and
regulation.

The Interest-drawing Class

The explanation appears to be simply this, that both
Marx and Lassalle, the " legislator " and the " prophet "
of modern Socialism in Germany, alike belonged to the
interest-drawing class, and were naturally not ready to
vilify it. In speaking of the cruel pressures of the manufacturing and trading system on the poor, Marx thinks
always of the bourgeois employer, never of the mere
capitalist behind the bourgeoisie, lending them his money
and living on his percentages. To that class, even now,
belong some Socialist writers to whom the word bourgeois
is as the red rag to the bull. In the personal devotion
which was felt by so many German workers for Lassalle
in his lifetime, and is felt retrospectively for Marx, there
has entered not a little of the handicraftsman's old rever-
ence for the " scholar and gentleman " who had " private
means," and who was positively esteemed for his unearned
income where the shopkeeper or the employer was disliked
for his trade profits. Yet the unearned income was
collected, broadly speaking, out of the surplus which
included those very profits, or out of rents.

Interest and Rent

A dispassionate view of the whole subject will soon reveal to any one the vanity of any moral hierarchy of " classes " which consigns whole millions of human beings to odium or promotes them to honour on the strength of the mere social classification in itself. The interest-drawing and rent-drawing class, concretely considered, will be found to pervade each of the others, inasmuch as rents and interest are paid not merely to persons of the " upper " classes but to persons of the " lower." When poor folk contrive to save and to invest successfully they draw rent and interest like the rest ; and they bequeath to their heirs the power to do the same. Insurance policies, annuities, benefit money—the whole system of individual self-help involves at every step the process of interest-drawing and rent-drawing ; and in large part it means the maintenance of widows and orphans, and the provision of industry for its old age. On the other hand, the " working " class, broadly so called, includes a percentage who work as little as may be—men who are partly or wholly supported by their wives and families—as well as men whose work is, in itself, either worthless or inimical to the common good.

Reciprocity of Service

Out of the confusion of the phenomena of class life, thus considered, we can reach one clear moral conclusion —that it is primarily the rendering of service that gives a true moral title to support ; and that reciprocity of service is the ideal social condition. And the gist of the moral case for Socialism is that only in a socialized state can such complete reciprocity ever be conceivably secured. On analysis, the category of citizens who live on rent and interest is found to include a multitude who have never rendered any social service ; whose " capital " was bequeathed to them ; and who have no thought of doing anything with their incomes beyond enjoying themselves and giving a fraction in charity. Granting even that this class-section might conceivably be " moralized " into regarding its wealth as a social trust, it is inconceivable that it could be "intelligized" into knowing how best to employ its wealth for social purposes. While the competitive system subsists, and while power of bequest and property in land remain, it is impossible to hinder the accumulation of great masses of income in the hands of more or less selfish idlers, who exist by the labour of all the rest, yielding little or no service in return. And this will never be reconcilable with a scientific ethic. Morally speaking, the old French Socialist formula, "From each according to his abilities ; to each according to his needs," is the highest of social ideals. And I have never been able to understand how professed Christians could denounce it, whatever might be their despair of attaining it.

Complete Reciprocity Unthinkable

No sooner, however, have we stated the moral ideal, than we begin to realize the utter impossibility of anything but a gradual advance towards it. Among men with deeply conflicting tastes and proclivities, complete reciprocity is unthinkable. Thousands of professed Socialists are in favour of forms or service and production which their more enlightened colleagues know to be, in some degree, anti-social. The formula, "From each according to his abilities," cannot permissibly be construed to mean "From each only the kind of service he prefers to render"; and "to each according to his needs" cannot be allowed to signify "to each whatever he thinks he needs." There must be reciprocal check all round ; and who pretends to be able to say what each ought to do and to desire in an ideal state ? The egotistic counterplay of bias and preference and faculty must and will be allowed a large measure of freedom for many a day.

Limitation of Bequest : Practical Liberalism

Meantime, out of the complexities of the problem presented by the phenomena of earned and unearned income, there emerges this safe principle : that the most just, the earliest practicable, and the least disturbing forms of taxation of unearned wealth are by way of taxation of the unearned increment in land values, surplus taxation of higher incomes, and limitation of the power of bequest. And while Socialists have been alternately spinning impracticable theories and vituperating Liberal politicians, these very discriminations have been effectually made by Liberal statesmen. The death duties imposed by Sir William Harcourt have become a copious source of national revenue, available for social betterment ; the first important innovations made by Mr Asquith consisted in increasing the pressure of the death duties in general, and differentiating taxation as between earned and unearned income ; and a further-graduated Income Tax and a tax on land values were added by Mr Lloyd George in 1909. Once more, what is just and practicable in the Socialist doctrine has been embodied in the Liberal policy and programme. What is sound in the moral sense for progressive Socialism is implicit in the principles upon which practical Liberalism proceeds.

CHAPTER IV

SOCIALIST MISCALCULATIONS

(1) *The Earlier Schools*

IT will not be denied, probably, by the saner Socialists of to-day, that the plans and forecasts of the founders of the movement, in whose day it received its name, were visionary and fallacious. Recent Socialism, indeed, has been only too ready to make light of the pioneers, dismissing them as " Utopian " in contrast with the attribute of " scientific," liberally bestowed by the modern movement on its own propaganda. Engels, whose book on *Socialism, Utopian* and *Scientific*, while it paid honour to his predecessors set the fashion of this terminology, had learned enough from his own blunders (though he never learned any humility) to recognize that error was not the monopoly of the pioneers. Writing in 1892 of the " Revival of the East End of London," which he hailed as a great renascence, he avowed that " undoubtedly the East Enders have committed colossal blunders ; so have their predecessors ; and so do the doctrinaire Socialists who pooh-pooh them." In some such spirit of sympathy, and with no unscientific animus, we may learn from a contemplation of early Socialistic miscalculations and miscarriages more than Engels ever did of the nature of his own and later errors of judgment.

Robert Owen

Though modern theoretic Socialism may be said first to take form in the writings of some French publicists of the eighteenth century, and in the Socialist conspiracy of Babœuf under the French Directory, it is in England that the movement first took anything like a durable and popular shape, and received its name. Modern

Socialism practically begins with Robert Owen, and was in effect baptized by him at an international conference. To dwell as we have to do here on his mistakes and failure, or even on his excessive self-esteem, would be both unjust and misleading if we did not from the first acknowledge his moral nobility and his fruitful beneficence. All subsequent social speculation and aspiration have been touched by his spirit. In his own day, while he had for a time a ready and friendly hearing from many highly-placed personages, he met at the hands of both Whigs and Radicals a stress of censure and criticism which to-day, on retrospect, seems ungenerous.

Marx was only too well entitled to point out, as Professor Marshall notes, " how the great Socialist invented and put into working the limitation of the hours of factory labour, the sending to school of factory children, and the system of co-operation ; how all these notions of his were called Utopian and Communistic, and laughed to scorn by almost all respectable people ; and how respectable these notions have since become." The second last phrase is indeed a bad exaggeration ; for Owen in his days of factory reform had a large upper-class support. And Marx, as it happened, had himself disparaged Owen, in the Communist Manifesto, on the score of his opposition to the Chartists. But Macaulay, girding at Southey, who was one of Owen's respectable backers, could find nothing better to say of the Socialist in 1830 than that he " is more unreasonably and hopelessly in the wrong than any speculator of our time." In his later period, apart from his own enthusiastic following, it was only the most aggressive of the Radicals who, themselves enthusiasts, mixed kindly recognition of his boundless benevolence with genial satire of his unpracticality. But when we realize his relation to the other progressive movements of his day, we see why he was thus assailed.

Owen, though he broke with orthodox religion and suffered much odium in consequence, had in him much of the idealism which inspired the quasi-communistic religious movements of earlier times. He was not merely an optimist, as was Adam Smith before him ; he was an à priori optimist, credulous of the potency of goodwill to regenerate the earth. And his own early

and signal success at New Lanark, the product of his
moral and administrative genius working under restraint
in a limited field, gave to his benevolent bias the fixity
of a conviction borne out by a great experience. That
experience is still one of the most wonderful tales of social
organization and felicitous captaincy. By sheer unwearying
persistence in methods of rational kindness, he transformed
a village of 2500 very ordinary workers, whom he found
mostly dissipated, disorderly, and larcenous, into a model
community, sober, cleanly, thrifty, and cordial. Starting
with a factory largely dependent upon miserable and
overdriven child labour, he contrived, under the headship
of capitalist partners bent upon large dividends, first to
lighten somewhat the burden of the children's toil, and
later to provide for the rising generation a kind of schooling
which to this day has not been bettered on the side of wise
loving-kindness and psychological insight. It was upon
this really beautiful success that he built his great miscalculation—a miscalculation possible only to a great
lover of mankind, who was at the same time a great dreamer
and a great doer.

The Dream

From his success in one well-organized enterprise,
conducted on competitive capitalistic lines, Owen inferred
the possibility of a similar organization of all the labour
power of the nation. The error was vital. His own
commercial success had been a competitive one, a success
as compared with the less success of rival establishments.
An enrolment of all the unemployed labour power of the
community in similar establishments was strictly a chimera.
It presupposed an unlimited demand for an unlimited
production of commodities. Owen, at first, could not see
the economic wood for the trees. He did, indeed, soon
begin to see that his ideal involved a communistic or
socialistic State ; and towards that ideal he directed
himself. But in his whole life's work on those lines he
failed, because he was not truly planning for society as it is. It
might seem no monstrous thing to ask that industry should
in detail be organized as he had organized New Lanark.
But he was asking a great deal more. Even as he demanded

that the warring sects should dissolve, he in effect required that all the myriads of competing cells of the social organism should enter into a quite new relation with each other.   His prescription to the world in general and to men individually was that they should get a new heart.   For the mediate readjustments of which alone communities are capable, he proposed to substitute a vast volitional transformation of which they are incapable.

Hence he found himself in radical, howbeit benevolent, opposition to all the other reforming movements of his time. He could see no utility in any of them.   Chartists on the one hand, and Free Traders on the other, he blandly dismissed as mistaken zealots, striving for mediate measures which could not regenerate society ; and in the doctrine of Malthus, which gave Darwin his basis, he could see no scientific value.   For mere political reform he cared nothing, telling the reformers that only a change of heart could change society.   Very naturally they, knowing too well how visionary was his plan and how essential was their own humbler programme, prescribed to him, genially or otherwise, a change of head, and their practical reforms went on without him.

The French Communitarians

While Owen was sowing his visionary but not valueless seed in England, other notable schemers and dreamers were at work in France, independently of him. The tracing of the psychic derivations on both sides has yet to be definitely done.   Owen is very elusive as regards his sources of inspiration, because, though he read much, he quoted little.   We now know that he was influenced by Rousseau and Godwin, but other possible French influences suggest themselves.   He and his French contemporary, Saint Simon, however, appear to have known little of each other, though they erred in similar fashion.

Saint Simon propounded a new non-supernatural religion which was to supersede Christianity ; and he, too, planned new cell-forms of society, so to speak, by way of altering the nature of the whole structure.   Of course, he and his followers after him failed.   For venturing to criticise, as did

Owen, the existing marriage laws, they were held in horror, and their innocent attempts at communitarian life were libelled. In many respects their ideals were far ahead of their day ; and in none more so than in the conception of an international federation, which Saint Simon passed on to his disciple, Auguste Comte. But he had no workable plan for French society as it then existed ; and the powerful brain of Fourier, which in the same period was working at a theory and criticism of social evolution and a plan for a new communitarian way of living, produced only an abortive experiment. In the atmosphere of political revival set up in France by the revolution of 1830, such schemes and ideals germinated hopefully ; and in the revolution of 1848 the idealists strove to realize, in " National Workshops " and otherwise, the larger socio-political conceptions to which they gave rise. But the large and the small, the particular and the general schemes, collapsed alike, and the second Empire rose on the ruins of the second Republic.

Causes of Failure

We need hardly ask why such plans failed. Without going into detail and tracing the counterplots and the recriminations, the exposures and the disillusionments all round, we can see at a glance that the failure followed inevitably from the nature of the human material. A greatly better society pre-supposes greatly better members. A state of all-round co-operation requires people fitted so to co-operate. The known average mass, self-seeking, quarrelsome, sectarian, prejudiced, may gradually be led to substitute in one or more socio-economic relations a simple and relatively-easy measure of co-operation for the methods of atomistic individualism. Such new and gradual combination is precious and educative ; and in giving rise to the English system of co-operative distributive societies, Owen did enough to leave his mark on social history if he had done nothing else.

But the broad law of social evolution is as plain as the laws of biological transformation. Even the Owenite community at New Harmony, save in so far and so long as it was magistrally ruled by Owen, with his special prestige, demanded more of average men and women than they were prepared to do. A general inclination towards brotherhood could not fuse a heterogeneous community, varying widely in culture, creed and character. Save under a semi-fanatical propulsion, involving much self-repression and virtual impoverishment of life, such as took place in some of the more lasting communistic groups in the United States and in antiquity, men and women must have individualistic elbow-room. Individual relations cannot in general pass under completely new laws of association with permanent comfort and satisfaction to the whole personality. Needless to say, what holds good of groups inclined to enter voluntarily into a new order of fraternity, obviously holds good in a much greater degree of entire societies. The economic relations of mankind, which are the most spontaneously individualistic and egoistic of all, can only by the most gradual processes, under slow pressures of partial combination on voluntary lines, approach to the state of things contemplated by theoretic Socialism. And the failure to see this is nearly as marked in the self-styled " scientific " Socialism of recent times as it was in the " Utopian " Socialism of its predecessors.

CHAPTER V

(2) *The Fatalism of Marx and Engels*

IT has been truly said by Émile Faguet that the special
achievement of Karl Marx was not his formula of
" surplus value," which had been made current
before his time by English Socialists of the school of Owen,
or his " iron law of wages," which was only an adaptation
of Ricardo's earlier doctrine as to wages and population,
but his teaching as to the inevitable emergence of Socialism
from the industrial evolution of the past. The " Utopian "
Socialists before him had all appealed to philanthropic
instinct and social sympathy. Owen had called upon men
to dismiss at once their sectarian hatreds and their plans
of political reform, and to join hands in a new brotherhood,
whereby alone could society be transformed. Saint
Simon had similarly prescribed a new religion and a new
combination in voluntary communities; and Fourier
had planned his Phalanstery, in which communism was
to be practised scientifically. All alike had insisted that
men should take thought for the morrow in a new fashion,
and shape a better world by general goodwill.

Marx, in the " Communist Manifesto " of 1832, had
propounded a very different doctrine. It made no demands upon benevolence and self-denial, co-operation and
fraternity. Religious considerations it simply ignored,
leaving them to whom they might concern. It did not
invite men to prepare for Socialism; it told them with a
blending of cold scorn and hot menace that Socialism was
coming, whether they wanted it or not. The whole industrial development, they were assured, was irresistibly
leading up to a crisis from which there was only one way
out. The industrial life was rapidly becoming more
miserable, more intolerable. The poor were becoming
poorer, the rich richer. One day the breaking-point

142

would be reached ; the unendurable misery of the toilers would be avenged in a frightful social explosion, and from the awful womb of revolution would be born the new society, in which " surplus value " would become the property of those whose labour had created it, and all things would begin to go well.

As the revolutionary character of Marx's doctrine is in these days often ignorantly and insolently denied by Socialists who profess to be Marxists, it may be well to cite the words of the Communist Manifesto, published by Marx and Engels in 1847 : " We have followed the more or less veiled civil war raging within our present society to the point where that war will break out into open revolution, and where by the violent overthrow of the bourgeoisie the proletariate will establish its dominion." Upon which passage M. Jaurès comments : " It is then, by a violent revolution against the middle-class that " [*i.e.* in Marx's doctrine] " the working class is to grasp power and realize Communism."[1] The matter is in fact put beyond all doubt by the closing paragraph of the Manifesto : " The Communists do not condescend to dissemble their opinions and their aims. They proclaim openly that these ends cannot be attained without the violent overthrow of the whole existing social order. Let the ruling classes tremble at the thought of a communist revolution. The proletaries have nothing to lose but their chains. They have a world to gain."[2]

The Folly of Prophecy

Such was the germinal doctrine of the post-Owenite Socialism, which calls itself " modern " and scientific. Engels, Marx's staunch comrade, filled as his friend was with the German fanaticism of theory, revolting at once against the English philosophy of rule-of-thumb and against the callousness of capitalist and competitive industrialism, indignantly preached the same gospel in the concrete. Where Marx in his larger work dwelt on the

[1] I quote here from the translation of M. Jaurès' " Studies in Socialism," published in *The Socialist Library*, pp. 48-49.
[2] From French trans. by Laura Lafargue, revised by Engels.

economic processes, as he interpreted them, Engels passion-
ately set forth the horrors and miseries of modern industrial
degradation, the ghastly death-roll of factory accidents,
and emotionally drew from the spectacle the same conclusion as was ostensibly reached by Marx on economic
lines.   The two men were at one in their faith in a bloody
revolution, at one in their rage alike against the bourgeoisie, whom they regarded as the odious architects of
social evil, and against the economists who contemplated
the economic problem with either calmness or complacency.
Nothing could be more precise than the prediction with
which, in 1845, Engels concluded his book on *The Condition of the Working Class in England in* 1844.

.   " The war of the poor against the rich, now carried on in detail
and indirectly," he affirmed, " will become direct and universal.   It is
too late for a peaceful solution.   The classes are divided more and
more sharply . . the bitterness intensifies . . . and soon a slight
impulse will suffice to set the avalanche in motion.   Then, indeed,
will the war-cry resound through the land : ' War to the palaces,
peace to the cottages ! '—but then it will be too late for the rich to
beware."

Over sixty years have elapsed since this prophecy was
penned, and mere time has turned it to naught.   As Jaurès
observes, " in whatever sense one may take it," the revolutionary doctrine of Marx and Blanqui and Engels " is
superannuated.   It proceeds either from worn-out historical
hypotheses or from inexact economic hypotheses."   " The
definite form under which Marx, Engels and Blanqui
conceived the proletarian revolution has been eliminated
by history."

Engels, himself, reprinting his book in 1892, airily
alluded to " the many prophecies . . . which my youthful
ardour induced me to venture upon.   The wonder is,"
he added, " not that a good many of them proved wrong,
but that so many of them proved right," ; and he goes on
to claim, in justification of the latter boast, that " the
critical stage of English trade, to be brought on by Continental and especially American competition, which
I then foresaw—though in too short a period—has now
actually come to pass."   He specifies no other of his
prophecies as having been fulfilled.   All the while the
" right " prediction was as vain as the others.   The course

of English trade has confounded the prophet, even as did the course of English politics. Unabashed by the knowledge that he had confidently given to the world utter delusion as scientific truth, he still posed as prophet and sought to " bluff " mankind in the name of science. So vain is the notion that an unscientific world can suddenly become scientific ; so unteachable can men be when possessed by the spirit of passion and self-assertion.

The Fallacy of Fatalism

To the very last, Marx and Engels failed to attain the evolutionary standpoint, or even to reach such a rational view of social causation as was possible to logical thinkers before Darwin and Spencer. They would presumably have called themselves determinists, as they always called themselves materialists. But their determinism was always at bottom unscientific, inasmuch as it was fatalistic. Fatalism is not determinism. Determinism involves the recognition of choice as the vehicle or proximate cause of the act. Fatalism is the assertion that choice does not count. And when Marx and Engels, repudiating previous Socialistic appeals to human volition, declared that volition could neither hasten nor hinder the social explosion, which they declared to be inevitable, they were talking neither determinism nor materialism, but a fatalism on a par with that of Islam.

To call a given political development " inevitable " is a favourite device of those who desire it but cannot morally justify it ; but no scrupulous man will ever use such a characterization as the defence of a disputed action. Of actions which result from choices, either all are " inevitable " or none are. On either view, the description is meaningless as applied to one willed action in particular, in distinction from others. Everything that has happened, every social evolution, may be said to have been inevitable when looked back upon. But no prospective line of human action or revolution is rationally to be singled out as " inevitable " when it depends upon choices not yet made, and events which have not yet happened.

In brief, the Marx-Engels doctrine was both philosophically and politically unintelligent, in so far as it was sincere. It might indeed be argued that when Marx laid down a strategy, a táctic, for the proletariate in the Communist Manifesto, he showed that he did not believe in the " inevitable." But though he may have been inconsistent, we must suppose him to have been in earnest in his quasi-philosophic doctrine. And it was radically fallacious. It meant failure to understand that history is a process of choices, of reciprocal adjustments. It was at bottom less rational, less scientific, than the appeals of the Utopists to men to choose another way of life. And it won adherents by force of its very irrationality. As Faguet remarks, men who are told that the evolution they would like to see is in course of irresistible accomplishment are very readily won to assent. The baffled enthusiasts of the generation before 1848 found a new stimulus in the doctrine of an irresistible social causation ; and when the revolution of that year came, the Marxists hailed it as the predicted cataclysm. When it failed, there was, for a time, despair ; but the next generation could in turn draw new comfort from the gospel of " the inevitable " ; and Marxism, profiting by the new pioneer work of Lassalle, came to be accepted in Germany in all its fallacious fulness.

Action checked by Theory

From the first, political progress has been partially arrested by the adoption of the Marxian error. It involved a policy of abstention from evolutionary measures ; and an alienation of forces which might have collaborated in such an evolution. Since Socialism was " inevitable," what Socialists had to do was not to take practical steps towards realizing it, but simply to be ready to take possession when the cataclysm came. Hence their policy of masterly inactivity as regards practical politics in Germany, which at length gave rise to the action of the Bernstein faction, who realized that a desired historic change is rationally to be made by voluntarily moving along a path instead of waiting for an earthquake which will hurl us across the desert. In consequence, the orthodox Marxian gospel has been at length modified by its very sworn champions. The false doctrine of " increasing misery " is officially abandoned, and as M. Jaurès again notes, the usual attempt is made to show that it was never held. The Marxians have had to unlearn, so far as they can, part of the A B C of Marxism.

But to this day the harm persists. To this day many Socialists waste their strength and generate reaction, even when they do not threaten a violent revolution, by declaiming over the ultimate ideal as if it were a programme, a course of action possible *en bloc* to the men of to-day. Still swayed by the original dream of a bloodily beneficent cataclysm, from which a new social order was to leap full grown, they argue as if political volition could enact such a change on appeal. From one extreme they have passed to the other. After denying that choice counted, they have come to believe that one set of choices can reshape the social cosmos, which is in sum the complex of innumerable warring and counteracting choices. The last thing they will learn is that from A to Z the way lies through the alphabet ; that from one definite social order to another generically different, the way lies through a slow series of intermediate stages, each one of which in turn is the fruition of a policy, a propaganda, a struggle, an adjustment of living people to a somewhat different environment ; that, in short, while Socialism means theory, action means Liberalism.

CHAPTER VI

(3) *Continental Compromises*

REFERENCE was made in the last chapter to the part played in Germany by Ferdinand Lasalle as the practical forerunner of the so-called " Scientific " movement of the school of Marx. That part was more important than some latter day Marxians are willing to recognize; and though Lassalle's ideal was, in some respects, less high than that of Marx, it is very doubtful whether the latter could have obtained its present following without Lassalle's pioneer work. Marx, of course, preceded Lassalle as a teacher, but it was the latter who first set up a strong popular movement. A boundless self-confidence, says his Socialist biographer Bernstein, was the bane of Lassalle's life, and it was the cause of his tragical death; but it was bound up with his qualities of initiative and organizing energy, and it built up a notable party.

He, on his side, was undoubtedly inspired by Marx's writings, but he was also inspired by those of Proudhon, who feared and hated everything communistic, and who, standing midway between Socialism and *laissez-faire*, proposed that the State should help associations of workers by lending them capital. It was on this line that Lassalle, after taking his part in a good deal of propaganda on Socialist lines, led the German Working Men's Association, which he joined in 1863, within a few months of its establishment. Previously he had sought to dominate the Progressist party, which was formed of democrats, who found the German Liberal party of that day impossible, by reason of the foolish middle-class prejudice that excluded working men from its membership. Having been placed under the ban for his revolutionary activities in the 1848 period, Lassalle was willing enough to take a " moderate "

course in politics; but when the Progressists refused to
concede to him the pre-eminence he craved, he was prompt to
accept the offer of leadership from the workers. It was
in this capacity that he made, or crowned, his reputation
as a political leader and Socialist prophet. Already, in
1862, a lecture by him to an artisans' association on
modern social and political developments led to his prose-
cution. After a brilliant defence he was sentenced to a
short imprisonment, which was commuted on appeal to a
fine.

Lassalle as a Practical Politician

It is some proof of his political breadth of view, as
well as of his energy, that within a year Lassalle was preaching the doctrine that the State should lend capital to associations of workers. Schultze-Delitzsch, supported by the
Progressist party, was leading a very successful movement
of voluntary co-operation. There was certainly personal
animus in Lassalle's scurrilous impeachment of Schultze-
Delitzsch, though the latter gave an opening for attack, as
well as ground for distrust, by openly associating himself
with the cause of capitalism. Lassalle's main case against
him—and even this he did not properly prove—was that his
system, however it might help artisans in regular employment and small tradesmen, could do nothing for the mass
of the people; and Lassalle in turn sought to justify his
leadership of the poorer workers by propounding a scheme
in their interest.

These, of course, are not the circumstances in which
economic science is most scrupulously handled, and Lassalle
took a dubious economic ground in order to justify an
impracticable proposal. His economic ground was " the
iron law of wages." This he rightly enough put in the
final Ricardian form that the average wages of labour always
remain reduced to the subsistence necessary, *conformably
with a nation's standard of life*, to the prolongation of existence, and to the propagation of the species. Thus he
admitted, by implication, that a nation may raise its
standard of life, whence it follows that the workers may
secure an increase of wages. He does not seem to have
explicitly propounded that false " law of increasing misery "

which was put forth by Marx, but he at times used language which implied the idea, though he also at times admitted that wages gradually rise. And, denying that the labourer could help himself under the competitive system, he demanded that upon the formation of voluntary Productive Associations by the workers the State should lend them capital, " first at low interest, and eventually free." It is a significant fact that the first really popular movement of Socialism in Germany proceeded for years on a plan which all Socialists now admit to be quite unworkable.

A Vain Dream

British workers and traders, probably, need little proof of the essential futility of the assumption that production could be successfully carried on for any long period by voluntary association of workers with capital either lent or given to them by the State. The experience gained in British attempts at voluntary co-operative production shows how great are the obstacles to success even when the experimenters, having their own capital at stake, will naturally do their best to handle it carefully. They have to face all the uncertainties of trade in competition with producers who either possess or hire the highest administrative capacity to run their businesses, and who are free to assume burdens and run risks which no group of co-operating producers could be expected to agree to face. Given a State supply of capital to such groups, they would in most cases merely take more hazards. Given even the same average administrative capacity as that possessed by their capitalist competitors, they would in a similar proportion of cases become bankrupt or be brought to a standstill ; and then would arise the question whether the State should supply fresh capital to an association which had lost a previous supply. That question would hardly be put twice. The King of Prussia, by Bismarck's advice, once generously advanced a sum of money as capital to a group of poor Silesian weavers ; but the experiment was not officially repeated.

So essentially visionary was Lassalle's scheme that it may seem difficult, in view of it, to regard him as a

man of real political capacity. Had he lived beyond
1864 he would have been shattered by inevitable failure,
and probably driven to yet wilder plans.   Men, however, are to be judged in comparison with their
surroundings;   and   Lassalle   figured   as   a   powerful
leader alongside of Bismarck, who in point of fact
had interviews with him, and, finding him " at heart
a true aristocrat," was not unwilling to coquet with his
schemes, though in the nature of things he could not
possibly work them.   Bismarck's economic insight was not
great, though in these matters responsibility restrained him.

The Lesson of Lassallism

Socialists to-day [1] are wont to argue that Marxism vindicated its " scientific " character by living down Lassallism,
with its recognition of the monarchic State and its
nationalist limitations.   They are entitled to say that
Lassalle was following the anti-Socialist Proudhon, rather
than the Socialist Marx.   But that is not the end of the
matter.   They make the old assumption that while previous
modifications of an ideal have been in turn seen to be
hopelessly fallacious, the last modification is final truth.
Men do not thus suddenly pass from utterly unscientific
ways of thought to scientific ways.   The German Socialist
movement, though latterly led by clearer-headed men than
Lassalle, is far from having got rid of its earlier chimerical
inspirations and its confusion between speculation and
science.   It still presents some of the main characteristics
of the Lassallean movement—credulous acceptance of
doctrine laid down by an admired personality ; uncritical
partisanship of an ideal ; impatience of the toil of analysis.
And all socialistic movements will continue to exhibit the
same characteristics until their adherents in general
learn to handle human troubles as problems in political
science rather than as themes for exercises in sympathetic
rhetoric.

[1] *i.e.*, in 1912.   The German Socialists of that period have largely
modified their views in the face of Bolshevism, which in turn has made
new converts.

CHAPTER VII

SOCIALIST MISCALCULATIONS

(4) *The Gulf between Theory and Practice*

SOME champions of old ideals might make a telling attack at one point at least upon the current lore of Socialism—that is, upon the entire self-satisfaction of so many of its adherents. So far as their propaganda shows, they are conscious only of the need for change in the social system and for reformation in the characters or annihilation of the property of all of those who are content to keep that system as it is. Of any suspicion of the need for a transformation in their own characters, or even a careful development of their own minds, they give no hint. The idealists of the past were seldom so uncritical upon this side of their problem. Owen, as we saw, insisted upon a moral adaptation first and foremost, though he was visionary enough in his expectation that it would be spontaneously made. And, with all his defect of political and economic science, he never missed, as did the Marxian school from the first, the essentials of his problem on the side of moral science. Always he was faithful to his ethical determinism. Teaching that " men's characters are made for them and not by them," he never lapsed into hate of those whose selfishness or prejudice stood in the way of his ideal. Preaching that brotherly love was essential to the reconstruction of society he never stultified himself by disseminating hate. Hence the fruitfulness of so much of his work despite the failure of his larger hope.

Of present-day Socialism, on the other hand, the great snare is precisely moral egoism. Professing to seek the material welfare of all, the Socialist tends to suppose himself immune from moral criticism. But it is possible not only to seek the ostensible common economic good in a spirit of egoism, but to miss any progress towards it by reason of lack of knowledge, lack of wisdom, lack of sympathy, and lack of justice. Some old ideals put the first condition of social improvement in self-reform. " Let me be more thoughtful, more scrupulous, more considerate, more patient ; and society will be to that extent at least the better," is one such form of aspiration. But it is possible to doubt, in view of much Socialist journalism and propaganda, whether many of its exponents have ever dreamt that any improvement in their own minds and tempers can be requisite to the production of a better social state.

" The Falsehood of Extremes."

Doubtless such absence of self-criticism is partly resultant from the tendency at the opposite extreme to insist that all reform must come from within. One school asks for better houses. Another retorts that better houses will be got when men have better characters. The truth to be recognized by the practical politician is that better houses help towards better characters, as do better characters towards better houses. But where, on the other hand, the social betterment demanded is far in advance of the capacity to retain and maintain it, the futility of the demand is sufficient to explain if not to justify the indignant or scornful revolt of those who protest that Paradise is not to be conducted by a community which in their view is abundantly composed of fools and knaves.

And this is the gist of the matter as regards those Socialists who, refusing the way of evolution, meet all schemes of gradual ascent by demands for the total embarkation of society in their balloon. It is sometimes denied that there are any such. The truth is that the same men, for sheer lack of mental coherence, will alternately denounce all plans for gradual advance and deny that they reject the notion of such advance. One of their catchwords is " Socialism the only hope " ; and they will meet every proposal for reform in detail by arguments to the effect that no reform in particular is attainable till the all-comprehending reform of Socialism has been attained. Yet when they are challenged to plan the achievement of

Socialism, they spontaneously set to sketching " steps,"
which are the refutation of their formula.

The Laws of Social Evolution

The cause of this incoherence is the inability or the
unwillingness to realize clearly that all social reform is
a social function, performable only in virtue of a balance
of the forces of co-operation over those of repulsion ; and
that for any great extension of co-operation, men must
be prepared by prior extensions. Society can become
capable of all-round co-operation only in virtue of a series
of experiences in widening co-operation. This holds good
as obviously on the side of the economic as of the moral
ideal. The amount of co-operative faculty—faculty as
distinguished from mere aspiration—required to conduct
a wholly socialized society is enormously greater than
anything yet evolved in any society whatever. Those
who fail to realize as much have simply failed to represent
to themselves in imagination, even faintly, the vast complexity of the control involved.

Even Mr. Bellamy contemplated complete socialization
only as an outcome of a process in which the organization
of all industry had passed through the stage of the syndicate.
Perhaps I should not say " even Mr. Bellamy," for some
Socialists talked of that amiable writer in his lifetime with
as much contumely as they are want to bestow upon mere
Liberals. My friends of the Fabian Society, I remember,
used to hold him up to contempt as a " bourgeois " and a
" Boston Sunday-school teacher." As it happened, the
Boston Sunday-school teacher achieved what they never
did, the exposition of an intelligible working scheme for a
Socialist society. If they are now capable of appreciating
a rational service to their own cause they will lay a wreath
upon his grave. He is, in fact, the only Socialist, with the
partial exception of Gronlund (who accused him of plagiar-
ism), that had so far propounded a thinkable detailed
system of Socialist organization for an entire community.
And he, avowedly, could not conceive of an effectual
resort to his system save after a prolonged evolution in
which organization was perfected and competition reduced
to unity upon individualistic lines.

It is difficult to gather what is the conception of social evolution now prevailing among the Socialists of Germany. Some years ago it appeared ot be, clearly enough, that of a process of competitive individualistic evolution ending in either a physical or parliamentary revolution, whereupon Socialists will proceed to run everything upon Socialist lines. What those lines are to be, Herr Bebel, able man as he is, has never attempted to sketch save in the vaguest way. It is sufficient to say, in comment, that Socialists will be no more able to pass from a state of slight and difficult social co-operation to one of complete social co-operation than the Britons of the age of Julius Cæsar were able to pass at will to the stage of constitutional government through a national Parliament.

The Moral Need

But the visionariness of the neck-or-nothing school of Socialists is best revealed by putting their own account of contemporary society in correlation with their own proposals. Upon their showing it is a " thieves' kitchen," a scene of selfish exploitation, in the maintenance of which Liberals and Tories are wholly at one. And it is out of this material that they propose in part to build their " New Moral World." To the task they bring, upon their own side, a moral gift as moderate as the faculty for ratiocination shown in their formulation of their case. To judge from their propaganda, their most constant inspiration is that of anger : it is mainly upon the exploitation of malice that they appear to rely in their appeals. It would be difficult to imagine a worse means of making good the lack of co-operative faculty noted on the economic side of the problem. Where the ideal society needs the ideal maximum of love, sympathy, patience and mutual comprehension, it is clamoured for by men who seem rather below than above the present modest average of those endowments. Want of co-operative experience is to be supplemented by an ingrained habit of hostility and viruleuce, which causes alienation even in the loosely related society of present-day politics, and which would reduce any scene of joint action to chaos in a day.

The truth is, that the most zealous holding of an advanced social ideal is no security whatever for fitness to live up to it. The old systems of voluntary Socialism set up by followers of Owen and others can be seen to have attracted to them men and women not more but less fitted for such modes of life than many who were content to take life as it is The " cranks," the people who got on rather badly with normal neighbours, and put the blame for it wholly on the neighbours and never on themselves, carried to the new communities their extra stock of incompatibilities, with the results that might be expected. " State " Socialists, it is true, might argue from this that separate experiments are no test of what can be achieved by the whole community, in which the normal control the abnormal. But when they themselves constantly assert the bad faith, the heartlessness, the anti-social bias of the mass of the members of the great political parties, what rational faith can they have in the optimistic accounts they give of what human nature is bound to achieve on a new footing ?

Granting, it may be replied, the extravagance of much Socialist abuse of the " bourgeoisie," are not those who give the bourgeoisie a better character committed to recognizing that it is capable of a much more ideal life than the present ? The answer is that the question is precisely one of degree. The sane account of human nature is that it is similarly faulty, at bottom, in all classes : that while labour sets up more wholesome conditions of moral life than does idle wealth, and makes men in some ways more sympathetic, it involves—and this is part of the very plea of labour for better conditions—limitations in culture which react on ideals ; and, further, that no conditions of life can rapidly eliminate egoism and prejudice. Assuredly there are some people much better fitted for the Socialist life than most of those who preach Socialism ; but if out-and-out Socialism is preached to a majority who by all accounts are either hostile or apathetic, which among these can derive confidence in the programme from the contemplation of a Socialist record which thus far tells in every page of bitter schism and strife among the idealists themselves, and a propaganda which utters three sentences of vituperation for one of persuasion ? And if the idea is seen to attract in particular the exasperated and neurotic types, the least capable of an orderly transmutation of life, who can thereby be made hopeful of the change ?

In short, the gulf between the theory of an ideal Socialist state and the actual moral and mental practice even of professed Socialists is too wide for the most optimistic imagination to bridge. The ideal State needs for its creation and maintenance at least a majority of decently ideal people. And these are apparently no more rapidly produced, on the moral side, by the Socialist movement, than they are on the economic side by the competitive industrial life.

CHAPTER VIII

THE FUTILITY OF THE THEORETIC DISPUTE

NO better illustration of the futility of most of the disputation over the ideal of Socialism could be given than is supplied by the reply of a Socialist to the speech of a leading Liberal in the autumn of 1907.[1] The Liberal opened his case by admitting, as so many Liberals willingly admit—and as has been not only admitted, but contended, in the opening chapters of this series—that the Socialist ideal is morally good, though beyond men's present capacity. He does not, indeed, seem to have made the further admission that the economic ideal is also theoretically the best ; but his argument on this head took the line of a demonstration—very clear and very convincing—that the ideal is utterly inapplicable at the present stage of industrial and commercial evolution ; and it is possible that his hearers took this for a confutation of the ideal, as ideal.

However that may be, the Socialist in an eloquent reply, delivered a few days later, granted both of the Liberal's main contentions, while urging, on the other hand, that the present industrial and commercial system is in process of obvious evolution towards one in which the multiform machinery of competition will be reduced to a much simpler structure by the agency of voluntary combination, as in the American trusts. This answer is, of course, quite valid, if the Liberal be understood to argue that the middleman will always play as large a part as he has played in the past generation, and that a State control of all production, distribution, and exchange will always be as far from practicability as it is now. But in thus arguing for the recognition of a continuous evolution and modification of the industrial system, which alone makes possible the

---

[1] The speakers were Sir William (later Lord) Robson, and Mr. Philip Snowden. Both spoke at South Shields.

ultimate attainment of his ideal, the Socialist is putting
himself, for practical purposes, on the same platform
with his antagonist.   He admits that present conditions
exclude Socialism.   And once more the question arises :
What is the use of politically disputing over the remote
ideal if it be admitted that it is NOT a political programme
for to-day ?

Socialist Admissions and Confusions

Nothing could be more explicit in its way than the
Socialist's admission as to the necessary tentativeness of
all advance, and the impossibility of realizing the moral
ideal at the hands of an unideal humanity.   " Socialism,"
he declared, " is nothing more or less than adapting our
industrial and social system to the forces of progress.
These forces are always moving."   And he was no less
explicit as to the limitations of character.   " If the
Liberal," he is reported to have said, " had taken a little
trouble to understand them, he would have known that one
of their axioms, or postulates rather, was that Socialism
would progress just as the intelligence of human beings
progressed, and that the advance of Socialism would be
made just as the moral character of the people developed."

Now, the Socialist is here putting as the doctrine of
Socialists in general what is only the doctrine of a section,
and a doctrine forced upon even that section by criticism
from without.   As we have seen, the " modern " Socialist
movement, as distinguished from the pre-Marxian, began
as a conception of a cataclysm, a revolutionary social
explosion, arising not out of advancing intelligence, but out
of the intolerable stress of popular misery.   That is still,
or lately was, ostensibly the doctrine of many, if not most,
members of the Social Democratic Federation.   I have
repeatedly heard the doctrine from members of that body.
Again and again, in past years, have I heard them talk
of the ultimate resort to weapons which they held to be
inevitable.   William Morris, as we saw, propounded the
same ideal.   My friend Mr. Belfort Bax still affirms the
" revolution " formula.   The Socialist just cited delivered
his speech at South Shields.   In the very week in which
he delivered it, I received from South Shields a challenge,

on the part of a branch secretary, to debate the question of " revolutionary " Socialism with one who would champion that ideal.

Possibly the challengers used the phrase with no clear consciousness of its meaning. A great deal of Socialist talk is so uttered. But the cause can hardly be helped by the Socialist champion demonstrating that his fellow-champions are much given to declaiming at random. Unhappily their habit is carried to lengths which invite charges of sheer unscrupulousness. About the same time I delivered to an Ethical Society a lecture on " The Fear of Socialism," one part of which was devoted to showing the value of the moral and economic ideals of the higher Socialism, and the hollowness of much of the current denunciation of the movement in general ; while the rest was given to pointing out the errors and extravagances by which Socialists earn discredit. In the discussion which followed I was told by one Socialist that I was setting up men of straw, only to knock them down, and that no Socialist now affirms the doctrine of revolution. This assertion was applauded by a number of the Socialists present. Within ten minutes another Socialist, referring to my criticism of the idea of a revolutionary war sketched by Morris, asked whether ten years of such war would not be better than the continuance of the present state of society ? and this question was still more loudly applauded by the same persons. They had implicitly endorsed the ideal they had just before repudiated. People so incoherent in their thinking should not be surprised if they are flatly accused of lack of common honesty. Certainly they are not likely to earn intellectual respect.

But even the Socialist debater, after making the explicit admission above quoted from him, is reported to have gone on to say that " human nature, so called, is very largely, if not entirely, the creation of external circumstances and conditions." This is put as if it were a vital qualification of the previous admission. But to what does this second postulate lead us ? If human nature be mainly the creation of external conditions, how is it to be so altered as to make it willing to recon-struct those conditions ? Must the " selfish rich " and the mere Liberal alike be subjected to a forcible change of

environment to make them better ? Or will the ignorant
and not very intelligent poor be made highly intelligent
and fit for a comparatively ideal society by simply improving their environment ? Either way, who is to begin
altering the environment—the rich or the poor ? The
Socialist has first of all admitted that the social change
will take place only step by step with the rise in intelligence.
Then the poor, on that view, can do but little at a time, and
the rich will be reformed only a little at a time.   This being
so, the plea about the overwhelming influence of the environment serves only to reinforce the previous postulate that
social change can be made but slowly, gradually, step by
step ; which is precisely our Liberal doctrine.   Some rise
in intelligence, and in sympathy, will lead to some material
betterment ;   and some material betterment will help
forward the movement of intelligence.   Where, then, is the
pretence of any radical difference between *such* Socialism
and other people's Liberalism ?

Back to the Clouds

The pretence of such radical difference can be
defended only by a return to the propounding of the
ultimate ideal, which has already been seen to be beside
the case.   Yet, thus it is that the debate is habitually
reopened on the Socialist side. Let it be granted that,
if the Socialist is beating the air in putting forward as a
programme for to-day the ideal which he admits to be
practicable only for a remote and much-evolved generation,
the anti-Socialist is equally beating the air if he seeks to
confute that ideal *as* an ideal for posterity.   And into this
error some critics of Socialism are constantly falling.   They
argue that the ideal must be bad, because for us to-day its
forcible realization—no other being possible—would mean
an intolerable restriction of Liberty.   Schaeffle argues so
after expressly contending, as against the Socialists, that no
generation can rationally hope to frame ideals for a posterity
hundreds or thousands of years off.   That is perfectly true ;
but the truth cuts both ways.   If Mr. Wells is moved to
derision, as a Socialist, by the limited ideals of many of
his fellow-Socialists, much more is posterity likely to be

set smiling by reading the prescriptions now written out for it.   But the chances obviously are that it will smile at least as much at the anti-Socialist of to-day as at the Socialist of to-day, should it be led to read the lucubrations of both.

Precisely because we cannot know what posterity will think best—save perhaps as regards some broad generalizations—we cannot say that ultimate Socialism will be felt by anybody as a restraint on liberty.   If an early Briton had been miraculously presented with a suit of twentieth-century clothes, he would have regarded it, we may reasonably infer, as a quite horrible form of bondage, beside which mere slavery were bliss ; and if a motor-car had been supernaturally produced and run in the Dark Ages it would have been regarded a a mere work of Satan.   Is it at all unlikely that our posterity will regard our economic " liberty " somewhat as we now regard that of savages ? The chances, philosophically reckoned, are that they may. John Mill averred in so many words that " the restraints of Communism would be freedom in comparison with the present condition of the majority of the human race."[1] What then can be more vain than the practical quarrel over the " idealness " of the ideal ?

In the words of Mill, yet again : " We are too ignorant either of what individual agency in its best form, or Socialism in its best form, can accomplish, to be qualified to decide which of the two will be the ultimate form of human society."   In formulating the conditions of maximum production, we cannot pretend to know whether posterity will desire maximum production under those conditions.   Is not the plain conclusion, once more, this, that political debate should turn upon what is good, and what practicable, for ourselves as we are to-day ?

[It is now fitting to add that Marxian Socialists in general have given all lovers of liberty the strongest grounds for dreading that their movement makes for the suppression of rational   liberty.   Challenged   to   defend   the   Marxian doctrine of violent revolution and dictatorship, Marxians

---

[1] The latest accounts of Communist life in Russia mark this as so far a false forecast, not merely as regards the life conditions of the non-Communists, but as regards many of the Communists themselves.

have habitually fallen back on empty rhetoric about the lack of " real freedom " in the existing state of society. Yet in that they themselves have had freedom to discuss to the full the whole problem ; and they have never pretended to show how, under a Socialist State, controlling all the means of production, there could be any free discussion of *its* procedure.   The absolute denial of freedom of criticism to opponents of the Bolshevik system in Russia is a black infamy, discrediting to the last degree all Bolshevik profession to seek freedom at all.   No worse tyranny has ever subsisted in Europe.   And the recent developments of systematic hooliganism in election meetings by zealots of the Labour Party, making free speech impossible at public meetings, give the gravest reason for regarding " advanced " Labourism as aiming at the Russian results.   The spirit of freedom has no part in such a movement.]

CHAPTER IX

UTOPIAS : THEIR VALUE AND THEIR VICE

TO some readers the thesis of the last chapter may have seemed to imply that systematic social ideals, as such, have no value, and should never be propounded in connection with politics. Being far from holding such a view, I will seek to indicate wherein I reckon the value of systematic social ideals to consist, and, *per contra*, wherein they seem to me to tend to frustrate the aspirations of those who propound them.

It would certainly be difficult to show, historically, that the framing and propounding of ideal systems of society has ever influenced men largely in their favour. Long after the publication of the *Utopia* of Sir Thomas More, which has given us the handiest name for such ideal systems, the term was almost invariably used as a synonym for a more or less absurd fancy. The word to start with meant " Nowhere," " the land which is not " : it was for centuries used to signify " the land which cannot be." Yet in our own time, I think, it is more and more frequently employed with the connotation, " the land which may be." And this fact seems to be in itself a proof of the propagandist value of Utopias, within limits.

Indirect Transmutation

A Utopia, in the first place, sets men speculating on the possibilities of social change ; and merely to do this is possibly to widen the range of political thinking all round. More's book comes into existence in the day of " the New Learning " : and the appeal it is seen to make to such an intellect as that of Erasmus is a warrant for its partial congruity with the widening thought of the time, and its power of furthering the love of light. It was a true Utopia

164

in that it was not at any point realizable by the age to which it was presented, or indeed, by any other ; and its repulsive aspects are such as to evoke the censure of modern Utopists. But who shall say that it availed nothing in stirring to wiser thought some of the better minds of that and succeeding generations ?   Merely to have thought of a new type of society, a type ruled by a higher order of reason than that which shaped existing societies, was to have taken a step in upward evolution.   Individuals must make the beginnings.

It would be impossible to say, without a very searching study of contemporary literature, how far More's ideal may have shocked or repelled contemporary minds ; but the fact that it never ostensibly affected More's credit in England as a practical statesman tells against any supposition that it directly set up reaction.   And there can be little doubt that Bacon's *New Atlantis* forwarded in some degree the general movement of scientific speculation which arose in the two generations following him, though it counted for little with his English contemporaries.

Without attempting to estimate similarly the influence of other Utopias, such as that of Campanella, *The City of the Sun*, we are entitled to hold further, I think, that the *Oceana* of Harrington, so highly praised by Hume in the next century for its speculative energy, counted for not a little in promoting political thought in the generation of Locke.   And, to come to our own time, whatever may have been the persuasive effect of the *Icarie* of Cabot in the first half of the nineteenth century, there can be no question that some stimulation has been given to the spirit of social reform by the series of imaginative projections, narrative and other, negative and positive, achieved by Mr. H. G. Wells.   The most impressive of all his books, *The Time Machine*, and the less remotely speculative romance entitled *When the Sleeper Wakes*, seem notably fitted to arouse men newly to the possibilities of evil germinating in a system of uncontrolled capitalistic production.   On the other hand the quasi-constructive picture presented by Mr Wells in *In the Days of the Comet*, a true Utopia, is so vividly suggestive of the need of moral regeneration as a means of economic reconstruction that it is impossible to doubt its having largely influenced a multitude of readers to new reaches of thought and new intimacy of self-examination. It is thus that ideals, Utopias, speculations, can affect the mental climate and temper of an age, leaving all men somewhat different who have been touched by them.

Direct Repulsion

But now comes the *per contra*. He who frames Utopias gives, in a special sense, hostages to fortune. He had need be keenly circumspect, if he would not give men new occasion to scoff. When Sir Thomas More failed to stand the test of the stress of practical politics in his own day, when the Utopist figured as a bitter persecutor, when the humorist gave way to malice, he had helped to turn many men's faces away from any sympathetic contemplation of the ideal of his younger and better days. No less, probably, did the scientific absurdities and erring dogmatisms of Bacon turn men even of a scientific bent against any reception of his best prescriptions for the conduct of the intellect. It is needless to say anything of the further obscuration of the great Chancellor's moral and intellectual influence by his formal lapse from judicial rectitude. He himself knew it only too tragically well.

And, to come to our own time, who shall say that Mr. Wells's formulation of a Samurai-ruled State has the same persuasive power as either his arousing visions of a downwardly evolving race or his romance of a race morally transformed by a cosmic miracle? The Samurai ideal at once gives pause and shock to every reader who has mastered the best lesson of Mill's *Liberty*—the lesson that a thoroughgoing benevolent despotism would be the most disabling of all conceivable human experiences; and that the sole security for social health is the safeguarding of initiative and self-rule in all. Perhaps no more arresting menace has ever been thrown out in the name of science than the doctrine laid down by Professor Metchnikoff in his *Studies on Human Nature*, to the effect that in the ideal future political choices will be left to experts, even as the practice of medical science is left to experts to-day. Such a deliverance at once forces the political student to say that the biologist is disastrously playing the expert where, in the terms of his own case, he has no *expertise*. In political science M. Metchnikoff, deep biologist as he may be, is a mere confident empiric. And though Mr. Wells is in no such case, being at the least an acute observer of social tendencies, he none the less sharply challenges criticism from those who have plied induction more and deduction less than he. I can well conceive that by his ideal of a Japanized future he has disillusioned not a few whom he had led to think hopefully of the measure of reconstructive agreement possible to men.[1]

The Snares of the Utopist

The Utopist, in fine, in his own way runs some of the risks besetting the propagandist who, by obtruding his ideal on normally practical people, convinces them either of his inability to understand life or of his menace as an unintelligent fanatic. Infallibly his own limitations, his own blindnesses, will be revealed by his dream, in the exact degree in which it is hortatory. Against the service done by Bellamy in respect of his economic sketch of a voluntary Socialist State, is to be set the disconcerting effect of his presentiment of his own commonplace æsthetic ideals as those of a perfected race. And not all the scorn of Morris for the average life of his day could hide the intellectual shallowness of his own scheme of the future. That a given tendency can be made newly repellent when its promoters crystallize it in an ideal, is made very clear by Mr Kipling, whose vision of a thoroughly militarized world, in which the very schoolboys deliriously practise strategy every Saturday

---

[1] Mr. Wells, I understand, has since, in whole or part, surrendered his Samurai ideal. In his *New Worlds for Old*, indeed, Mr. Wells seems much concerned to conciliate all manner of types, which formerly (or since) he has flouted—assuring the orthodox Christian that Socialism has been associated with Secularism only as early Christians happened to be thrown into the same jails with criminals ; and hinting at openings for flag-worship under Socialism to the Jingo —to say nothing of a promise of " wholesome bottled ales " to the average Briton. Utopia-mongering has strange vicissitudes.

Mr. Wells's later experiments in Utopia-making, it is to be feared, tend to set up the impression that he writes for a certain literary market as little concerned as he to understand practical politics.

afternoon, is the most repulsive Utopia ever dreamed. A hater of militarism wants no better warning-board against every militarist measure. And even so may the extravagances, the egoisms, the miscalculations and fanaticisms of Socialists, reduced to the form of Utopias, utterly repel many to whom a step or two of Socialistic progress would not be unwelcome.

Above all, where the Utopist, as he is so apt to do, prefigures a sudden or convulsive political change as introducing his ideal State, he renews the old and evil misguidance given to thoughtless zealots by every doctrine of revolution. Mr. Wells frankly makes his last Utopia[1] turn on a vast miracle, as it were, telling men that nothing less will adequately alter human nature;[2] but others are less subtle. Morris, a man essentially unscientific in his thinking, was so possessed by the notion of a sudden or violent new birth that it appeared in his political poetry, even as it did in his romance. " The day of days is here " is the crowning line of one of his songs ; and multitudes have sung it in the belief that verily a great day of transformation is coming. Thus are ill-instructed men and women placed in a visionary relation to the whole problem of life. They had better have had no such pabulum save after a common-sense account of social science. Utopias may stimulate them ; but surely they need science a great deal more.

[1] Written in 1912.
[2] All along, indeed, Mr. Wells is a catastrophist in his sociosophy. No less than six times he has romantically figured the destruction of human society. (*Time Machine, When the Sleeper Wakes, War of the Worlds, Days of the Comet, War in the Air, Food of the Gods.*)
In his recent work entitled *Men as Gods,* Mr. Wells contrives even to make his useful advocacy of Birth Control appear visionary, by putting it on a par with a puerile picture, of leopards educated to vegetarianism. Unscientific science is Mr. Wells's bane.

CHAPTER X

IT is told of a Labour Member who witnessed the ceremony of the opening of Parliament by the King, that he was moved to give the verdict, " All this will take a lot of shifting." He had suddenly realized at once the *vis inertiæ* of institutions, conventions, and traditions, and the extent to which these take the place of ideals for multitudes of people. It is probable that Labour Members, like others, further learn from the daily round in the House of Commons as to the amount of resistance, reasoned and unreasoned, that is evoked by every species of reform, however reasonable it may be or appear. It was Lord Derby, the colleague of Disraeli, who met a complaint from a friend as to the small amount of legislative achievement in the House of Commons with the answer : " If you knew how confoundedly hard it is to get through anything at all here, you wouldn't wonder that we don't do all you want." The truth is that every important change in the legislative structure of the State affects innumerable persons in unanticipated ways, and sets up unforeseen reactions. And it is the inevitable fate of reformers to be ahead of the immediate possibilities with their theories, even as it is the fate of the rule-of-thumb politicians to be behind the problem with theirs. The whole task of politics is to bring about approximations between the forces of propulsion and repulsion.

The Lesson of Failure

Victor Hugo, in *Les Misérables*, makes one of his characters avow the perplexity which overtook the best friends of the French Revolution, when they saw, again and again, the social organism react in utterly unexpected directions from their most vigorous pressures. " What is this strange thing," they asked, " which never moves as it is pushed, and develops new tendencies as fast as we go about to control the old ? " Herbert Spencer, noting the same proclivity in things, cites the problem of the iron plate with a bulge in it, as an illustration and an apologue. Your first thought, if you want to flatten the plate again, is to hammer on the bulge. The result is simply to transfer the bulge to the other side. Only the expert knows how to reduce it by hammering round about.

In a certain Greek State, history tells, it was enacted that every citizen who proposed a change in the laws should do so with a halter round his neck. That dramatic stipulation expressed the painful experience of the community in respect of numerous plans to cure social evils, which not only failed of success but called new evils into existence. Spencer has made a collection, depressing but instructive, of a multitude of instances in which our own legislature has had to confess, tacitly or explicitly, the futility of its schemes of reform. It is the plain duty of every reformer to study and profit by that sinister record ; and it is for the conscientious legislator to ask himself : Are we guiltless when we add fresh miscalculations to the roll of failures, fresh abortions to the miscarriages of the past ? Does not every reform miscarried make new reactionists ? Are not Liberal failures the seed of Conservatism ?

So painfully true is this that Spencer might fairly be credited with generating by his *Man versus the State*, if not by his *Introduction to the Study of Sociology*, a very large amount of the more rational Conservatism of our time. So few men will take the trouble to think out the problem. Most are content to note the miscarriages and decide against further experiments, forgetting that if the failures are evils, they still stood for attempts to remove evils more intolerable. Spencer took this short cut to his political conclusions, falling short of true philosophy like all Conservatives before him. But the way to refute him will never be that of mere railing. His negative science must be overpowered by a positive science that goes deeper and looks further, profiting by the truths in the negation to frame more victorious plans. And science is never generated by mere prejudice and passion ; it is the offspring of brooding and patience, the foster-child of " slow time."

Recent Advances.

One of the most comforting symptoms of modern politics is the recent development of schools and movements which aim at truly radical innovations, realizing that one really scientific fiscal change may do work which has been vainly sought to be done by a whole series of empirical measures. One of these planned reforms is the taxation of land values, which is calculated to effect far-reaching benefits in the way of housing, provision of employment, increase of agricultural production, and relief of congestion in the labour market, that can be compassed by no " frontal attacks " upon these evils.   And while the neck-or-nothing Socialists, as usual, deride or disparage the plan on the score that it will not cure all social evils, those of the progressive school put it forward almost as if it were their own invention.   It is the cue of some of the more spiteful assailants of Liberalism, from the side of democracy, to denounce the entire Liberal party for not having already accomplished this vital reform, giving no credit to those who have striven hardest to bring it about.

But some of us can remember how, when Mr. John Morley, in the 'eighties, pleaded eloquently for this very cause, the Socialist section of that day, instead of seconding him, furiously denounced him because he did not concur with them in their demand for a universal Eight Hours Bill, on which they were then concentrating all their activity. The universal Eight Hours Bill came to nothing.   The Fabian Society framed a Bill, which it soon withdrew, tacitly confessing that it was a futility.   Meanwhile, the cause of taxation of land values has been steadily advanced by Liberals, into the fruit of whose labours many Socialists seem now very ready to enter.

So, too, with Old Age Pensions.   Liberals began the modern movement.   Long ago the late Dr. Hunter, as editor of the then Radical *Weekly Dispatch*, elaborated the principle in the name of Liberalism, while Mr Chamberlain was characteristically scheming to exploit it on behalf of Toryism.   One compensation, indeed, for all the harm Mr Chamberlain has wrought, lies in the change he set up in the Conservative camp, where, for purely strategical reasons, acceptance was given to certain of his proposals, so that latter-day Conservatism can no longer play whole-heartedly its old part of sheer negation.   But it is no mere impulse of " concession to Socialism," still less one of concession to Conservatism, that has brought about the nearly unanimous rally of Liberals to the doctrine of Old Age Pensions.   It is, on the one hand, the deepening recognition of the scientific importance of the principle, and on the other, the strengthening resolve to grapple with the problem of poverty in a comprehensive fashion, putting aside the policy of small palliatives.

New Complications

It is true that even among the supporters of Old Age Pensions there are still many who have not realized the reasons in economic science for the measure, being moved mainly by simple sympathy with poverty, or by an *a priori* moral conviction of the right of all workers to State support at old age.   And this jostling of *a priori* with *a posteriori* motives will probably set up trouble when the scheme comes to be developed.   So, too, in regard to the taxation of land values, it is found that some of the Henry-Georgian pro-moters, proceeding on abstract theories of right and wrong in property, talk on the one hand as if it were just to abolish all property in the land without compensation, and on the other, propose to abolish all taxation, limiting State revenue to the exaction of the economic rent.   Such doctrines, if pushed far, will certainly generate reaction.

There is a risk, too, that the doctrine as to the expediency of forcing all land to its best economic use may propel us towards a new form of *laissez-faire*, which will evolve new evils.   But happily, the very forwardness of the new doctrines, and the latter-day development of methods of critical analysis on the side of what now purports to be *laissez-faire*, tend to meet all such overbalancing tendencies with a resistance which, being reasoned, promotes reasoning on the side of the reform.   And so, in the face of all the retardations and casualties of progress, its friends may say with Goethe and Carlyle, " We bid you be of hope."

CHAPTER XI

THE LINE OF ADVANCE

WHEN apparent differences of theory are reduced
to avowals of different degrees of faith in the
possibility of rapid progress, there remain
abundant difficulties in the way of practical co-operation.
And these difficulties at times threaten to become acute,
as between what may be termed the " centre " and the
" left." Not so much in the House of Commons—where
the education of the Council Room modifies, in some degree,
the asperities even of direct hostility, and still more the tone
of disputants heading in the same direction—but on the
platforms outside, where the restraining influences of opposition are replaced by the urgencies of partisan heat, and
above all, by the demands of " the gallery."

The problem alike for Liberals and Labourites (Socialist
or non-Socialist) is : How can the ideals and convictions
of both parties be respected without a degree of conflict
which jeopardizes the common interest ? In both parties,
be it confessed, there are types who are only too ready to
sacrifice that common interest to dogmatic or egotistic
affirmation of their special ideals. Some Liberals are prone
to a kind of language about " Socialism " which is condemned by the very fact that it is so nearly identical with
the Tory rallying-cry of the moment. Yet those who use
it are ostensibly firm in their hostility to Tariff Reform
so-called, the triumphant defeat of which, at three General
Elections, has been the result of a combination of the
Liberal and Labour forces. To do anything to shake that
combination is to give a gratuitous advantage to the common
enemy. On the other hand, some Labourites are given to the
use of language concerning Liberals in general, which
amounts to an eager aspiration for the discredit of the
Liberal cause. And in the way of direct and specific
attack, so far as I can see, far more is done on the Labour
than on the Liberal side.

173

Elements of Strife

During the General Election of 1906, whatever may have been the local strifes of the past, the Liberal tone towards Labour was perfectly friendly. For years, indeed, the Labour party, as such, had little or no experience of criticism on the political platform, while constantly criticizing both of the other parties. The plain truth is, of course, that Liberal and Conservative alike wanted to get the support of Labour ; and the Labour party so-called was perfectly entitled to hold an independent attitude. But one of the elements in the Labour party which has a considerable effect on its platform policy is the presence of a rather large number of ex-Tory working men, who, in the past, had been in an attitude of constant and bitter hostility to Liberal measures and to the Liberal party. This section, far from being penitent for its past resistance to good causes, is apt to be zealous chiefly in the vituperation of the party whose programme it used to oppose ; and there can be no doubt that some Labour orators are incited by its cheers to a denunciation of Liberals which takes no account of the fact that the cheerers have been in the past tools of oppression and reaction.

Now, the Labour party is fully entitled to claim credit, as some of its members often do, for having won to the side of progress Tory working men, who could not have been won over by Liberals. But that credit is no good ground for pandering to the old passions of reactionary workers, whose past political record is bad. It is a plain danger to the Labour party to be thus tempted to play down to what is, on the face of the case, the least enlightened of its own elements. The fact of his being a worker is no vindication of the past opposition of any elector to good and progressive causes. A Tory working man is as much an enemy to democratic progress as a Tory capitalist ; and the judicious Labour leader will lead rather than be led by him.

The Rights of the Labour Party

Let it not be thought that this is an appeal to the Labour party to sink its independence. Nothing of the sort is

suggested.   By its very nature it is bound to maintain a
critical attitude towards the Liberal party.   But if it is
led by the example of " the Opposition " in ordinary party
strife to asperse the men it is criticising, it will simply end in
being in as direct hostility to the Liberal main body as is
the Tory party.   In that case the cause that will benefit
will assuredly be that of the common enemy.   Extremists
in the Labour party do not disguise the fact that, to spite
Liberals, they would rather see a Tory elected, if they cannot
win themselves ; and some Liberal extremists are equally
bitter in their opposition to Labour.   That way madness
lies—and defeat for both.

This temper of the extremists is partly reflected in the
official decision of the Labour leaders to make no kind of
" deal " by way of averting three-cornered fights.   If the
same temper prevails in future, the result may be at least
as disastrous to the Labour party as to the Liberal.   The
trouble will, it is to be hoped, be partly averted by the passing of a measure giving a second choice (which is better
than a second ballot) to the electors in all three-cornered
fights—an arrangement absolutely fair to all parties, inasmuch as it alone can ensure that the candidate elected
shall be chosen by a majority of the electors.   But recent
experience on the Continent warns us that hate between
Liberals and Socialists, if not brought under the discipline
of good sense, may, under any system, lead to lamentable
sacrifices of the common good.   Forewarned should be
forearmed.

The Case of Labour against Liberalism

So far as can be gathered from the utterances of responsible speakers, the political grievances of the Labour party
against the Liberal Government are reducible to these :
(1) That it did not promptly enough at once establish Old
Age Pensions and abolish the Sugar Duty ; (2) that it
nevertheless made a remission of Income Tax (involving a
small loss of revenue) on earned incomes up to a certain
amount ; (3) that it uses the forces of Government to
prevent or suppress industrial riot.   That is to say, most
of the grievance is not as to direction of policy but as to
rate of advance.   Hardly any Socialists, however, have

argued against Mr. Asquith's policy of rapidly paying off
national debt ; many of them, to my knowledge, approve of
it.   Yet their critical case is of the weakest unless they
formulate an argument of that kind ; and if it were formulated it would still be a difference in method, not in aim or
ideal.   What they want is a quicker advance—precisely
what Radicals have always wanted as compared with moderate Liberals.   But both Radicals and Labourites need the
votes of moderate Liberals to carry their point and to hold
the ground gained.   The problem is, to preserve that co-
operation.   If Labour cannot employ criticism without
falling into rancorous enmity, it will confess itself unable
to conduct political life with the measure of wisdom necessary for success and compassed in the past by those whom
it now opposes.

As regards, finally, the quarrel over the employment
of military and police force in the suppression of Labour
riots, the issue can surely be narrowed down to one of
executive judgment.   Too many Labour leaders habitually
speak as if all rioting were innocent, and as if only the
resisting police and soldiers were ever blameable.   Habitual
denunciation of the latter, without a word of blame of the
rioters, is not the way to a right understanding all round.
Blame of precipitate or unnecessary resort to official force
is one thing ; constant championship of forces of disorder
is another.   There must be agreement on the guilt and
folly of all disorder before the ground can be clear for fair
investigation of the conduct of a sorely-tried police, upper
and lower.   But in the very latest Socialist utterances
on the subject, we find appeals made to soldiers not to shoot
rioters (whether with or without exhortations to " shoot
the other fellows,") accompanied by no appeals to the other
side not to use missiles or weapons to begin with.   A
rational Socialist might be expected to see that the appeal
to the soldier not to shoot is without moral excuse or decent
plausibility save on a prior assumption that the demonstrating proletariate uses no violence on its part.

And the rational Labour leader must surely admit that he
ought to police his own demonstrations if the interference
of the police is to be unnecessary.   In these matters, the
Labour party has something to learn.   Some of its members
have repeatedly denounced such a measure as the placing

of soldiers at railway stations under apprehension of their being wrecked during a railway strike. Such a precaution has been described as an act of "intimidation" towards strikers. The words are meaningless save with the implication that either strikers or outsiders should be free to wreck railway stations if they wished to. All such perverse and sinister reasoning is a gratuitous hindrance to a right understanding between Labour organizations and the general public.

Let it be freely granted, however, that the Labour party has already exercised a useful forward pressure on the Liberal party, and in so doing has been an invaluable ally of the Radical section. The practical ideal is that that pressure should usefully continue. Socialism apart, there is hardly one collectively avowed and concrete aim of the Labour party which it does not hold in common with the majority of Liberals. [1] The next important scheme thus far mooted in its name is, as aforesaid, that of nationalization of railways—an old Liberal proposition, to which not only many Liberals but many business men, who are in other respects Conservative, are known to be favourable. To prepare the country for such a measure, and to carry it completely into effect, will be the work of years. It is the business of rational men who desire it, to promote the combination of the required forces, and to minimize their friction. [2]

---

[1] A recent exception is the Capital Levy. And of course recent vote-catching devices of Labour candidates far outgo those of twelve years ago.

[2] The ideal of railway nationalization has had an instructive history. Before the war, a number of Liberals who formerly entertained it began to see that the reorganisation of railway systems and the consequent rise in stock values had made impossible a good national bargain. During the war, all the railways were practically under national control ; and the experience then gained seemed to turn business men in general against any notion of nationalization ; though it was after the War that, as a Coalitionist Minister, Mr. Churchill proposed such a course. To-day, with the old systems reduced to a few groups, the pretence of national gain derivable from a complete unification is quite unimpressive.

CHAPTER XII

THE DANGERS OF REACTION

THE last thing that zealous innovators are disposed to reckon with is the danger of setting up a fatal reaction by their extremer demands. And yet a condensed history of politics is almost in the main a record of such reactions. They chequer the pages of the social history of Republican Greece and Rome ; of Republican Italy in the Renaissance ; and of England in the pre-constitutional period. From 1660 to 1688, English history on the political and social side is largely one of triumphant reaction ; and the greatest of all historic reactions is that which visibly triumphed in Britain, as elsewhere, from 1790 till the passing of the Reform Bill, and lasted more or less effectively for twenty years more. It meant the arrest of nearly every kind of progress in social and mental freedom ; and it was rooted in the deep revulsion of feeling set up by the rapid lapsing of the French Revolution from a movement of generous liberalism to one of terrorism, plunder, slaughter, and tyranny. In that period the very idea of radical social change had become a stone of stumbling for the majority of men.

To say this is not to single out for blame the reformers who miscarried. The best of them were better than those who resisted them ; the worst of them were hardly worse than the worst of the reactionists. If, however, history is ever to teach us anything, the fact that they miscalculated, and were not only defeated but discredited, should serve to put us upon doing better than they, avoiding their mistakes and escaping their fate. But who among our extreme innovators to-day shows any intelligent recognition of the lesson ? How many Socialists seem to be taking precautions against repetitions of the so-called " anti-Socialist " triumph at the London County Council

election of 1906 ? How many have thoughtfully considered
the history of English Chartism ?

Reactions in the Nineteenth Century

Chartism, it may be replied, was not socialistic, but
purely political in its aims. True ; but it stood for advanced democracy in its day ; and in its methods it
had many points in common with the Labourism and
Socialism of to-day. It had a not unreasonable, almost
a scientific, programme. And yet of its " Six Points,"
three are not yet carried ; one—payment of Members—
was carried but yesterday ; and two more—universal
suffrage and equal voting districts, with one man one
vote—are important desiderata now.[1]

Why did the Chartist movement collapse ? It is
not easy to give an answer that shall be both just and
comprehensive ; but if we are to draw our conclusion
from the record of Gammage, it must be that the failure was
the result of the errors and follies of the Chartist party as a
whole. Gammage is censorious, but seems honest ; and on
all hands we find him revealing faults and weaknesses among
the men who had the faculty of leading. Their leading,
accordingly, was largely wrong. In some, the defect was
want of character ; in others, want of political intellectual
capacity ; in others want of wisdom. As Gammage says :
" If Chartism has had its virtues, it is at the same time but
too painfully evident that no small amount of folly has
been mixed up with the movement."

Specially instructive is the mistake made by the Chartists
in opposing the movement for the repeal of the Corn Laws.
Gammage, who shared the general Chartist hostility to that
indispensable reform, and to Cobden and Bright as its
champions, tells how they were challenged to public debate
by Feargus O'Connor, and how O'Connor utterly failed on
the ground he had himself chosen. Such tactics placed
Chartism in practical opposition to the Free Trade movement, with which it should have co-operated ; and the
fundamental liberalism of the Chartist doctrine became

[1] Written in 1912. The " equal districts " and the enfranchisement of women have since been substantially attained.

lamentably associated with illiberal courses. Physical-force doctrines, though preached only by a few, helped to complete its discredit ; and to this day its aspirations are mostly unrealized.

Our optimistic Socialists, with their happy conviction that the " Utopian " period is past and done with, take it for granted that they cannot fail as the Chartists failed. But they would find it hard to show that their own outlook is essentially different from that of the French Socialists of 1848. Those men had a progressive scheme of State industries much more practical than that of nationalization of all the means of production and distribution. Yet they not only failed to sustain their system in its beginnings : they set up through the whole of French society a reaction so powerful that it established the second Empire, and retarded all French political progress for a generation. The men of the Commune, a generation later, had equally failed to read the lesson of history ; and they in turn added reinforcement of reaction to the horrors of civil war in the very hour of national disaster.

Current Symptoms

I have already spoken of the possibilities of serious resentment, involving counter-abuse, set up by a mere policy of personal vituperation against Liberals on the part of politicians who are not in any serious degree opposed to Liberal principles and policy. But over and above such influences there goes on the more general growth of opinion as to the utter visionariness of Socialism, in the stricter sense of the term, taken as a political programme. Ninety-nine business men out of every hundred, to say the least, are as certain of the impossibility of nationalizing the means of production in their day as they are of their own existence. Practical Labour politicians, whether directly or indirectly associated with Socialism, see as much ; and still the exigencies of the platform, and of party organization, force them into association with the " absolute " doctrine. If they repudiate it, if they discountenance the formula of " class war," they incur the rancour of the zealots, for whom that formula is a working motto. Thus the cause

of Labour tends to be identified for large masses of " bourgeois " and other electors, including even masses of working
men brought up under Conservative influences, with the
creed of revolution and violence.

Any one who has calmly studied the history of British
politics in the past twenty-five years must realize that
there is an immense potency of reaction in the electorate
of all grades.   Myriads of working men must have voted
repeatedly against Home Rule for Ireland ;   myriads
more voted for khaki in 1900 :   and in 1906 and 1910,
many thousands of them still must have cast their votes
for Toryism and Protection.   It may be that a recognition
of the undue sanguineness of Gladstone in 1886 and 1892
has made a number of Liberals over-inclined to hedge
and temporize.   It is not in that direction that safety
and success lie.   Prudence is not stagnation ;   and the
doctrine of masterly inactivity, laid down by Lord Rosebery
after the defeat of 1895, is one by which Liberalism cannot
live.   But the very fact that past miscalculation and
consequent reaction turned so many Liberals into mere
weather-watchers, is a reason for guarding against the risk
of setting up new reaction by a far more gratuitous attempt
to force the pace of the community as a whole.

On practical questions the vast majority of Liberals
and Labourites are agreed ;   and on none of them can
Socialists be in rational opposition.   And if, in resentment
of the mere slowness of the attainment of these common
aims, the extremists take a course which can effect, if
anything at all, only the success of the party most opposed
to all of them, we shall but be experiencing once again the
fate of frustration which unteachable men have so often
brought upon themselves and their fellows in the past.

PART III

CAPITAL, BRAINS AND LABOUR

CHAPTER I

FUNDAMENTAL FACTS AND PROBLEMS

OF late we have become more and more accustomed to two war-cries or formulas, each of which is supposed to contradict the other, and both of which profess to embody a vital sociological truth. One is that " All wealth is the product of labour " ; the other, " All labour is maintained by capital." Both formulas are of old standing ; both have been supported with a good deal of ability, and both have come to the front afresh in the national battle over the Budget of 1909. The second formula, which had somewhat lost vogue, even among capitalists, since Mill abandoned the doctrine of the wage fund, has been propounded by Lord Rosebery, who has revived that doctrine with no sign of suspicion that it had ever been discredited. The first formula is the standing maxim of the Socialist platform, and is a main part of the foundation of the Socialist case, as commonly put.

To any one who looks at the two war-cries dispassionately but judicially, the first criticism they suggest is that neither shows any concern for precision of statement, and that neither, therefore, aims at telling the whole truth. On the face of the case they apply the terms " capital " and " labour " in the broad general sense of " the capital of capitalists " and " the labour of labourers." It is in these senses that they are commonly understood. Yet a very little reflection will serve to show that in these senses they cannot possibly be true. All existing wealth arises out of previous wealth, and so on back through the ages. And the production of wealth may easily be traced back in history to a stage in which the labour of labourers is not wage-paid, and therefore is not in any sense maintained by the capital of capitalists. We may, if we like, call the early labourer's tools capital, and we may say the same of the fruits or roots or meats which he accumulated in order to have the leisure

185

to make tools or undertake some further task which would only after a long time yield him an economic return.   But that is not the sense in which " capital " is used or understood in the formula before us.

In the same way, noting the fact that the capitalist sets himself to find markets, without which a given amount of labour could not be employed, we may include him under the first formula by calling his activity " labour."   But that, again, is not in intention avowed by the first formula which we have been considering.   I have heard an audience of Socialists deride the idea that the work of the employer counted for anything.   Both sides, in short, shut out essential facts, and this not by oversight, but from prejudice.

Capital and its Champions

There is nothing to choose between the opposed extremists in point of one-sidedness or crudity of thinking.   The land-owners, Lord Rosebery tells us, are " centres of employment and bounty and civilization."   He does not dream of asking whether they are not also receiving centres of the fruits of other men's labour.   A French academic, Professor Guiraud, in an essay on the evolution of labour in Greece,[1] pronounces no less naively that " one of the reasons which contribute with us to protect riches is the social function which they fulfil.   The rich man to-day enjoys his fortune ; but he also conveys enjoyment from it to the poor man by the employment which he gives him.   All the gain of the poor man, under whatever form it reaches him, is derived from the capital of the rich man."   Evidently it has never occurred to M. Guiraud to suspect that labour does anything in the way of sustaining capital.

Beside these entirely serious deliverances we may usefully set the utterance of a great satirist.   In his *Isle of the Penguins* M. Anatole France has pictured a primitive popular assembly in which the presiding saint proposes that for the sustenance of the church and the carrying on of communal administration, the owners of cattle—the main form of property then existing—shall allot one in every ten

---

[1] *Etudes Economiques sur l'Antiquité*, 1905, p. 73.

of their beasts.   He is answered by one of the cattle-owners
with a triumphant demonstration that the public interest
" commands that too much be not demanded of those who
possess much.   For in that case the rich will be less rich and
the poor poorer.   The poor live upon the property of the
rich ; that is why that property is sacred."[1]   And the man
of property further shows that the true way of raising
revenue is to tax all food.   What is said in dead earnest by
Lord Rosebery and M. Guiraud, with the subsequent support of Lord Hugh Cecil, passes perfectly as pure satire when
so applied.

Captains of War and Industry

The spectacle might suffice not only to sober the titled
assailants of the Budget of 1909, but to move to reflection
those capitalists who are still capable of regarding themselves, first and last, as the real sustainers of all industry.
But perhaps another illustration may more effectually
bring home to them a perception of the total reality of
things.   In Julius Cæsar we see a captain with whose
efficiency the most self-satisfied captain of industry will
hardly propose to compare his own.   In Cæsar we have the
consummate imperator, whose genius alone can forge into
a triumphant weapon the myriads who form his host.
Without Cæsar the legions can avail nothing, can neither
conquer Gaul nor rout Pompey.   Nay, without Cæsar they
had not been even legions, but merely a helpless series of
scattered units, at best capable of extorting a scanty livelihood from an ill-guarded soil.   And yet what were Cæsar
without the legions ?   Not less dependent than they upon
him is he upon them.   His towering fame and his treasure
alike are piled up at their hands ; without them he had been
not Divus Julius but a needy adventurer, the prey of any
robber gang or pirate crew.   And Cæsar, like Alexander,
confessed his debt and provided for his veterans.   Can the
captains of industry in the twentieth century be less enlightened, less alive to the nature of their problem, than the
captains of swordsmen and spearmen in remote antiquity ?
In sooth, they mostly are.   It is because most of the

---

[1] *L'Ile des Pingouins*, p. 67.

modern captains of industry have never contrived to give their veterans either steady subsistence during their fighting years or security for old age that their legions are in large measure distrustful, semi-hostile, disparaging towards their captains, and bent on evoking some system which shall provide for the mass collectively some such security of comfort as the captain takes to be his sure heritage. They are less like to the trusted legions of the old conquerors than to the distrusted plebs of earlier Rome and earlier Athens—a mass at the mercy of the landowning patricians whose possessions they maintained against the enemy, with no certainty of being themselves maintained in sufficiency of food.

The Fatality of Class Hatred

From which class may a deeper insight be most fitly demanded ? From which might a wise lawgiver most reasonably demand patience and magnanimity ? On one or the other side these qualities must be evolved if the problem of modern civilization is to be any better solved than that of antiquity. In many States of the ancient world the fundamental opposition of workers and capitalists—the have-nots and the haves—came to a head without solution. Greece perished of perpetual tribal strife, complicated by class strife within each community so-called ; and Rome did but perish more slowly and more terribly because the domestic problem was transformed by the degeneration of imperialism into the more hopeless one of preserving civilization without liberty. In the day of Aristotle, at the highest point of Greek intellectual evolution, we find the youth of the aristocracy still swearing to " hate the demos," even as centuries before, in the day of Theognis, they vowed to " drink the blood of the demos," to trample on them, and to smite them with the sharp goad. Class hated class as bitterly as Athenian hated Spartan or Syracusan. The oracular lesson, " Know thyself," was not to be learned. To learn it would have meant the recognition by the aristocrat of the purely accidental, non-moral, non-intellectual basis of class and wealth. On such points the average

Athenian " gentleman " could not think ; he could but hate.

And inevitably the question arises : How far is that temper transcended to-day ? The problem would be hopeless indeed if we did not know that by many, if not most, of our captains of industry it is transcended almost entirely, thanks as much to the continued pressure of labour organization setting up a habitual relation of adjustment as to the direct effect of modern culture on the commercial mind. Trade unions, as they now exist, originated in the perception by the British workers of several generations ago that most of their masters cared for them only as for hired machines, getting out of them the utmost possible for the least possible outlay, leaving them idle and unfed in times of bad trade, and throwing them to the scrap-heap in the end. Masters and men alike growing more civilized, the former are more sympathetic, while the latter, seeing their subsistence still insecure, scheme in varying tempers for a further hold on the machinery of wealth-production. And here lies the crux. If the workers can see no prospect of security of comfort, in vain will they be asked to content themselves. The more they think, the more will they concern themselves for safety ahead. And the masters in mass do not come forward with any comprehensive scheme, though many honestly seek to make some independent provision. A comprehensive scheme must be produced in concert, else we shall have more and more scheming of the kind that runs to discord.

Hopes and Fears

Thus the situation is one of persistent unrest ; and in the political strife over the Budget of 1909 we have an index of the forces which make solution so difficult. In varying relations to the class of captains of industry stand the investing and landowning classes, who rather live upon than lead industry ; and of many in these classes the temper is hardly better than that of the old Roman patricians of the last age of the republic. Irrationally zealous for dominion abroad,[1] they have no unselfish heed for the

---

[1] I leave the criticism standing, not as a description of post-war conditions, but as a statement of the situation before the War, fitly to be kept in mind.

building up of a sound and happy society at home.   In the cries of rage at the prospect of new taxation of their unearned wealth we seem to hear the very voices of the mindless aristocrats who contrived to assassinate one after another the series of reformers who sought to cut out the deadly cancer of Roman life by sharply reforming the land laws, which maintained perpetual and ever-widening poverty alongside of ever-accumulating ownership of wealth.   Were it not for the immeasurably greater patience, science, and circumspection of the modern reformers the outlook would be indeed black.

And the problem, hard as it was before, is being complicated by the resort to a new quackery on the part of the anti-democratic class of to-day.   To workers craving for the bread of security they offer the drug of a vicious fiscal system, promising that it will bring welfare and peace.   Thus far the workers have shown by far the greater sanity, most of them refusing the proffered quack medicine, whatever hasty prescriptions some frame on their own account.   But not a few among their masters, moved mainly by mere concern for private profit, throw in their lot with the cause of quackery, putting all industrial and social progress in hazard ; while some who formerly shunned that course avow that they will rather take it than submit to being taxed in new ways.   What is needed to save the cause of progress is a coalition between all the friends of just taxation, all of the masters who care alike for economic science and for the elevation of their workers, and all of the workers who can discern between practicable evolution and the planning of Utopias on paper.   And this is our social problem in a nutshell : Are there sane citizens enough, sane masters enough, and sane men enough to conduct the State by the safe channel between the whirlpool of civil strife and the rock of fiscal error ?

CHAPTER II

SO much more progress in social science has ostensibly been made by the working class than by the employing class in recent times that the former inevitably runs some of the risks of vainglory. Working men, looking back on modern history, have seen every claim on their part for political justice stubbornly resisted by large sections of the landowning and capitalist class, and every step made by them towards self-organization denounced as fatal to their own best interests. And they now see their gains not only acclaimed by the most qualified students of social science, but even tacitly or outspokenly endorsed by many of their employers. Knowing themselves to have been wiser than their masters in these matters in the past, they are naturally apt to assume that they have the greater wisdom as regards all the problems of the present and future.

But the problems are vitally different. Men standing for their political rights against political privileges have a much simpler issue in hand than have men who propose to alter the social machine, applying new principles. Workmen seeking to organize all industry have an incomparably harder task before them than that of workmen seeking to organize their own groups for the purpose of bargaining with their masters. And when it comes to the wider and deeper problem, " labour " has no advantage from moral right and aspiration. One of the hardest lessons for all mankind to learn is this, that " nature," the vast complex of things, shows no lenity or docility to mere goodwill. Only by patient science is it ever controlled. A false step by society means broken legs, so to speak, as surely as it can in the case of the heedless man or animal upon an unsafe path. And the need to earn his bread by the sweat of his brow gives no man any special insight into the larger problems of social science. There the labourer is on a par with the

capitalist ; and if he cannot realize this he has sore trouble
before him. Too often he cannot realize it. Even as the
rich man so often fails to see that he is but as another man
with wealth added, the worker often fails to see that he is
but a man without wealth, with the passions, illusions, and
endless fallibilities of the natural man of all ages. And in
this folly he is apt to be confirmed by the flatteries not only
of his own leaders, but of some of the spokesmen of other
parties. Too often do they speak as if " labour " implied
a double share alike of original righteousness and of common
sense.

The Snare of Passion

From day to day the risks are apparent. *In the name
of labour* we see freshly committed the old political errors
of the average Englishman of the days before the Labour
party. We hear thoughtless demands for intervention
in the affairs of foreign nations, impossible proposals to
redress the wrongs suffered by foreigners at the hands of their
own people. They come, be it noted, from men with a
creditable record for the promotion of peace and for resistance to militarism. Men who would have hotly resented
any foreign demand for the punishment of the Jameson
Raiders, any foreign protest against the tragedy of Den-
shawi or the execution of Scheepers, appear to suppose that
it is for us by open intervention to prevent in Spain such
judicial outrages as the mock-trial and execution of Ferrer.
That way chaos lies.

The first promptings of feeling are no better guides for
democracy than for aristocracy, and are no more infallible
in home affairs than in foreign. And it cannot be but
that a great deal of the opinion current among the working
multitude is ill-grounded in knowledge and reflection.
Looking back, Labour leaders can see all manner of short-
sighted action on the part of the leaders of other parties in
the past. They should bethink them that no party can be
purged of error and safeguarded from delusion by the mere
fact of its consisting of men who work with their hands.
Strictly, they had need be more righteous than the Whigs
and Tories. But let them not lightly fancy themselves so.
A survey of the mere strifes of trade unions among them-

selves will reveal exactly the same forces of egoism, jealousy and folly as have been at work in the politics of the middle and upper classes in all times. Labour groups have quarrelled among themselves as blindly as parties ever did, and have shown at times in the narrow field of local industry as much tribal prejudice as do any of the self-seeking " interests " of to-day. Behind the Labour leaders is a multiform mass, including multitudes of men who are no wiser than the dukes, and in some respects no more scientific than the Tariff Reformers among their employers. The Tory working man of a few years ago, the willing tool of Tory clubmen and agents in disturbing Home Rule meetings, and the zealous retainer of the drink trade, does not become enlightened by merely transferring his allegiance to the Labour party. The motive of simple class sympathy cannot of itself conduct men to political wisdom. And what thoughtful and candid Labour leader will deny that the self-will of masses of workers has wrought as perversely in some industrial strifes as ever did the selfishness or obstinacy of employers ?

" They will not consider markets," confessed a Labour leader to me once, at a crisis in which a strike was being prolonged by a small majority of young men, to the disgust of their elders and the sore distress of subsidiary groups. In these words are conveyed the history of much past trouble and the promise of much to come.

Masters and Men

We should indeed be far astray if we supposed that such waywardness had no show of justification in the past procedure of employers. When masters are impatient over ill-timed demands for a rise in wages, or refusals to acquiesce in a forced fall, they might chasten themselves by asking whether they, the masters, ever offered a rise to their men, however great might be their profits. The certainty that every advance has to be extorted is the basis of every effort to force an advance and to resist a decrease. And thus on each side the air is darkened by vivid and resentful reminiscences of the sins of the other side, uncorrected by recollections of the counterbalancing errors.

To speak as if either side had more to learn than the other

would be unwarrantable.   There is no good prospect unless
both can learn.   But the danger is that where employers
may continue to be swayed by simple selfishness the workers
may be carried into new error by visionary hope.   That
Labour leaders are in the main as reasonable as employers,
I have not the slightest doubt ; and that the status of
labour is more favourable to some intellectual virtues than
the status of the professional and moneyed classes is, I
think, demonstrable.   Working men are relatively innocent
of snobbery, cant, and make-believe.   But of the critical
sanity which comes of knowledge they cannot well have
the larger share.   In point of fact, they tend to set up a kind
of inverted snobbery inasmuch as they think in terms of
class feeling where they should be guided by dispassionate
science.   And herein lies a new danger.
   There is, perhaps, no better general guide to political
action than a comprehensive ideal, involving a strict scrutiny
of the moral basis of conventional ideals and the economic
basis of the existing system.   But there can be few worse
guides than a remote ideal held as a programme.   An
abstract theory or loose generalization as to the relations of
capital and labour can be as illusory on the labour side
as on the capitalistic ; and to think of capital solely as
perpetually " exploiting " labour to its own advantage is to
become capable of taking all manner of wrong turnings.
Obviously labour in general is recreating capital faster than
it draws subsistence from it.   At the week's end the productive worker has generally placed in his master's hands
more capital than he receives in wages.   But on the other
hand plenty of fluid capital is annually lost in the vain
effort for fresh profit ; and this not merely in new undertakings.   Nothing can be more idle than to denounce as an
" agitator " every Labour teacher who exhorts working
men to secure a better share of the product of their labour :
were it not for such " agitation " in the past they would
certainly be worse off than they are.   But the agitator can
err like another ; and if he misstates industrial facts he is
as guilty as another.   And not a little of working-class
opinion is at any moment founded upon misstatements of
industrial economics by irresponsible critics who affect to
know beforehand concrete facts which can be known only
by investigation.

The Economics of Industry

An illustration may make the trouble clearer. I have before me[1] a case in which a Socialist teacher—a clergyman, not a workman—tells a working-class audience that of, say, 14s. paid for a ton of coals in a town not far from the colliery, only 1s. goes to labour and the rest to capital—1s. of it as royalty to the landowner, something more for wayleaves, and the bulk as profit to the coalmaster. From first to last the teacher is in error. He forgets that an ill-situated or infertile mine may pay as little as 3d. a ton in royalty, though its coal sells at the same price as that which pays 1s. He forgets that there is much labour done in and at the mine besides the coal-hewer's. In reality the labour cost per ton in the mine is over 4s., and the further costs of transportation, storage and distribution—processes which employ much further labour—are such that in the case in question the coalmaster during the past nine months has undergone a dead loss of 1d. per ton. This, of course, is exceptional ; but it is not further from the average actuality than the fancy picture drawn by the theory-primed " agitator." And without accurate knowledge of actualities, there is no safety in theories.

High-flying theories seem to win a specially ready acceptance among the youngest workers ; and, as a result of this, we find among them a special proneness to headlong action in the way of strikes and stoppages, all tending to lessen the total product, of which their wages are their share. The ideal is to maximize (without individual overstrain) the total product and the worker's share. And while it is certain that higher wisdom cannot be attained on one side without an approximation to it on the other, it is fitting to point out to the worker that, as he has most to hope for, it behoves him to be specially wary alike as to his thinking and his action. Betterment is to be attained by political and industrial co-operation ; and it is precisely where industrial collaboration has been carried furthest between masters and men that there is the greatest readiness on the part of the former to go further still. The theory that employers in general are to be driven forward by exasper-

[1] Written in 1909.

ating blows, and that there is no other way of advancing, goes hand in hand with the practice of wasteful strife and reckless quarrelling.   And the outcome of that whole way of thought and action is the theory of revolutionary Socialism properly so-called—the old theory of Marx and Engels, discredited by history, and now in process of slow abandonment by older Socialists, but still apparently fascinating to many of the younger.

The Employer's Advantage

It is a reasonable conclusion that while employers in general cannot be trusted to be more unselfish than their men, and must therefore be always faced by labour organizations, they are likely, on the whole, to have a clearer insight into industrial possibilities.   The history of the attempts at co-operative production tells as much.   It may be answered that the frequent failures of individual capitalistic enterprises prove the abundant fallibility of the employing class ;   and that this fallibility brings much distress upon the workers whom such failures throw out of work.   But it must not be forgotten, on the other hand, that the enterprise which has failed has spent its lost capital in employing labour ;   and that in the existing social system alike the successful and the unsuccessful enterprises constitute the channel through which the bulk of employment is given, and the bulk of production is achieved.

The capitalist is certainly looking out for himself ;   but it is not merely part of the process of his moral education to learn to look more and more to good relations with his workers as a condition of success ;   it is part of his economic necessity at times to subordinate his immediate to his future gain.   It pays him ultimately to keep a good staff around him ;   and it pays him ultimately to run his works for periods at a loss.   The coalmaster who makes a net loss of 1d. per ton on nine months' trade is presumably acting on sound business principles.   He keeps his mine going because to close it would involve an ultimate loss which, by bearing a present loss, he may hope to escape.

Given all these motives to sympathetic action on the part of the employer, it surely behoves the worker to beware lest under the spell of a remote ideal, and the inaccurate estimates of present fact to which it so easily lends itself, he puts all social progress in jeopardy by ill-conceived action. Before he and his fellows can successfully control the industrial system, he or his leaders must assimilate the commercial knowledge and trained judgment of the average successful employer. And mere self-interest, or even a generous conception of class-interest, cannot supply such insight. Class-interest, like so-called patriotism, can easily be a mere channel for crude instinct and natural malice. I have a sad conviction that the majority of English Socialists at this moment are men and women who, had they been born in the moneyed class, would have been no more sympathetic with popular interests and aspirations than the majority of that class actually are. It remains quite true that, none the less, popular class-interest is a great motive power towards social betterment. But surely, even on that view, it is a motive power that needs enlightenment and constant correction.

CHAPTER III

IT is over the problem of unemployment, as aforesaid, that the political struggle between labour and capital, in the conventional senses of the two terms, most naturally and most justifiably arises. Whether or not, as Ruskin has it, all wealth is to be measured in terms of life, certain it is that the end of all labour is self-preservation. And it is not conceivable that when once the mass of working men have attained a conception, however loose, of the fundamental relation of capital and labour—the ultimate dependence of capital on labour for its renewal, with whatever immediate dependence of labour on capital for access to food—it is not conceivable that after this has once been realized, the mass of the toilers will be content with a relatively precarious tenure of life. They may go further than the demand for either security of subsistence or " right to work " ; but one or other of these they will infallibly seek until they get it—unless our society is to sink like the civilizations of the past.

For it is quite clear that unemployment is a standing feature in the industrial life. It may be conceived either as a disease of modern commercialism or as a simple form of the phenomenon of poverty, which is a political factor in all societies further evolved than those wherein subsists the primitive tribal law of mutual sustenance. The moral charm of that way of life, abstracted from other considerations, leads some moderns to lament all civilization as a further receding from brotherhood. In reality all that constitutes civilization has been reached by the hard way of competition : and even the ethic of the primitive communist is sympathetic only as regards the fellow-tribesman. The larger view of humanity, like the larger knowledge of the universe, has been obtainable only through the casting-off of the primitive fraternity ; and in the slow

198

advance poverty has been the malady of every form of society.

The truth is not fully conveyed by the familiar formula which ascribes industrial distress solely to " production for profit." Poverty is normal long before the stage of systematic industrialism. As soon as a tribe has passed beyond the primitive communism, poverty must arise through the bad luck, bad health, or bad habits of the less fortunate or less fit. Only the primitive communal organization ever precluded it for any length of time—it could be no great time at best—and only organization ever will. Probably even the primitive tribe had ways of eliminating the plainly unfit ; and it is the half-reasoned, half-instinctive recoil from the burden of the unfit, who so tend to multiply in the more advanced stages of civilization, that has retarded in modern times the growth of an aiding organization adequate to the evil.

In the pre-commercial period unemployment can arise through mere local over-population. Peasants are limited by house-room, and artisans by the restrictions of their guilds. In the early commercial period it arises through displacement of farm hands by shepherds as a result of " production for profit " of sheep. As the industrial system develops, unemployment recurs like the influenza, for reasons often as hard to trace as the causes of the epidemic. Some seek still to trace the trouble in all cases to deficient harvests, but it can demonstrably be set up by a good harvest. A very large crop in England, a generation ago, threw idle much of the shipping before employed in carrying wheat cargoes from America ; idle shipping meant idle shipyards ; many idle workers meant restricted demand for the product of others, and so on indefinitely. Such contrarieties are only special instances of the economic process through which good harvests may impoverish the farmer, while scarcity enriches him.

The Quack Medicine

Perhaps the worst aspect of the current movement of " Tariff Reform " is the very general pretence of its promoters that it will make an end of unemployment. Even those more scrupulous leaders who repudiate that pretence are wont to affirm that their policy would "lessen" un-employment. As a matter of fact, there was chronic and grievous unemployment in the protected silk and woollen industries of England throughout the eighteenth century ; and enormous and oft-recurring unemployment in many industries during nearly the whole of the first half of the nineteenth century, under a system whether of complete or of modified protection. In the United States, alike in "good" and in "bad" times, there is demonstrably more unemployment than in Britain in corresponding periods ; and in Germany during the trying year 1908 there was greater superfluity of labour than in almost any year since 1880. All this must be known to the leaders of the party whose official organization sends broadcast the promise of "work for all" under a tariff. Only the dullest or the most venal of the workers are swayed by it. But the very fact that such charlatan promises can find currency proves the standing need for a true remedy.

That true remedy is to be found only on the lines of a national provision of insurance, on the lines latterly laid down by the Government. No conceivable organization could so regulate employment that no able-bodied person should ever be unemployed. Under the most theoretically perfect system of Socialism workers in given industries would be idle at times, whether by reason of the weather, the seasons, fires or accidents to machinery. A good industrial education might make all workers much more capable of transferring their labour from one industry to another. So much may be achieved without Socialism. But no worker could conceivably be made capable of transfer from any one industry to any other ; and all that Socialism could accomplish would be the securing of his maintenance whether he was at work or not. And that is precisely what is aimed at under a system of insurance. Displacement of labour cannot be provided against ; but destitution from unemployment may be. That is at once the ideal, the pressing need, and the practicable course.

Risks of Collision

Here, however, emerges the risk of conflict between practicable and impracticable courses. The Labour party have of late been much disposed to make a test question of the " Right to Work " Bill; and the immediate issue is whether they will abandon that entirely unworkable scheme for the insurance scheme of the Government. The " Right to Work " Bill is the standing proof of the danger set up by the failure of working men to realize the nature of the work done by the skilled employer. It proceeds, in effect, upon the assumption that the skilled employer performs no special service whatever. Proposing as it does that any man or men unable to find work shall be entitled to call upon a local authority to provide work and wages, it virtually assumes that " making work " is a thing which any body of inexpert persons can successfully undertake. It does not propose or contemplate " relief works " of the old kind, which are avowedly non-economic. The very phrase, " the right to work," points to productive work, as distinct from any form of mere " relief." With a warmth which cannot but evoke sympathy, its supporters protest that they really want work and not charity for working men. But as to how economic work can be provided on the lines of their Bill, in times of industrial distress, they can offer no elucidation.

One has only to set forth mentally the situation which the Bill would create, to realize its utter impracticability. Let us suppose the best possible arrangement, that is to say, a local authority composed of business men, accustomed to manage industrial concerns. In the terms of the case, many or most of them are unable to find economic work in their own businesses for the men unemployed. Yet they are called upon collectively to find economic work for these very men. Now, it is not to be denied that a local authoirty might provide some kinds of work which individual employers could not give, such as road-making, coast preservation, etc. But to make such " public industries " dependent solely upon the ups and and downs of unemployment is, by the repeated admissions of Labour leaders, to discredit every ideal of State-regulated industry. Any kind of work provided under the " Right to Work " Bill would eventually be mere " relief work " of the old and unsatisfactory kind. True economic work could not possibly be so provided.

The ideal underlying the Bill, I repeat, is worthy of all

sympathy.   Perhaps Mr Oscar Wihl, in his excellent pamphlet on *Unemployment,* is a little too severe on the fore-
thoughtlessness of its promoters.   They could plead that
before their Bill appeared nothing adequate was being done.
But they must learn that labour legislation is to be gone
about not less but more circumspectly than any other.
The cause of democracy is in some degree on trial in every
important new measure planned in its interest, and history
is studded with the records of collapses and retrogressions
resulting from hasty or incompetent plans of that order.
It is not too much to say that the immediate future of
social and industrial progress in this country turns upon the
choice between a right and a wrong method of dealing with
unemployment.

CHAPTER IV

THE CREED OF "ALL OR NOTHING"

TO those who have learned to think of society as a kind of mosaic which can be taken to pieces and reset at will in a better pattern, such a plan of betterment as insurance against employment is repellent, just because it is a "palliative." Though professed Socialists are wont to speak of "the social organism," they appear in general to think only of a social machine— something that can be radically remodelled and recreated by a few edicts. People who realize what an organism is would understand that a palliative is all that is possible, at any given time, in the case of a serious organic malady that has lasted for the greater part of the organism's lifetime. But it is noteworthy that even medical men, when they turn Socialists, are apt to lose all hold of the analogies of biology, and to think of society rather as a building than as a living structure. They assume that by closing certain doors and opening others, adding new wings and pulling down old, you can, in a generation, transform the very plan and purpose of a society, as you might turn a farmhouse and its outbuildings into a country house, or a cotton mill into a concert hall. And this is pure delusion.

To be sure, the metaphor of "the social organism" is not in itself perfect. A society can in time be modified as no single organism can, even in the great changes made from infancy to maturity. A truer analogy would be that between a society and an animal species. The species can change greatly from age to age by the hereditary trans- mission of accumulating modifications, as the horse of to-day has been evolved from an animal very little like him, and man himself from a sort of gorilla. And in the case of a society, to say nothing of the developments of function set up by changed economic conditions, there is the element of intelligent and calculating will, enlightened by scientific knowledge, which makes possible a far more rapid evolution than that of an animal species. But still the quasi-biological fact remains that no society can stably pass through radical changes of structure and purpose in a generation.

Even changes of a purely political kind, if they are fundamental—as the change from a monarchy to a republic —are nearly sure to be unstable if rapidly made. And the change from a regimen of merely partial co-operation to one of universal co-operation (which is the definition of a change from the present state of partial socialism to one of universal socialism) is simply impossible in a short period of time. It involves a complete readjustment of nearly all the social functions. In the evolution of a species, every step or phase between one marked type and another means an age of adaptation. Granted that a society can modify itself by will, the process is still one of a thousand successive adjustments. From partial to complete co-operation, let us say once more, the way can be only through the whole series of individual steps in co-operation. The evolution of society consists in such graduated progress. Cataclysm is not evolution but dissolution ; a process which leaves society less progressive than before ; and to dream of hastening progress by it is to plan for frustration.

This is the answer at once to those who scout as " mere palliatives " what are really acts of social modification, and to those who denounce every step as preparing the way for further steps. Both sets of extremists alike are vainly flouting the law of evolution. The rabid anti-Socialists are really as blind as the Socialists. The remote ancestors of the horse, could they have met him, would have regarded him as a portent wholly alien to them. They would have refused to mate with him, as early Romans would have refused to mate with Virgil, supposing him to have been seen by them in a vision, or as the Normans would have put aside, like a bad dream, the vision of a vast society of unarmed " clerks." Denunciations of " Socialism " as a wild attempt to impose a paper Utopia of mutual help on a world of competing traders and mutually vituperative politicians are as such valid, albeit blatant. As denunciations in advance of any future form of society, merely because it will be inevitably different from the present form, they are gratuitously and irredeemably ridiculous.

That is, in brief, the theoretic and scientific answer alike to the " all or nothing " and to the " nothing at all " schools. The practical answer consists in showing how neither can hold its ground in practical politics, upon any immediate issue. The out-and-out individualist vainly talks of curing the evils of poverty by " thrift " and " self-help." In spite of him, we have already initiated Old Age Pensions and State insurance against invalidity and unemployment. Such deeds are the mission, and their achievement is the vindication of our Liberalism, and the task never ends. If political science does not put its hand to the task, political quackery will be called in by a tormented proletariate. To propose to cure industrial poverty by the simple expedient of ever-increasing " saving " among the mass is blindly to counsel an actual worsening of the disease. " Bad trade " means lack of demand for industrial products and services, with a correlative lack of field for safe investment of saved capital. Extra saving at such a stage would simply mean for the time being a further restriction of the demand for products, with a further correlative curtailment of the field of investment.

It is vitally important, again, that the insurance premium for unemployment shall not come wholly out of the workers' income. A fund so raised under the worker's own management could not be safely invested. The process must be in large part a matter of national revenue and expenditure. But it is essential that they shall contribute. If indeed the workers could be trusted to spend wisely their whole earnings, the State might safely bear the whole burden of unemployment—given, of course, a scientific system of taxation. " Contributory " Old Age Pensions would have been as bad a blunder on the economic as on the political side. But contributory insurance is a quite different problem. The task of insurance against unemployment can only gradually be gone about, the more precarious trades being the first to be dealt with ; and contribution by the benefited workers is of the essence of the scheme.

As regards the contrary demand to abolish " production for profit," the negative case is equally clear. Supposing it to be certain that the human race will one day be vegetarian, it is none the less certain that no community can be made vegetarian by law. Dogs may be, not men. To expel from the whole industrial field, by edict, the fundamental instinct of competition, is as hopeful an undertaking for this age as to set about abolishing all games of chance.

The " Bill " Test

The House of Commons, with all its impotences and ineptitudes, natural and artificial, inevitable and remediable, is a great touchstone of legislative conceptions.

If a theoretically well-conceived measure entirely fails to impress that body, there is to be inferred a clear need for preliminary popular propaganda : the people in the mass are not ready. If a given theory is unworkable, the demonstration of that is furnished by the failure to produce a workable " Bill." " Table your Bill " is a test which sobers or corners declaimers of all schools, from the advocates of pure beer to the advocates of national production. The Labour party has demonstrably failed to plan even a non-socialistic remedy for unemployment that would work for a week. Of anything in the nature of a scheme for national ownership and control of all the means of production, there is not even an adumbration.

Even the tentative of a scheme for the nationalization of railways—an incomparably simpler thing—has never been seriously taken up by a Labour representative, though the party has moved resolutions on the subject, calling for immediate decision and action at impossible moments. Men who have actually done legislative work soon realize that it is a measure to be considered and sketched and planned for years before a Bill can be plausibly drafted. It is thus worse than idle to talk to the workers of a possible transformation of industrial society in a few years' time ; and hardly less idle to ask their votes for a measure which will not stand an hour's discussion in detail. Even the conception of a " right to work " is a mental confusion. No " right " can vest in any one to call upon society to do at once what society cannot demonstrably do.

But if, putting aside the idle affirmation of " right," all sincere reformers unite to call for a systematic effort to cure the great social disease of poverty, great as the

task undoubtedly is it may in time be accomplished.
It will certainly never be done by taking the whole enormous
industrial machine to pieces and refashioning it on entirely
new principles. The spectacle of the development of such
simple new departures as motor-cars and flying machines
might suggest to enthusiasts the impossibility of re-arrang-
ing all industry from top to bottom by edict. For years
after their first appearance, motor-cars could not be trusted
to go ten miles without a breakdown. The flying machine
is now [1912] in that tentative stage. But the breakdown of
a new industrial organization would mean something immeasurably worse than individual inconvenience or injury.
It would mean social ruin, anarchy, the breakdown of
civilization.

Possibilities and Dangers

If any friend of the cause of labour supposes that there
exists in that or any other section of society the capacity to
run a new social system without any of the mishaps which
attend the application of any single new invention of
importance, he miscalculates insanely the present development of human faculty. Assuredly there is a great fund of
potential capacity in our working mass which at present
comes to little or nothing because of the frustrations of a
social system that embodies a hundred evils surviving from
the past. This is a reason why every rational employer
should desire to see on the one hand a great improvement in
the educational machinery of our own country—still so
lamentably deficient, and so lamentably retarded in its
development by the eternal feud of the sects—and on the
other a systematic provision of security of life for all. But
precisely because the educational machinery is so bad
and the available directing faculty so precarious, it would be
madness to dream of any experiment that it is not within
the known power of society to carry through.

Needless to say, it will be hard to develop to the full
even a feasible enterprise for the establishment of industrial
security by insurance. Not only will many theorists
undertake to show that the non-socialist scheme is " Socialism," and to set against it all the imbecile terrors which
that name can conjure up, but there is a risk that the whole

machinery of so-called " Tariff Reform " will be turned against any systematic reform which admittedly tends to " side-track " that egregious movement by putting something sane and efficient in its place.   Deprived of the opportunity of promising a " cure for unemployment," the quacks will be apt to denounce with their utmost virulence, and counterwork with all their powers of electoral corruption the sound scheme.   It will lie with the mass of the workers to determine their own fate.   If they yield to the perversity of the self-seekers in their ranks, and withhold from the party of practical reform the force required to carry out its legislative plans, they will pay the full penalty in postponed betterment, if not in absolute retrogression.

CHAPTER V

THE EVOLUTION OF CAPITALISM

IT is some sixty years since there emerged in politics, at the hands of Marx and Engels, the conception of capitalistic production as proceeding inevitably to an irretrievable overthrow, in which society would be violently disrupted, whereafter a new and better system would promptly be raised upon its ruins. Things were bad, said the theorists, and would have to be worse before they were better. On the one hand, capitalism was conceived as a blindly egotistic force, ruthlessly exploiting life ; on the other hand, the " iron law of wages " kept the workers for ever at or near the bare subsistence level of comfort ; and their misery was ultimately to force them to work their own salvation by the socialization of all things.

The course of events has callously falsified this theory of social destiny. Framed before the biological law of evolution had been established, it presents the Hegelian view of development as operated by or in an " idea " or abstract momentum, in which the adaptations of historic life counted for nothing. The " iron law of wages," as we have seen, was an exaggeration of an early thesis of Ricardo, which Ricardo himself effectually qualified. Its basis was the tendency of the workers to propagate up to the level of subsistence. But, as Ricardo proceeded to point out, the workers could raise their ideal of necessary comfort ; and when pressure of population was relieved by wholesale emigration to countries of large free land area and high wages, the standard of comfort did rise all round. Trade unions and factory laws did the rest. Wages slowly but surely rose ; and, be it said, the moral standards of employers rose with them.

True, the total rise has not been exhilaratingly great or rapid ; but it has been enough to dispose of the theory that reform is to come by mere explosion of accumulated misery. At the same time, various failures of schemes of co-operative production, and the observed limitation of the

area of those which succeeded, has shaken popular faith in
the possibility of the public control of all manner of industry.
The more practical have realized that the head or " entre-
preneur " is as necessary a factor in industry as the
" hands " ;   and that the fluid capital which he either owns
or controls is a determinant of employment.   And while
the devotees of theory insist the more on the nationalization
of capital, the work-a-day world realizes that no single
industrial State can conceivably resolve itself into a
Socialist community while the rival States carry on world-
trade in the old way of individual enterprise.   Social
evolution, it becomes clear, must be a far more gradual
process than that imagined by the Marxians.   Commerce
is as complicated a thing as production, and commercial
faculty must continue to command its price in trading
communities.

It is, in fact, more of a monopoly than is " capital."
Capital, helpless without him, seeks the organizer no less
than the organizer seeks capital ; and for more than half a
century industry in Europe has been more and more a
matter of combinations of capital furnished to " heads " of
concerns whose shareholders or bankers are more or less
passive.   Often the organizer becomes a capitalist-in-chief,
in virtue of his primary indispensableness.   In the United
States we see the evolution carried to lengths which stagger
British experience, individual organizers becoming the
masters of whole groups of railways.

Socialists, if they think of utilizing this kind of capacity
at all, appear still to dream of socializing it by force.
Many of them evidently still conceive of a social conquest
either by votes or by weapons, the result of which is to be a
setting of the feet of the people on the necks of their former
masters.   It is notable that no Socialist Utopia sets out in
any detail the process of peaceful transition.   Mr Bellamy,
the most persuasive of the schemers, left virtually blank in
his forecast the steps from the competitive to the non-
competitive State, save for the suggestion that it would be
reached through the general development of capitalist
syndicates.   Other Socialists resented and disparaged even
his presentment of the machinery of the latter, protesting
against any forecast of a concrete kind.   Mr Keir Hardie
still repudiates scornfully the duty of " showing how it is

all to be done." William Morris could but scheme an ideal community—his particular ideal—as something Mosaically constructed after the existing industrial society had been reduced to utter wreck by a long civil war. It would probably be difficult to find anywhere a Socialist who has anything but the most nebulous notion of how the existing world of competitive production is to transform into the ideal world of his theory.

It may be taken as reasonably certain that, whatever is in store for us, the " heads " as well as the " hands " will play their part in deciding the evolution. The process will not be one either of putting the heads in gaol and supplanting them by committees of workers who will successfully fill their place, or of keeping them at their posts with pistols held to their backs. On neither plan could industry be long carried on. Every conception of a social change in which mere coercion rectifies existing inequality is dismissible as a dream either of envy and ignorance or of puerile optimism. Political change is hard enough when it is simply a matter of correcting the bases of taxation : witness the struggle over the 1909 Budget, and the menace of constitutional revolution at the hands of its enemies in the Upper Chamber. Structural changes are very much harder. Capitalists and organizers will go on playing their parts under a series of modifying conditions, to be set up by fiscal and other legislative measures, which will operate directly as well as indirectly.

" Production for profit " will assuredly continue for centuries, profit being not merely the condition of the furnishing of fluid capital, but the test of industrial efficiency. Fluid capital is about as far from the stage of collective management as the tides. Society will in the near future deal with capital as it deals with marriage and the family— not communalize it, but prescribe for it legal conditions. And the capitalist class will share in the framing of the prescription. They clearly cannot be the sole controllers. Comte's conception of a society in which the capitalist class, guided by a class of " priests of humanity," moralizes itself, playing the part of a new and more conscientious aristocracy, to which a docile proletariate for ever looks up in well-fed contentment, is as far from actuality or fitness as any dream of Socialist coercion. It ignores alike the facts of heredity and the forces of democracy. Such a society would ossify in a generation. The demos will neither subside in permanence nor merely coerce the " upper " classes. It will continue to look after its own interests as against masters who merely look after theirs. It will continue to react upon them as it is doing now, modifying them as it modifies itself. Even this, indeed, is an unduly simplified statement of a process in which the demos is rightly to be understood rather as a multiform mass, traversed by manifold forces, than as an organism or entity with one will or ideal.

But no harm wrought by ill-conceived ideals can make an end of the need for ideals among men. We live by them, and " not by bread alone." Civilization would be a failure indeed if the mass of workers could not rationally hope for a better lot for their children than that they were born into. The employer who does not sympathize with that hope is no good citizen. He would count it a calamity for his own children after him to have to live the life of factory hands ; and if he has a spark of sympathy—the instinct which is the germ of all morality—he must wish that the lot of the hand-worker shall improve as rapidly as may be through the generations. To cherish, as some do, the wish for a perpetual abundance of ignorant poverty, as a source of cheap labour, on the score that " somebody must do the dirty work," is to exhibit the moral attitude of one who well deserves to have to do the kind of work in question.

No really rational man can fear that any feasible elevation of the life-conditions of the mass will bring about a state of things in which everybody will be qualified for " refined " work, and nobody willing to do any other. The fewer people there are, indeed, who can do only the lowest work, the better ; their wages will rise. But if there is any truth in Darwinism,. there will always be plenty of people of small capacity and small gifts. What every man of the people may and should hope for, on behalf of all his fellows, is that on the one hand men of small capacity shall not for ever be able to lord it over others by reason of possessing much wealth ; and that, on the other hand, even small capacity shall not doom any to lifelong penury. An ideal thus marked out is justified by all social science, and its systematic pursuit is the plain quest for all rational reformers.

CHAPTER VI

THE IDEAL OF EQUALITY

BEHIND the movement of modern Socialism, as behind all movements for popular betterment, there is at work the primary craving for " equality." At all stages of history we find inequality, whether of human standing, as between master and slave in antiquity and in barbaric societies, or of social status, as in all monarchic and aristocratic communities, or of wealth. This last and least artificial differentiation of men's lives has survived from the most primitive societies, as seen duplicated among contemporary savages, into our own world, where it is the one decisive factor of social inequality. The others have been removed or undermined, and this in the first instance by an economic process. The most desperate slave wars in antiquity failed to put an end to slavery, which arose out of the primeval process of war and conquest. The slaves who revolted were always defeated, lacking as they did the power of cohesion no less than material resources. As little did religion avail to destroy the principle. The Christian Church itself owned slaves as long as mediæval slavery subsisted. Economic pressures alone sufficed to substitute, first, serf labour for absolute slave labour, and later, hired labour for that of serfs.

Once the worst and oldest form of inequality was destroyed, popular progress took the form of new struggles against the more oppressive forms that remained. Peasant wars were on all fours, morally and economically, with slave wars. All along men strove for what, with a true and deep instinct, they called " rights," generally giving fallacious reasons for the claim, and making legal claims where the law was not yet with them. The true " right " of suffering men is to the sympathy of those who profess to do as they would be done by. Given the profession of sympathy— and it is ostensibly made by all Christians, whatever their politics—some obligation follows. And some sense of obligation on the part of the " haves " towards the " have-nots " has entered into all political reforms which reduce differences of status, though the claim was never conceded without long pressure.

As the jurist put it, the progress made in men's legal relations has been " from status to contract," that is, from one of compulsory to one of voluntary service ; in other words, from greater to lesser inequality. More and more completely the conception of legal inequality has been eliminated from the normal life of civilized peoples. Adult suffrage will mean the removal of the last vestige. But even before the systematic formulation of the claim to the political franchise for all men—a claim followed in due course by that of women—there arose the aspiration for that further extension of equality which is attainable only through a better distribution of wealth. And it is this aspiration for economic equality that motives the proposals of Socialists, who are wont to speak of the ideal of mere political equality as an obsolete delusion. The contemporary instance of the women's franchise movement might reveal to them the fact that the two desires spring from the same root of self-preservative instinct ; and that the priority of the political claim is both natural and wholesome, were it only because it is so much the more easily justifiable.

When men propound the ideal of equality they rarely think of an absolute equalization of property or anything else. Very little reflection will show any one that the theoretic absolute is as impossible as equality of physical and mental endowments. Even a nominal equality of income, per adult or per family, could not secure equality of material enjoyment. What the idealists are thinking of is simply an increase in the share of wealth available to the majority. All men know that there can be moral and social equality in all respects between the very rich people and others of moderate means. Community of culture counts for more than equality of income. The more intelligent Socialists know, too, that mere division of existing credit capital could not result in a high level of wealth for all. Hence their resort to a scheme of nationalization of all the means of production, to which they look for a much enlarged production of wealth.

For those who realize the futility of the paper plan, save as a mere Utopia to steer towards, the practical question is, How can the existing society be raised in the way of a better distribution alike of wealth and of culture ? That is how alone the ideal is to be worked out in practice, and, thus made practical, it is impregnable to the simple syllogisms of those Conservatives who daily explain to us that equality is impossible. Their own dialectic processes demonstrate the fact : nothing can raise their thinking above the level of complacent platitude. But the very fact that Conservatives of the most meagre intelligence have no misgivings about criticizing opponents far superior to them in every way is one of the proofs that the instinct of men towards equality is indestructible. For ever will they energize towards the unattainable : the very effort is a condition of healthy life. And the instinct is as indestructible in " the masses " as in " the classes."

For one thing, though working men are still at some obvious disadvantage in their dealings with the employing class, by reason of difference alike of commercial and of social training, many of them have tasted enough of the higher culture of books to be conscious of the artificial nature of the difference. I have known working men much more widely read than the average manufacturer ; and, comparing the cranial aspects of the occupants of workmen's trains with those of the train-loads of business men who travel in first-class carriages to " the city," one is led to suspect positively higher potentialities for artistic and mental evolution in the majority of the " hand-workers " than in the so-called " head-workers " whose activities are purely commercial. Commercial success is apt to stand for a mere overplus of the acquisitive faculties.

None the less, acquisition is the need of the workers— acquisition both of income and of culture. And how is it to be effected ? Once more, by a series of steps and safeguards, steps in education, such as the raising of the school-age and the provision of facilities after that age ; safeguards against destitution, such as State insurance against unemployment and sickness ; sanitary safeguards, such as housing laws ; and, last but not least, safeguards against the hereditary transmission of incapacity by the breeding of the unemployable. For the last we must one day have something in the nature of " labour colonies," were it only to put the problem of unemployment on a manageable basis.   Given a raising at once of the mental and of the physical standard of life, we may count on a progressive curtailment of the economic and moral waste in drink-consumption, and a further curtailment of the birth-rate among the poorest.   Even now, with chronic outcry over the curtailment that has taken place, population increases almost in proportion to the improvement in the distribution of wealth.

For the financing alike of the educational steps and the legislative safeguards, provision must be made by a system of taxation which lays wealth under reasonable contribu-tion.   At the same time, it should be the aim of democratic reformers to increase the real wage of the workers by a removal of all taxes upon their wholesome consumption. Those who insist that all " ought to contribute something," forget (1) that most workers as such are producers of wealth in excess of their consumption, whereas mere income-spenders render in comparison only a negative service ; and (2) that it is fixedly wrong to reduce below a fair level the standard of popular nutrition.   By sparing the small margin of the toiler, and drawing on the large margin of the wealthy, and especially of the idle rich, the State is promoting in things fiscal " equality of sacrifice," and so doing on per-fectly ethical lines something to further that striving " away from inequality " which is the irreducible element of life in all ideals of equality.

CHAPTER VII

THE DISTRIBUTION OF WEALTH

WHEN Aristotle said that many States had been brought to anarchy and ruin by inequality, he was not thinking of that mere difference in human capacity, and that mere impossibility of absolute equality in material as in mental possessions, to which empirical Conservatives complacently point as proving that " equality is impossible." Aristotle knew that at least as well as they. He was thinking of the injurious extremes of economic inequality which divide communities into hostile halves—one hating, the other combining a reciprocal hate with fear. Ancient civilization went chronically aground upon that rock, and would have gone on doing so if it had not been ultimately wrecked upon the deadlier reef of militarism and conquest. And it behoves us to-day, running both of these risks, if happily in a less degree, to look closely and constantly to our navigation if we would escape them. Men are not so very much better in the mass to-day than were the Greeks and Romans. What they may hope for is to be better politicians. The ancients, even with Aristotle to help them, had little of the accumulated material upon which alone a science of society can be built. They had little written history ; that of Greece having begun to be written only a century or two before Aristotle wrote his politics. We have a hundred times their store of experience. The problem is to apply it.

Having eliminated from our social system the rotten foundation of slavery, we are evolving, as aforesaid, on a basis of legal equality. This, the idealists tell us, is futile ; the economic inequality is as dire as ever, and involves even more misery than did the older system. Admitting much misery, but denying that it is unreduced, the practical reformers answer that our task is to bring it under control ;

and this they claim to be doing.   The economic footing of Labour is being slowly but steadily improved.   Education is being developed.   Add to this the new provision by insurance against destitution from sickness and unemployment, with a system of semi-paternal employment for the " unfit " and a reconstructed poor-law, and the plague-spot of misery will be cleansed away.   And this is substantially what is asked for by those Socialists who profess to want simply to " abolish poverty."

But whatever these may say, others will continue to insist on the vital and injurious inequality which remains. While the majority are condemned to nearly continuous toil, with at best security for maintenance, a large minority will continue to enjoy all that wealth can give—leisure, travel, culture, all forms of luxury and pleasure—without rendering any service in return.   To the mass the envied joys of unlimited ease and leisure and culture can never be known, save as things unpossessed and unattainable, and envy, overrating the joys of idleness, yearns to penalise their possessors.   For, say the Socialists, it is the toil of the mass that provides all these things for the labour-consuming rich.

If they added, " the skill of the organizer, using the fluid capital of the rich," they would be right ; and the moral involved would be valid.   No deeply thoughtful person can pretend to think that idle enjoyment of wealth is a satisfactory feature in any social system.   What alone thoroughly moralizes life is reciprocity of service.   In the old case of the shipwrecked crew and passengers landed on an uninhabited island, with no hope of being taken away, the formerly rich man who should expect to be supported while doing no service would be a farcical figure.   And if in time some of the islanders grew rich by skill or craft, and left to their children wealth whereon to live idly, the situation would be none the less irreconcilable with any thorough-going ideal of life.   The social problem of the islanders would be ours.   What is needed is a control alike of wealth and poverty, tending always to promote reciprocity of service and to minimize idle living, whether among poor or rich.

Seeking for the slow and sure way, and discarding the futile expedient of violent revolution, we resort, first, to fiscal methods. Already all wealth is laid under special fiscal contribution in most civilized States, albeit with a very imperfect attainment of " equality of sacrifice." Where revenue is largely raised by indirect taxation, that is, by a tariff on imports, the inequality is gross. To tax equally the consumption of necessaries by poor and rich, is to negate equality of sacrifice altogether. Under our own system of progressive direct taxation, the Income Tax, now in large part graduated, though roughly, modifies the evil. The death duties work in the same direction. By those sound and essentially scientific expedients, idle wealth is laid under a larger contribution for public needs than it ever made before in human history.

Some Conservatives affect to see in both death duties and the new taxes a repetition of the finance of decadent Athens, in which the mass blackmailed the rich by making their public comfort depend upon large donations for public uses. But between such black-mailing and regular taxation there is even a greater moral and economic difference than between the earning of income by regular service and the extortion of vast prices from communities and individuals by the owners of much-needed land. The new taxation proceeds upon, and imposes, a moral and social law, which in time builds up a new moral sense. Recognition of the special taxability of unearned wealth is a step towards a recognition of the ethic of reciprocity of service. If only the revenue is used for building-up, not for destroying, for schools and public works and productive training and Old Age Pensions, not for furtherance of the eternal waste of militarism, it is wholly healthful.

And, short of revolution, there is yet another way of increasing Labour's share in the total production of wealth. Allusion has been made to the failure of many attempts at co-operative production, and the visible limits of the field within which there has been success. The great success of co-operation thus far has been attained in the field of distribution of the products consumed by working men. But who shall say that the share in invested capital which has actually been secured by co-operative thrift may not be increased as the workers gradually learn the lesson of the past ? The standing drawback is still their common failure to realize the vital importance of the part played by

the organizer, the captain of industry. One hears of the
collapse of a series of " Self-help " undertakings in the
textile-making districts by reason of sheer indiscipline.
Workmen running such concerns feel that they ought to be
their own masters, and so, defying the rule of manager and
foreman, work in their own business with a slackness of
which competitive industry does not permit.

To point to such collapses as a proof that " nothing but
Socialism will serve " is a mere refusal to face the facts.
Socialism itself, if ever tried, would infallibly fail if the
members of the community were less conscientious for
the commonwealth than they are compelled to be for the
employer. When all is said as to the necessity of social
control, scientific taxation, and constructive institutions,
the eternal fact remains that " 'tis in ourselves that we are
thus or thus." In fine, the capacity of working men to
enter into and maintain profit-sharing relations with masters
and capitalists will be the most essential proof of their
fitness, as citizens, to take part in a social system which shall
progressively eliminate idle living. And it will be no less
welcome a proof of that moralization of capital which
Comte vainly hoped to bring about by the precepts of a
caste of priests, and which a recent writer hopes to see
attained by some spontaneous development of moral
imagination. Of late years the instances on both sides
are increasing in number. Mr Carnegie, speaking from
the point of view of a great capitalist, has told how the
method of sympathy and " synergy " redounds to profit on
both sides ; and what he and others have achieved under
a system of vicious Protectionism can surely be improved
upon under the nobler and sounder regimen of Free Trade.

Slow, alas, is the upward progress of collective mankind,
or even of the most progressive community. The main
cause of retardation, since the stage of civilization has
been reached, has been strife—the purely destructive expenditure of human energy. With the control of strife,
international and industrial, are bound up all the hopes of
humanity. But the very recognition of the necessity is
new, is modern ; and herein lies the new foundation for
hope. Given the recognition of the problem, goodwill for
its solution surely cannot be lacking. In the failure to see,
to understand, lies the great danger, alike to the weal of

nations and to the common weal of each. And the main comfort of the reformer lies in the conviction that to maximize thought as against passion, knowledge as against blind zeal, sympathy as against egoism, is to promote understanding, vision, and accomplishment.

APPENDIX

THE PROMISES OF SOCIALISM

A Reply to Six Articles by Mr. Philip Snowden
(1923)

I

IT is to be feared that the voluminous articles of Mr. Philip Snowden, under the title of " If Labour comes into Power," have elicited from many readers in private the classic appeal to " cut the cackle and come to the 'osses." That will be the aim of the present comment.

What " Labour " Will Not Do

Mr. Snowden occupies much space with intimations of what " Labour " will not do. At the outset he even seems anxious to have us feel that it will do nothing out of the way of past politics. In this connection he assures us that " a Labour Government would certainly contain many men " of the orders of " lawyers, doctors, university professors, teachers, ministers of religion, consulting engineers, manufacturers, journalists, and even landed proprietors." Nine orders are here named, and nothing is said at this point of trade union secretaries. Thus, it is in effect promised that the first " Labour " Government will not be a " Labour " Government in the sense which that term naturally bears for plain men of all classes. And thus it is incidentally admitted that the visible Labour party of a few years ago was as ill qualified to constitute a Government as Liberals then declared it to be—to the great indignation of some of its then " leaders."

At the same time, Mr. Snowden is " confident " that the Labour Government will be " less of a class Government than any Government of the past has been," though it will, of course, "be concerned in the main in improving the condition of the working classes." Mr. Snowden gives his reasons for hoping that gradually the trade unions will lose their preponderance in the running of the party ; but cautiously adds that even if this does not happen, " it is not likely " that trade union interests will override " national considerations."

When, for instance, Mr. J. H. Thomas is made President of the Board of Trade, he will have to resign his position as secretary of the Railwaymen's Union. It is with perfect seriousness that Mr. Snowden gives this assurance, apparently on the assumption that outsiders would expect the contrary. And thus, he tells us, he disposes of " the only objection to Labour government brought forward by our opponents to which I attach much importance." He avowedly takes it for granted that the trade union secretary, once promoted, will be absolutely impartial in dealing with disputes between employers and employed.

Thus far, Mr. Snowden anxiously balances his appeal to other " classes " with his promises to the " working classes." There are to be " many " middle-class Ministers, including ministers of religion, and manufacturers, and and landed proprietors ; but it is not suggested that any of them will go to the Board of Trade. But the rest of us are to be quite tranquil on the subject because Mr. Snowden thinks it is " not likely " that a former railwaymen's representative would be anything but impartial.

What Labour Will Do

Now, however, Mr. Snowden must reassure his Socialists. While avowing that the Labour party, like others, has sections which pull different ways, and blandly inviting us to disregard any sections which may not agree with him, he declares without reserve that it will act as a Socialist party. It collectively believes, he tells us, that " private ownership and private management of productive concerns " is " inherently wrong, and that no amount of tinkering with it can make it permanently tolerable for the majority."

Therefore, the Labour party will apply to every " ameliorative proposal " the " acid test "—the question whether it " gets down to the root causes of economic and social ills "—the root causes being as aforesaid, private ownership and private management. Any ameliorative measures, then, which do not get down to those conditions will for the Labour party be of no account. Ownership must cease not merely as to mines, land, and railways, but as to manufactures generally.

But no sooner is the fiat pronounced than it is recalled. The adherents of the Labour party, Mr. Snowden assures us, are rather conservative than otherwise. (They are, indeed, as regards their modes of propaganda !) Therefore, the party will not be ruled by its " extremists." So, then, there are extremists who go further than the socialisation of all the means of production and some of the means of distribution. Who are they, and what do they want ? Mr Snowden will but tell us that they are young and inexperienced, and that some of them will in due time turn Tories—which, indeed, is not unlikely.

As to his own practical aims, we get this clue in his second article :—

" It is ridiculous to assume that the Labour party believe that capitalism is the cause of *every* ill which afflicts mankind to-day. But it does believe that *general* poverty, and all the evils which *arise* from that, are due to capitalism, and that the abolition of the private monopoly of the means of life would ensure conditions *where poverty would not be the compulsory lot of the vast majority.* When such conditions had been established it would depend upon the character and will of the individual whether he made the best of his opportunities, and if he failed to do so economic conditions would not be responsible."

Then we get this clue in the third : " Its [Labour's] legislation and administration will be directed to the gradual supersession of the capitalist system by the public ownership and democratic control of the essential industries and services." But soon afterwards comes the pronouncement that the Labour Government will proceed "*tentatively* and gradually to nationalise those *industries* and *services* which have reached the most advanced stage of *monopoly* and concentration. The industries and services ripe for this transformation are *land,* mines, railways, *electric power, banking, and insurance."*

Thus far has Mr. Snowden got in three or four prolix and discursive articles, in each of which he raises and drops the same topics, saying and unsaying, soothing and scaring, defining and cancelling his definitions. After the explicit statement that the task of Labour will be to nationalize the means of production, we get a programme which professes to nationalize services, and puts " land " first on a list which ends with " banking and insurance." There is no word now of " production," and not an allusion to the great manufacturing industries, which, by implication are to remain under private ownership. These industries, apparently, are not " essential." And, as to land, what is to take place, apparently, is a mere nationalization by purchase, leaving production to proceed on competitive lines as at present. There is, Mr. Snowden assures us, " a growing appreciation in the Labour party of the vital importance of the agricultural problem." That is to say, the theory of Socialism upon which the Labour party is founded was framed without any due recognition of that important problem. Only now has it " committees at work which are trying to evolve plans." It is so reassuring.

All that is so far clear is that there is no more substance in the promise to nationalize " services " than in the promise to nationalize " production." What are to be nationalized are railways, land-rents, mining-rents, electric power, banking, and insurance. All other services are to go on as before ; the production of food, wool, clothing, leather, coal, and all metal work, and the distribution thereof, is to proceed by way of competition ; and the weakest will, as before, go to the wall ; but now " the economic conditions will not be responsible ! " The Labour Government having done what it sees fit to do, nobody can blame the Labour Government for bad trade, unemployment, low wages, or low profits. Such, so far, is the programme.

How food and raw material are to be produced, while the Labour Government is busy with nationalizing banking and fire and life and marine insurance, we are to imagine for ourselves. How coal is to be competitively sold abroad while the Labour party is presumably controlling wages and limiting output is also considerately left to our imagina-

tion. It is not the business of the Labour champion to
make such things clear.   His task is to conciliate sentimen-
tally humane people, and elicit " Labour " support by
broadly glowing promises.   Alike as to what Labour will do
and what it will not do we are left in the vague.   But
happily we can frame inferences for ourselves.

II

Mr Snowden, it will be remembered, promises that a
Labour Government in action will " tentatively and gradually " nationalize certain " industries and services " on the
ground that they have reached an advanced stage of
" monopoly and concentration," the list including land,
mines, railways, electric power, banking, and insurance.
But inasmuch as agriculture, the actual work of food
production, is *not* to be nationalized, the " services " dealt
with work down to the four last named.   If agriculture is
not to be nationally worked, mines, presumably, will not
be.   It is only the " monopoly " that is to be nationalized.

No Confiscation

And, be it observed, there is to be no " confiscation."   On
this he is emphatic.   Capital, he warns his comrades, must
not be scared off.   The State is to *purchase* what it national-
izes.   That is to say, it is to act as a board of directors,
paying interest on the vested capital just as boards of
railway directors do at present.   And when it is asked
wherein the new system will differ from the old, he replies,
in effect, that just as railways save administrative costs by
amalgamating, so will the State.   By " saving waste," as
he puts it, " a sinking fund would be created which would
ultimately repay the purchase."

One can imagine the laughter with which this prospectus
will be received by the surviving adherents of Marx.   How,
one wonders, will it be received by Socialists of the newer
schools, including those advisory committees of doctors,
lawyers, clergymen, and others who, as Mr. Snowden

boasts, provide his party with plans. All landowners, mineowners, railway and banking and insurance shareholders are first to be bought out with State scrip. Then a vast sinking fund is to be built up. How? Is it to be invested in either State scrip or private scrip? Or is the State simply to proceed by way of progressively buying up its own scrip out of its profits? If so, what is the meaning of the phrase " sinking fund? " Has Mr. Snowden, or have the Labour party's advisory committees, one asks, any clear idea of what they are talking about?

The Repayment of Capital

Since the Socialist sinking fund defies cogitation, let us suppose that the procedure will be a simple progressive buying-up of the State scrip. How is *that* to be done? At present, scrip is bought by the tendering of other or fresh scrip, or cash credits. Since the Socialist aim must be to abolish scrip, the State must pay in cash. And as the total purchase price of land, railways, mines, electric-power plant, and banks and insurance offices, must amount to thousands of millions, we are in effect promised that for an indefinite period the State will go on paying out annually scores or hundreds of millions from its administrative profits to meet the capital claims of all the former owners and shareholders concerned. For at least some generations, then, in addition to whatever payment of interest is still made on war debt, an immense revenue will be annually spent on maintaining the " idle class." And just as fast as the idle class gets through its repaid capital (which it will then be able to invest only in the non-nationalized services, whatever they may be) its members will be provided with posts of some kind. For under " Labour " there is to be no unemployment. Indeed, all the men paid-off in the process of " saving waste " by State amalgamation of existing concerns will have to be provided with new work by the beneficent State.

And how is *that* to be done? Amalgamation, be it observed, is to mean *less employment*, whether for head workers or for hand workers, in the " services " nationalized. But always the disemployed must be newly employed, else the Labour Government will be the most unpopular on

record. And how is the new employment to be provided ?
Is it to be *profit-yielding* for the State ? This dilemma Mr
Snowden never faces, because he does not see it. If the
State is to " save waste " by amalgamation, it must employ
fewer people. But the Labour-ruled State is committed
to finding employment for all. And what are the means
of *profitable* employment of labour that Capitalism has not
yet sought to exploit ? In their absence, what can the
Labour Government do but pay out as doles to the unemployed what it " saves " by amalgamation ?

The Capital Levy

But we must not forget the financial panacea which has
won so many votes for the Labour party—the Capital Levy.
Mr. Snowden, it will be observed, makes no use of that
formula in connection with his proposals to nationalize land,
railways, banks, and so forth. These are to be *purchased*—
by implication, at their market value. It is only in his
fourth article, and there in connection with taxation policy,
that he comes to the levy. And, reaching it, he puts it
exactly as it has been put by a number of Liberals in recent
years—as an expedient which *will benefit capitalists.*

> " The proposal of a capital levy is just a business
> proposition. . . . It could not be justified except for the
> purpose of debt reduction. It would be most unwise to
> impose a capital levy for ordinary revenue purposes. *It
> is a thing which could only be done once.*"

Such is the language of the Socialist leader to the general
public. Let it be compared with the advocacy which has
won most of the seats gained by the Labour party. And,
above all, let that advocacy be compared with this avowal
by Mr. Snowden :—

> " If of course . . . those who would have to contribute
> to a capital levy *will not have it,* but prefer to go on paying
> a high income tax . . they must bear it, and a Labour
> Government *would have to look in other directions than the
> capital levy for revenue. . . .*"

There is to be no compulsion ! The " owning " classes are to have their own way in finance, even under a Labour Government ! The only threat is that in that case death duties will have to be increased and super-incomes more heavily taxed, while the beneficient Labour Government will actually reduce taxation on the lower, especially the earned, incomes.

The Residuum

Need we go further on that line ? As all students are aware, neither the higher incomes nor increased death duties can be made to yield any such revenue as will materiallylighten the income tax for the main body of payers, especially if, as Mr. Snowden proposes, the mass of small incomes now taxed are to be in a material degree exempted. In a word, the Labour party has no financial policy worth serious consideration. It will not enforce the capital levy against capitalist resistance. Its one alternative hope is in the heavier taxation of inheritances. And thus once more we are back to the crudest and poorest of all the formulas of Socialism—the appeal to the envy felt by the masses for the money-claim of the small body of the really rich, without regard to the vital fact that all increase in general national well-being must come from *largely increased production of real wealth*, relatively to population.

Like Mr. Webb, and like Socialist propagandists in general, Mr. Snowden makes a deep division between all who " live on interest " (or rent) and all who " live by working." That division is notoriously a false one. Among the receivers of interest are not only the retired middle-class men who in their working lives toiled at least as hard as Mr. Webb or Mr. Snowden ever did at *their* occupations, but multitudes of working men who provide for their old age by investments in shares or house property. And, knowing this, Mr. Webb and Mr. Snowden make their " class " attacks to no consistent purpose, since they are professedly resolved to confiscate nothing. They use the " class " cry to catch votes, knowing how useful it is in that way ; and to the same end they talk of increased taxation of inheritance. That will please the " have-nots." But of a policy by which a State can live, what outline do they give us ?

III

After all the parade of Socialist theory, it is to mere " palliatives " (as Socialists themselves style such measures) that we come, in Mr. Snowden's Labour programme. After the pose about " the acid test," by which all ameliorative measures are to be tried, we have the explicit admission that all the great root-and-branch measures are a long way off. The nationalizing measures first to be tried are those proposed in the past by many Liberals—notably, the nationalization of railways, ostensibly proposed by the late Coalition Government, and abandoned because too many of its supporters objected. And, Mr. Snowden confesses, " the advantages of nationalization would not be immediately obvious ! "

A Policy of Palliatives

So the Labour Government would have to turn its hand at once to " palliatives " which admittedly cannot pass the " acid test."

" The complete solution of the unemployment problem is not possible within the capitalist system. But its *worst evils* may be eliminated by State action. . . ." As if they had not been already eliminated ! Or—if it be argued that the worst evil is not wholesale starvation, but the demoralisation of having nothing to do—as if State action had not been already tried to make work for the workless !

The new palliatives are to be " extensive schemes of public works of a *necessary*, useful, and *remunerative* character," ; and those put foremost are (1) " a big housing scheme," which is to employ for years to come all the skilled labour in the building trades, and much unskilled labour besides ; and (2) " work for years to come for hundreds of thousands of men in remaking the roads and adapting them to modern requirement." All this work, then, is to be *remunerative*. And how is that to be attained ? Hardly has Mr. Snowden entered upon the problem when we find him, in effect, admitting that his

housing policy will not be remunerative in the honest
meaning of the term! The Labour Government, he an-
nounces, is not to build houses on present lines : it " will
bulid up the ideal. *If this cannot be done on an economic
basis*, then the State, under a Labour Government, will
subsidize housing as a part of the Public Health Service.
And that *will not be an economic loss* to the nation, but in a
hundred ways a direct gain."

The Economic Collapse

A gain, yet " not on an economic basis ! " Mr. Snowden
knows as well as the rest of us what this really means.
In plain language, a vast public expenditure will be undertaken which will make short work of any Sinking Fund
for the repayment of the capital of the vendors of banks,
land, railways, mines, electric plant, and insurance cor-
porations. Houses are to be built wholesale, for which
the tenants will be unable to pay rents that will cover
costs, and the Labour Government will be well on the
way to bankruptcy before it can pretend to go about the
business which its advocates declare to be *alone* worthy
of recognition as going to the root of social evils. Meantime new social evils on the most colossal scale will have
been wrought by the insensate policy of vast expenditure
that is confessedly non-economic, on the pretence that it
must somehow be beneficial.

Long ago, John Stuart Mill pointed out that any State
which undertook under all circumstances to provide occupa-
tion and subsistence for all its population would have
to regulate the number born. Mr. Snowden, speaking for
present-day Socialism, not only ignores blindly the crux
which Mill faced, he promises on behalf of the Labour
party a line of action which, so long as it is allowed to
go on, will stimulate population as it never was stimulated
before. With " ideal " houses provided for all, at sub-
sidized rents, within the means of all, irrespective of the
cost of building, and with " work " provided on similar
financial principles, the marriage-rate and the birth-rate
will mount until the not-distant day when the Labour
Government faces on the one hand bankruptcy, and on

the other the outcry of a starving people awake to its
incompetence and their own past delusion.

Disillusionment First ?

Whether all this is ever going to happen is, of course,
a " contingent " question. These very articles of Mr.
Snowden's go far to suggest that he and his colleagues
are already becoming conscious of the hollowness of their
case. Within the past year or two there have appeared
several serious books by former Socialists avowing dis-
illusionment. The gist of their confession is that while
they personally were moved by unselfish ideals, there was
forced upon them the discovery that Socialist politics in
general turns upon the sheer egoistic envy felt by the " have
nots " towards the " haves " whose wealth tantalises
them. Out of those " leaden instincts," the disillusioned
ones see, you cannot build up a golden world. If ever
mankind is to be industrially socialised, it will have to be
on a basis of enlightened good will.

But no less important than the ethical awakening is
the economic one. Long ago, even Socialists of the Fabian
school were able to see that the political economy of Marx
was radically false ; that he did not understand the current
economics which he vilified ; that his theory of value
was a chimera ; and that his doctrine of progress by social
catastrophe was a mere surrender to anarchism by a system
which professed to combat anarchism. Thus within the
ranks of Socialism so-called there awoke perceptions of
the futility of Socialist dogma as a lever to change an
ignorant world into an instructed one. Social science,
it was felt, must come before there could be Socialism ;
and current " Socialism " was the negation of all science.
The principle of population, the new idealists began to see,
must be faced instead of being flouted as it had been by
Marx. Marxism was felt, by men trained in it or allured
by it, to be out of date.

The Continental Collapse

And now has come the virtual abandonment of Socialism
as a working scheme for the existing world, by the saner

Socialists of Germany and Austria, faced by the frightful ruin of Russian Bolshevism.   And it is at this stage that the British Labour Party, earnestly protesting its anti-Bolshevism, sees ahead a chance of coming into power, and hurriedly strives to translate into passable political formulas the vote-catching cries with which it has been doing business ever since, during the war, the Liberal party suspended party propaganda in maintenance of the Coalition truce (for which loyalty to truce the Liberal party received its reward in the general election of 1918).

The British Labour Dilemma

The British Labour party has, in fact, been living at the polls on cries which have become largely obsolete in the countries in which they were first framed, and have for over 70 years been mainly propounded.   Intelligent Socialists in Germany know that Socialism cannot be worked in the present stage of evolution, whatever they may hope for in the remote future.   But our Labour leaders are committed by their vote-catching to the manufacture of a programme which shall at once reassure the sane political majority and retain the allegiance of the " stalwarts " of Socialism.   Hence the articles of Mr. Snowden, which seek to do both, and will do neither.

Mr. Snowden is courageous enough to say that, among his own backers, there is a common illusion about a lifting of " labour " in general by way of " preparing all promising children for the black-coated professions " ; and that this notion is futile.   But when he talks vaguely of " educating " all workers up to an ideal level he is but paltering with the issue.   All over the country, Labour candidates, or their henchmen, have promised " university education for all." Mr. Snowden knows this to be empty nonsense ; but it is by such empty nonsense that his party wins ignorant votes, and he must seek a compromise.

The Future of Parties

Thus " trimming " to the best of his power, Mr. Snowden reassures his backers by announcing that in no circumstances will " Labour " ever make a Coalition with Liberalism. It is distressing to have to obtrude upon him the proverbial reminder. A Labour Government, as described by Mr. Snowden, would be an organized hypocrisy, yet with ruinous commitments ; and Liberalism certainly will not coalesce with such a concern. Its task will be to avert the catastrophe. And on the whole the probabilities would seem to be that while Mr. Snowden's party sweetly spreads its net in the sight of the bird, the occulted common sense of the electorate will come to its rescue, and force the Labour party back to common sense.

Postcript.—Those who remember the " Right to Work " Bill of the Labour Party before the War, and who collate it with the performance of the Labour Party in office, need no further testimony as to the ineptiude of that movement for the tasks of actual government.

INDEX